Discovering Literature Series

CHALLENGING LEVEL

To Kill a Mockingbird
A Teaching Guide

by Mary Elizabeth

Illustrations by Kathy Kifer

Community Strand

To Kill a Mockingbird
by Harper Lee
is available in many editions.
This study guide was prepared
using the following:

To Kill a Mockingbird
Warner Books
1271 Avenue of the Americas
New York, New York 10020

All page references in this guide are to the Warner Books edition of *To Kill a Mockingbird*.

A Bridge of Childhood: Truman Capote's Southern Years, ©1989 by Marianne Moates. Reprinted by permission of Henry Holt and Company, LLC.

Writing Fiction: A Guide to the Narrative Craft, © 2002 by Janet Burroway. Reprinted by permission of Longman Publishers.

Teaching Guide published by:
Garlic Press
605 Powers St.
Eugene, OR 97402

www.garlicpress.com

ISBN 0-931993-74-1
Order Number GP-074

Table of Contents

Note: The chapters in this book are untitled; the phrases after each title are placed as guides.

NOTES TO THE TEACHER

The Discovering Literature Series is designed to develop a student's appreciation for good literature and to improve reading comprehension. At the Challenging Level, we focus on a variety of reading strategies that can help students construct meaning from their experience with literature as well as make connections between their reading and the rest of their lives. The strategies reflect the demands of each literary selection. In this study guide, we will focus on beginning a book, setting and mood, plot, foreshadowing and flashback, characterization, forming hypotheses, point of view, irony, symbolism, rereading, theme, and consulting outside references, among others.

The following discussion explains the various elements that structure the series at the Challenging Level.

THE ORGANIZATION OF THIS LITERATURE GUIDE

Chapter Pages

Each **Chapter Page** is organized into three basic elements: Chapter Vocabulary, Journal and Discussion Topics, and a Chapter Summary.

Chapter Vocabulary

The **Chapter Vocabulary** is introduced on each chapter page in the order in which it appears in the book (with page numbers from the Warner Books edition). You can display the list on an overhead projector before the students read each chapter and guide them in using one of the vocabulary exercises from below to preview the chapter vocabulary. Introducing the Chapter Vocabulary prior to students' reading ensures that their reading is not disrupted by the frequent need to look up a word.

The Chapter Vocabulary includes definitions of key words from each chapter. To save time, students need only to copy, not look up, definitions. The more meaningful the vocabulary exercises are, the more easily students will retain vocabulary. Suggestions for teaching vocabulary include:

1. Have students create a web or other graphic, showing the relationships between and among the vocabulary words. Encourage them to add other related words to their web. Finding relationships between and among words helps students learn the words better than treating them separately.
2. Have students label a picture with a group of words that is primarily nouns.
3. Have students use the words in a piece of writing, for example a poem, a one-act play, a diary entry written from the point of view of one of the characters.
4. Have students research and record the etymology of each word.
5. Have students make and exchange crossword puzzles created with the vocabulary words.
6. Have students write and exchange a cloze exercise using the vocabulary words. A cloze exercise has a blank for each vocabulary word, and the surrounding context is carefully constructed to indicate which word belongs in each blank.

Because there are so many important vocabulary words having some legal meaning, these words have been pulled out and placed at the end of this introduction (pp. 12–17). You may wish to do separate exercises with these words, either prior to or during reading of the book, such as showing how certain subgroups of words are related, or putting some groups of words in time-order sequence (e.g., change of venue, postponement, trial, testify, cross-examination, verdict).

Journal and Discussion Topics

The **Journal and Discussion Topics** include questions for the students' Reader Response Journals and questions for Discussion to help the students become engaged with the literature. Warner page numbers are used to help locate references.

One or more of the Journal and Discussion Topics can either be displayed on the board or on an overhead projector before each chapter is read. The selected Journal and Discussion Topics will help to focus the students' reading of the chapter. Choose questions that will not give away important plot elements.

Answer Pages are provided at the back of the book for each set of questions. Answers to complex questions are of necessity often incomplete and only suggestive. Students' answers should be more fully developed.

Students will benefit by reading with their **Reader Response Journals** beside them. This will allow them to easily note any unfamiliar vocabulary that was not presented before the lesson, questions they have about the literature, and their own reactions as they enter into the experience of the story. Journals can also be used for written dialogue between you and students. If you wish to do this, periodically collect the journals and respond to students' comments. It is important for students to know beforehand whether their journals are private or public. In either case, journals should not be corrected or graded, but only recorded for being used. You may wish to keep your own reading journal.

Discussion can take place between partners, in small groups, or with the entire class participating. Students may wish to reflect on the discussion by writing in their journals. Discussion starters include:

1. A group retelling of the chapter.
2. Each reader telling
   a. the most striking moment in the chapter for him or her;
   b. a question she or he would like to ask the author or a character about the chapter;
   c. what he or she liked most or least about the chapter.
3. A discussion of how the chapter relates to the portion of the book that preceded it. Discussion can end with predictions about what will happen in the next chapter. Each student should note predictions in her or his journal.

Always ask students to retell (or summarize) the material to check comprehension and encourage integration of material. The retelling can be oral, artistic (for example, a storyboard), or in written prose. Retelling can take place in the discussion groups or in the journals.

Chapter Summary

The **Chapter Summary** for each chapter is included for teacher use only. It provides an at-a-glance scan of the chapter events. Use it to refresh your memory about the contents of each chapter. Identifying phrases for each chapter have been used in the table of contents and at the top of each chapter page, to help you recall the events in each chapter.

Strategy Pages

Strategy Pages throughout the series have been developed to increase students' understanding of strategies they can use to enhance their understanding of literature. Some important examples are:

- Monitoring (e.g., adjusting reading rate; consulting outside sources for further information, using context and referring to illustrations to help clarify meaning, and rereading)
- Identifying important information (e.g., marking a text)
- Summarizing
- Evaluating
- Understanding the tools that writers' use to make meaning—the elements of literature such as theme, plot, character, allusion, symbolism, and metaphor

The pages for each literature selection reinforce the strategies important for engaging deeply with that particular work of literature. You may copy and distribute these pages. Students can answer on the back of the page or on a separate sheet of paper.

Answers are provided at the back of the book for each Strategy Page. Answers to complex questions are of necessity incomplete and only suggestive. Students' answers should be more fully developed. Some Strategy Page questions require ongoing attention as the students continue reading.

Tests

At the end of groups of chapters, a comprehensive closed- or open-book **Test** has been provided for your use. Each test includes vocabulary exercises and short essays. You may copy and distribute these pages.

Answers are provided at the back of the book for each Test. Answers to essay questions are of necessity incomplete and only suggestive. Students' answers should be more fully developed.

Writer's Forum Pages

Suggestions for writing are presented under the **Writer's Forum** heading throughout this guide. You can choose from these suggestions or substitute your own creative-writing ideas.

Each Writer's Forum includes both instruction and directions for a particular writing task. Students will write a variety of genres relating to the text and their own experience of the text. As you plan lessons, allow enough time for students to engage in the writing process:

- Prewrite (brainstorm and plan their work)
- Draft (give a shape to their ideas on paper)
- Review (revisit their work with an eye to improving it, on their own as well as with peers, with you, or with others)
- Revise (make changes that they feel will improve their draft)
- Proofread (check for accuracy in grammar, mechanics, and spelling)
- Publish (present their work to others in some way)

Answers are provided at the back of the book for each Writer's Forum. Answers are of necessity incomplete and only suggestive. Students' answers should be more fully developed.

History of Social Thought Pages

One of the challenges of reading sophisticated works as a young adult is recognizing where the author's thought fits in the history of ideas. Even if the author is explicit, it can still require some research to understand where the author stands on particular issues. Lee's book addresses ideas about social, racial, and gender inequality. Certainly, *To Kill a Mockingbird* can be, and is, read with only a general knowledge of the issues. If you would like to address more deeply some of the issues Lee brings up, you may wish to use these pages. They are grouped at the end of the book, but can be used before the students begin the book, as the individual topics become important in the narrative, or after students' reading is complete.

Theme Pages

This study guide offers two different ways to approach theme. First is the standard Theme Strategy Page used in every work in this series. If, however, you would like to treat the themes in this work in more depth, the **Theme Pages** at the end of the text focus more deeply on some of the themes that Lee explores in the novel. You may wish to use them while students read, introducing them either as the individual topics become important in the narrative or after students' reading is complete.

THE GROUPINGS OF LITERATURE

We have among our titles a group of works that could be presented as part of a unit called "Community." We present groupings of literature so that you can easily present works as a unit. The works of literature in the "Community" unit resonate with each other, providing a multifaceted look at a variety of **themes** such as

- Equality
- Individuality
- Justice
- Responsibility
- Freedom
- Education
- Belonging
- Diversity and Unity
- Family
- Integrity

Since no substantial work of literature has only a single theme, "Community" is not the only possible grouping for these works of literature. Reference to themes can help focus students' attention as they read and help link works of literature together in meaningful ways. Similarly, a grouping of books can throw light on **Big Ideas**. Big Ideas worth considering include the following:

- What makes a community?
- How does the community context (familial, cultural, social, etc.) affect individuals?
- How can individual and community goals conflict or coexist?
- What does the community owe the individual and vice versa?
- How can we contribute to our community?

INTRODUCING THE LITERATURE

Students will be better prepared to become involved with the work of literature if they can place it in a context. The process of contextualizing a

work of literature begins with accessing their **prior knowledge** about the book, the author, the genre, and the subject. A class discussion is a good forum for this exercise. After you have found out what, if any, familiarity students have with the book and author and what they have been able to discern about the genre and subject, you can provide any necessary background knowledge and, if it seems appropriate, correct any misapprehensions students have. See Strategy 1: Beginning a Book (p. 22).

Explain that in a work of fiction, an author creates an imaginary world. An important task in beginning a literature selection is to come to terms with that world. Point out that it is possible to consciously assess one's own understanding and that this process is called **metacognitive reflection.** You may wish to model this process applied to understanding of literature using a **think-aloud** approach as you go through the material on pages 22–24 of this teaching guide. To do this, simply read aloud the portions of *To Kill a Mockingbird* needed to answer the questions, and speak aloud your thoughts as you formulate your responses, making explicit the connections and prior knowledge you are using in developing your thoughts.

After students have a beginning notion of the context of a work, you can proceed with the prereading activities that students will use prior to every chapter.

SAMPLE LESSON PLAN

Engaging **Prereading** activities include:
- Previewing vocabulary and doing a vocabulary exercise
- Reviewing the events of the previous chapter
- Leading students to examine their expectations about what will happen next based on what they already know, but be ready for surprises Have students consider any illustrations as they make predictions but preview the illustrations to make sure they don't reveal too much. If you wish, you can use a prediction guide. Students can fill in the guide as a class, in groups, or as individuals

During Reading, students read with their Reader Response Journals. (You may wish to give them some of the journal and discussion topics before they read or after they read a particular portion of text.)

Remind students of the questions that can help them to begin to understand a work of literature (see pp. 23–24). You may wish to have students address these questions in their journals as they begin the book. Encourage students to continue using this kind of self-questioning in their Reader Response Journals.

Additional journal activities they can use with every chapter include:
- A summary of the events of the chapter
- Evaluations of the characters and/or text
- Questions about what they have read
- Associations they have made between the text and other texts, experiences, or situations
- Notes on the images the text evoked
- Notes on the feelings the texts evoked

After Reading, students complete the Journal and Discussion Topics, the Writer's Forum and Strategy Pages, and the Test, if any.

Legal Vocabulary
Quick Find

BOOK ORDER

Page	Word	Definition
4	chattels	slaves; property
5	alleged	accused but not proven
5	detention	holding in custody
9	culprit	person guilty of a crime
10	disorderly conduct	less serious legal offenses including disturbing the peace and behaving inappropriately
10	disturbing the peace	acting in defiance of law and order; also appears on page 196—Jem does not seem sure of the import of Judge Taylor's remarks. Judge Taylor is concerned that Link Deas's unsolicited remarks could result in a mistrial
10	assault and battery	threat to use force on someone and carrying out of the threat
10	abusive	insulting or vulgar
10	profane	showing contempt for God or sacred things
17	illicitly	unlawfully; against the rules
20	entailment	restriction on how property can be inherited
21	mortgaged	borrowed against and held as security until the loan is paid back
27	truant	child who fails to attend school as legally required by the state
31	misdemeanor	crime less serious than a felony, carrying a punishment of a fine or local imprisonment
31	capital felony	serious crime punishable by death
67	perpetrated	committed
67	libel	defamation of character; harming someone's reputation using writing or representation so that the injured person is identifiable and a third party knows of it. Libel must be intentionally malicious.
74	defended	represented the defendant in a court of law
75	come to trial	be scheduled for a hearing by a judge and jury
75	postponement	delay granted in hearing a court case
88	evidence	material or testimony legally submitted to a tribunal and accepted as part of a court's inquiry into the truth of some matter
88	jury	group of people summoned and held under oath to decide on the facts at issue in a trial
125	Blackstone's *Commentaries*	important book on British law
135	rape	in this book it refers to a particular sex act: forced heterosexual intercourse by a man with a woman, involving penetration of the vagina by the penis—today *rape* has a wider meaning, including other kinds of sexual assault with force and without consent and the wording of the laws in many states has been changed to be gender neutral
135	carnal knowledge	sexual intercourse (literally, "knowing someone through the body"); in the book, defined as heterosexual and involving penetration of the vagina by the penis
136	penitentiary	prison
144	defendant	one charged with a crime; the accused; the person against whom a criminal proceeding is begun; to be distinguished from *criminal*, which refers to a person who has been convicted of a violation of the criminal law
145	trial	the procedure by which a judge or jury makes a finding of fact concerning a lawsuit
145	change of venue	change of the location in which a trial is to be held; often requested when the defendant is considered to be in danger
146	chair	the electric chair by means of which capital punishment (death sentence) was carried out in Alabama at that time
160	subpoena	legal document requiring one's appearance in court
160	picking the jury	the process of deciding which community members will hear a particular case; both the lawyer for the defense and the prosecuting attorney have a role in the selection

163	solicitor	the chief law officer of a municipality
163	circuit clerk	clerk for a circuit court—the circuits are judicial divisions of a state
163	probate	the court whose main business is wills and estates
164	circuit solicitor	the representative of the state; the prosecutor
165	equity	justice applied to circumstances not covered by law
165	champertous	as in a proceeding in which someone not party to a lawsuit bargains to carry on the pursuit of the case in exchange for a share of any profits
165	connivance	consent to wrongdoing
165	litigants	the parties engaged in a lawsuit
166	testifyin'	dialect for *testifying*; giving sworn testimony in a law court
166	witness chair	the place reserved for the witness to occupy during testimony; it is placed on the witness stand
166	convened	assembled to begin official business
166	witnesses	those called upon to testify in a court; an eye-witness made personal observations at the time an event took place
167	objection	opposition to a question or line of questioning by the opposing counsel; there are rules governing the criteria for finding a question objectionable; the judge may sustain (admit) or overrule (reject) the objection
167	took advantage of her	raped her (see definition of *rape*, p. 135)
167	took him in	brought him to the local police station or court to charge him with a criminal offense
168	court reporter	court official in charge of recording court proceedings
169	opposing counsel	the lawyers for the defense and prosecution respectively
169	title dispute	disagreement over the legal ownership of some property
169	corroborating evidence	evidence that supports a claim
170	. . . so help me God	part of the oath taken by witnesses in which they swear to "tell the truth, the whole truth, and nothing but the truth, so help me God"; the form of the oath includes placing the left hand on a Bible and raising the right hand
171	recess	official break in court proceedings as ordered by the presiding court officer
173	gavel	judge's mallet, used to command attention in the courtroom
174	contempt charges	charged with open disrespect for or disobedience to the authority of a court of law
174	sexual intercourse	see definition of *carnal knowledge* (p. 135)
176	testimony	evidence given under oath in a court of law
176	on the stand	giving his testimony (while standing on the "witness stand" in the courtroom)
176	irrelevant 'n' immaterial	inapplicable and of no substantial importance (to a particular situation)
177	overruled	the judge's rejection of the objection raised by a counsel to the opposing counsel's question or line of questioning
177	cross-examination	requestioning of a witness by the opposing counsel on matters discussed in the *direct examination* carried on by the lawyer who called the witness in the first place
181	state	the party initiating a criminal suit; same as the prosecutor
182	let the record show	a request to the clerk to enter something into the record outside of the counsel's questions and witness's responses
186	browbeating	intimidating; overpowering
188	rested	finished its case
189	reversed	found a judge's decision to be erroneous and changed a "not guilty" finding to a "guilty" finding or vice versa
190	convicted	found guilty
190	serve	complete an assigned jail sentence after being found guilty
190	fine	amount assigned as restitution upon being found guilty
192	volition	will
195	under oath	having sworn in court on a Bible to "tell the truth, the whole truth, and nothing but the truth," with God's help

196	expunge	delete; strike out
196	told the jury to disregard	in a court proceeding, the jury's finding must be based on the evidence and testimony that has been presented in the case; anything outside this system (whether true or false) is not to be part of the jury's considerations in reaching their verdict, so they must disregard it
201	fraud	deception; twisting of the truth
202	capital charge	a charge for which one can receive the death penalty if found guilty; same as *capital felony*
204	swore out a warrant	obtained, by making a charge under oath, a document from a judge allowing an officer to search, seize, or arrest
207	verdict	opinion of a jury on a question of fact
207	acquit	bring a finding of not guilty
208	charged the jury	entrusted the jury with their responsibility by giving them instructions concerning the guidelines they should apply as they seek a verdict
209	jury box	location in a courtroom reserved for jury members during the trial
211	foreman	the chairperson and spokesperson for a jury
211	polling the jury	asking the jury, one by one, to verify their individual findings in the case that led to the joint verdict presented by the foreman
213	appeal	request for a new hearing of a case by a higher court which reviews the lower court decision in hope that the higher court may reverse the lower court's decision or call for a new trial. (see definition of *reversed*, p. 189)
215	court-appointed defenses	attorneys appointed by the court because the plaintiff is too poor to hire one
217	threatened	declared an intention to inflict damage or injury to another by a wrongful act
218	put . . . under a peace bond	impose a bond on a person who has threatened to breach the peace in order to guarantee the person's good behavior for a period of time; can only be done by a judge
218	credibility	believability; trustworthiness
219	commutes	alters; reduces
219	acquittal	a finding of not guilty; setting free from the charge of an offense
219	statute	law
219	circumstantial	evidence that proves a fact—not directly, as in an eye-witness account—but by inference
219	eye-witnesses	those who see and report their observations pertaining to the matter at hand
219	reasonable doubt	the technical term guiding jurors in the degree of uncertainty about a defendant's guilt that they must have in order to vote for acquittal
221	excuses	relieves from the civic duty of serving on a jury in a particular case according to set criteria
222	strike him	remove a prospective juror that counsel thinks may have an unfavorable view or bias in the case
244	prosecutin'	dialect for *prosecuting*; bringing legal action for alleged criminal or law-breaking activities
249	assault	threat or attempt to hurt someone that either puts a person in physical danger or causes him/her to fear harm
272	self-defense	the legal right to protect oneself against violence with reasonably necessary force

ALPHABETICAL ORDER

Word	Page	Definition
abusive	10	insulting or vulgar
acquit	207	bring a finding of not guilty
acquittal	219	a finding of not guilty; setting free from the charge of an offense
alleged	5	accused but not proven
appeal	213	request for a new hearing of a case by a higher court which reviews the lower court decision in hope that the higher court may reverse the lower court's decision or call for a new trial. (see definition of *reversed*)
assault	249	threat or attempt to hurt someone that either puts a person in physical danger or causes him/her to fear harm
assault and battery	10	threat to use force on someone and carrying out of the threat
Blackstone's *Commentaries*	125	important book on British law
browbeating	186	intimidating; overpowering
capital charge	202	a charge for which one can receive the death penalty if found guilty; same as *capital felony*
capital felony	31	serious crime punishable by death
carnal knowledge	135	sexual intercourse (literally, "knowing someone through the body"); in the book, defined as heterosexual and involving penetration of the vagina by the penis.
chair	146	the electric chair by means of which capital punishment (death sentence) was carried out in Alabama at that time
champertous	165	as in a proceeding in which someone not party to a lawsuit bargains to carry on the pursuit of the case in exchange for a share of any profits
change of venue	145	change of the location in which a trial is to be held; often requested when the defendant is considered to be in danger
charged the jury	208	entrusted the jury with their responsibility by giving them instructions concerning the guidelines they should apply as they seek a verdict
chattels	4	slaves; property
circuit clerk	163	clerk for a circuit court—the circuits are judicial divisions of a state
circuit solicitor	164	the representative of the state; the prosecutor
circumstantial	219	evidence that proves a fact, not directly–as in an eye-witness account–but by inference
come to trial	75	be scheduled for a hearing by a judge and jury
commutes	219	alters; reduces
connivance	165	consent to wrongdoing
contempt charges	174	charged with open disrespect for or disobedience to the authority of a court of law
convened	166	assembled to begin official business
convicted	190	found guilty
corroborating evidence	169	evidence that supports a claim
court reporter	168	court official in charge of recording court proceedings
court-appointed defenses	215	attorneys appointed by the court because the plaintiff is too poor to hire one
credibility	218	believability; trustworthiness
cross-examination	177	requestioning of a witness by the opposing counsel on matters discussed in the *direct examination* carried on by the lawyer who called the witness in the first place
culprit	9	person guilty of a crime
defendant	144	one charged with a crime; the accused; the person against whom a criminal proceeding is begun; to be distinguished from *criminal*, which refers to a person who has been convicted of a violation of the criminal law
defended	74	represented the defendant in a court of law
detention	5	holding in custody

disorderly conduct	10	less serious legal offenses including disturbing the peace and behaving inappropriately
disturbing the peace	10	acting in defiance of law and order; also appears on page 196—Jem does not seem sure of the import of Judge Taylor's remarks. Judge Taylor is concerned that Link Deas's unsolicited remarks could result in a mistrial.
entailment	20	restriction on how property can be inherited
equity	165	justice applied to circumstances not covered by law
evidence	88	material or testimony legally submitted to a tribunal and accepted as part of a court's inquiry into the truth of some matter
excuses	221	relieves from the civic duty of serving on a jury in a particular case according to set criteria
expunge	196	delete; strike out
eye-witnesses	219	those who see and report their observations relating to the matter at hand
fine	190	amount assigned as restitution upon being found guilty
foreman	211	the chairperson and spokesperson for a jury
fraud	201	deception; twisting of the truth
gavel	173	judge's mallet, used to command attention in the courtroom
illicitly	17	unlawfully; against the rules
irrelevant 'n' immaterial	176	inapplicable and of no substantial importance (to a particular situation)
jury	88	group of people summoned and held under oath to decide on the facts at issue in a trial
jury box	209	location in a courtroom reserved for jury members during the trial
let the record show	182	a request to the clerk to enter something into the record outside of the counsel's questions and witness's responses
libel	67	defamation of character; harming someone's reputation using writing or representation so that the injured person is identifiable and a third party knows of it. Libel must be intentionally malicious.
litigants	165	the parties engaged in a lawsuit
misdemeanor	31	crime less serious than a felony, carrying a punishment of a fine or local imprisonment
mortgaged	21	borrowed against and held as security until the loan is paid back
objection	167	opposition to a question or line of questioning by the opposing counsel; there are rules governing the criteria for finding a question objectionable; the judge may sustain (admit) or overrule (reject) the objection
on the stand	176	giving his testimony (while standing on the "witness stand" in the courtroom)
opposing counsel	169	the lawyers for the defense and prosecution respectively
overruled	177	the judge's rejection of the objection raised by a counsel to the opposing counsel's question or line of questioning
penitentiary	136	prison
perpetrated	67	committed
picking the jury	160	the process of deciding which community members will hear a particular case; both the lawyer for the defense and the prosecuting attorney have a role in the selection
polling the jury	211	asking the jury, one by one, to verify their individual findings in the case that led to the joint verdict presented by the foreman
postponement	75	delay granted in hearing a court case
probate	163	the court whose main business is wills and estates
profane	10	showing contempt for God or sacred things
prosecutin'	244	dialect for *prosecuting*; bringing legal action for alleged criminal or law-breaking activities
put . . . under a peace bond	218	impose a bond on a person who has threatened to breach the peace in order to guarantee the person's good behavior for a period of time; can only be done by a judge

rape	135	in this book it refers to a particular sex act: forced heterosexual intercourse by a man with a woman, involving penetration of the vagina by the penis—today *rape* has a wider meaning, including other kinds of sexual assault with force and without consent and the wording of the laws in many states has been changed to be gender neutral
reasonable doubt	219	the technical term guiding jurors in the degree of uncertainty about a defendant's guilt that they must have in order to vote for acquittal
recess	171	official break in court proceedings as ordered by the presiding court officer
rested	188	finished its case
reversed	189	found a judge's decision to be erroneous and changed a "not guilty" finding to a "guilty" finding or vice versa
self-defense	272	the legal right to protect oneself against violence with reasonably necessary force
serve	190	complete an assigned jail sentence after being found guilty
sexual intercourse	174	see definition of *carnal knowledge*
. . . so help me God	170	part of the oath taken by witnesses in which they swear to "tell the truth, the whole truth, and nothing but the truth, so help me God"; the form of the oath includes placing the left hand on a Bible and raising the right hand
solicitor	163	the chief law officer of a municipality
state	181	the party initiating a criminal suit; same as the prosecutor
statute	219	law
strike him	222	remove a prospective juror that counsel thinks may have an unfavorable view or bias in the case
subpoena	160	legal document requiring one's appearance in court
swore out a warrant	204	obtained, by making a charge under oath, a document from a judge allowing an officer to search, seize, or arrest
testifyin'	166	dialect for *testifying*; giving sworn testimony in a law court
testimony	176	evidence given under oath in a court of law
threatened	217	declared an intention to inflict damage or injury to another by a wrongful act
title dispute	169	disagreement over the legal ownership of some property
told the jury to disregard	196	in a court proceeding, the jury's finding must be based on the evidence and testimony that has been presented in the case; anything outside this system (whether true or false) is not to be part of the jury's considerations in reaching their verdict, so they must disregard it
took advantage of her	167	raped her (see definition of *rape*)
took him in	167	brought him to the local police station or court to charge him with a criminal offense
trial	145	the procedure by which a judge or jury makes a finding of fact concerning a lawsuit
truant	27	child who fails to attend school as legally required by the state
under oath	195	having sworn in court on a Bible to "tell the truth, the whole truth, and nothing but the truth," with God's help
verdict	207	opinion of a jury on a question of fact
volition	192	will
witness chair	166	the place reserved for the witness to occupy during testimony; it is placed on the witness stand
witnesses	166	those called upon to testify in a court; an eye-witness made personal observations at the time an event took place

Quick Find
Chapter Index

 # Bibliography

As you and your students immerse yourselves in this work of literature, you may wish to consult other works by the same author, thematically related works, video and/or audio productions of the work, and criticism. Here is a brief list of works that may be useful.

WORKS OF LITERATURE
Short Stories
Capote, Truman. "A Christmas Memory" in *Breakfast at Tiffany's.*
Capote, Truman. "The Thanksgiving Visitor."
Capote, Truman. "El invitado del Dia de Accion de Bracias."
    (in Spanish; Editorial Lumen).
Keyes, Daniel. "Flowers for Algernon."
Vonnegut, Kurt. "Harrison Bergeron."

Novels
Adams, Richard. *Watership Down.*
Golding, William. *Lord of the Flies.*
Lowry, Lois. *The Giver.*
McCullers, Carson. *The Member of the Wedding.*
Twain, Mark. *The Adventures of Huckleberry Finn.*
White, T. H. *The Sword in the Stone.*

Scripts (Play, TV, Screen)
Blinn, William. *Brian's Song.*
Cunningham, John M. *High Noon: A Screen Adaptation.*
Foote, Horton. *To Kill a Mockingbird, Tender Mercies and*
    The Trip to Bountiful: Three Screenplays by Horton Foote.
Rose, Reginald. *Twelve Angry Men: A Screen Adaptation.*
Sergel, Christopher. *To Kill a Mockingbird* (full-length play).
Serling, Rod. *The Twilight Zone, Script Twenty: The Monsters Are*
    Due on Maple Street.
Shakespeare, William. *Julius Caesar.*
Shakespeare, William. *Romeo and Juliet.*
Shakespeare, William. *The Tempest.*
Sophocles. *Antigone.*

Biography
Moates, Marianne, & Carter, Jennings Faulk. *A Bridge of Childhood:*
    Truman Capote's Southern Years. (Henry Holt Company, 1989)

Autobiography
Angelou, Maya. *I Know Why the Caged Bird Sings.*
Frank, Anne. *Diary of a Young Girl.*

History
Carter, Dan. *Scottsboro: A Tragedy of the American South.*
Hamilton, Virginia Van der Veer. *Alabama: A Bicentennial History.*

A FEW WORKS OF CRITICISM
Collections of Critical Comments

Bryfonski, Dedria (ed.). "(Nelle) Harper Lee," *Contemporary Literary Criticism*, Vol. 12. Detroit: Gale Research Company, pp. 340-343. 1980.

Matuz, Roger (ed.). "Harper Lee," *Contemporary Literary Criticism*, Vol. 60. Detroit: Gale Research Company, pp. 239-250. 1990.

Two Works by a Critic with Whom Lee Spoke About the Work

Johnson, Claudia. "The Secret Courts of Men's Hearts: Code and Law in Harper Lee's *To Kill a Mockingbird*." *Studies in American Fiction*, Vol. 19 , No. 2. 1991.

Johnson, Claudia. *To Kill a Mockingbird: Threatening Boundaries*. New York: Twayne Publishers. 1994. Includes parallels to the Scottsboro Trial.

Review of the Movie

Campbell, Virginia. "To Kill a Mockingbird," *Magill's Survey of Cinema: English Language Films; First Series*, Vol. 4, Frank N. Magill (ed.). Englewood Cliffs, NJ: Salem Press, pp. 1756-1759. 1980.

PERFORMANCES

If you want to experience *To Kill a Mockingbird* in another medium, this list will help you. I strongly urge you not to show videos or play audios until students have completed their reading.

VHS

To Kill a Mockingbird. MCA Home Video. 1991. Directed by Robert Mulligan, starring Gregory Peck.

Audio Cassettes

To Kill a Mockingbird (Unabridged). Read by Sally Darling. Recorded Books. 1988.

To Kill a Mockingbird (Abridged). Read by Maureen Stapleton. Random House and Miller-Brody Productions. 1975.

To Kill a Mockingbird (Unabridged). Read by Roses Prichard. Audio Partners. 1997.

Part One
STRATEGY 1
Beginning a Book

Directions: Read the explanation, then answer the questions.

When an artist or craftworker sets about creating a work, he or she has available a set of standard tools, techniques, and products. The theatre director, for example, can choose from a wide variety of styles of dramatic presentation: improvisation, one-act play, classical play, musical, and so on. The director can draw actors from an established company or hold auditions and will complement the acting with lighting, scenery, make-up, properties, and perhaps music to create an impression, set a mood, make a statement, or tell a story. The choices in these areas may be guided by the time and place in which the piece is set, or they may be an eclectic collection based on some other principle. The director cannot and does not use every technique and style in each piece, and each director's choices are guided by his or her goal, which might be the answer to a question such as, "How can I effectively communicate my vision?" The audience watching the performance perceives it over time and most likely is not able to take all the details in one viewing. There may or may not be an opportunity to see the production again. Attending to detail, movement, words, and the effect of the whole, the viewer brings his or her experience to bear and can come to understand the performance in some meaningful way.

The writer is an artist who works in words, which create images, thoughts, and feelings in the reader. Like the director, the writer works to communicate a vision to people without speaking to them directly in conversation. The reader's understanding of the standard tools, techniques, products, and conventions of the writer helps the reader to comprehend the writer's vision. But at the same time that we try to understand the writer's communication, we must acknowledge that each reader also brings an individual and unique understanding to the act of reading. As a result, no two readers will experience a book in exactly the same way, just as no two viewers will have identical experiences of a theatre piece. Individual readers will have different insights and feelings, so discussion between and among readers can enrich the experience of all.

Beginning a book is particularly important because readers starting a book are entering a new and uncharted territory. When you are starting a book, paying particular attention to the writer's use of tools, techniques, and conventions can help.

Title. It is a convention for a novel to have a title, found on the front cover, the spine, and the title page. The title of the book may explicitly tell what the book is about, may hint about the story, or may seem very mysterious. Depending on the title, you may feel interested, curious, or hopeful. The author's name follows immediately after the title. If you already know something about the author or the book—for example, that Harper Lee was a childhood friend of Truman Capote on whom the character of Dill in the book is based or that the book won the Pulitzer prize in 1960 or that an Academy Award-winning film was made from it—you might make predictions about the content of the book.

Book Cover. Most books have a picture on the cover. The writer may or may not have had a voice in what appears, so the illustration may not represent the writer's vision.

Copyright Page. The copyright page tells the dates of the book's publication. It can help you know whether the book is recent or older.

Other Books By. Sometimes there is a list that names other books by the same author. If you are familiar with any of these other works, you may have some idea of what is to come. This is also true if you have heard about the book from friends, read a book review, heard the book on audiotape, or seen a movie version. This is some of your prior knowledge about the book.

Table of Contents. Some books have unnamed divisions, but sometimes authors title their chapters. Lee divided the book into two parts, but the thirty-one chapters are untitled.

Inside Illustrations. Some books are illustrated throughout with drawings, paintings, photographs, and the like. This book is not.

Book Cover Blurbs. The notes on the back cover are advertising, meant to give away enough of the story to pique your interest and convince you to buy the book. The back blurb for the Warner edition of *To Kill a Mockingbird* carefully avoids giving away the story, unlike many other back cover blurbs, which (in my opinion) you should skip because they give away part of the plot and will interfere with your reading of the book.

Reviews. Some editions of the book have quotations from book reviews. Like the book cover blurbs, these can give away plot, and I suggest that you skip them.

Epigraph and Dedication. Not every book has either of these; this book has both. The epigraph is a quotation that relates to the theme of the book. The dedication offers the book as a gift to a person or persons whom the author wishes to honor. Harper Lee dedicated her book to family members—her father, a lawyer himself, and her sister.

Forward. Some editions of this book have a forward in which Harper Lee requested that the book not be given an introduction.

First Few Paragraphs. The first few paragraphs of the story provide the writer with the first opportunity to introduce the characters, plot, setting, and theme(s) of the story. Read carefully to learn as much as you can about the world of the book.

1. What is your reaction to the title of the book?

2. Based on the title, what do you think this book will be about?

3. Describe the jacket illustration. What can you gather from it?

4. How long has it been since this book was first published?

5. What, if anything, do you already know about Lee or *To Kill a Mockingbird*?

6. What literary award has the author won? What does that signify to you?

7. What meaning do you find in the epigraph?

Read to the break in the text (p. 5) after the sentence ending, "Atticus was related by blood or marriage to nearly every family in the town," and answer the following questions:

8. What do you think of Jem? of Simon? of Atticus?

9. The narrator's father is referred to by his first name. What do you make of this?

10. What is the narrator like? Can you trust the narrator's perceptions? How did you decide?

11. Where does the story take place? Is it a real setting or a setting created by the author? What special characteristics does the setting have?

12. What clues are there to the genre of this story?

13. What does the focus of the story seem to be?

14. What do you predict will happen next in the story?

15. What more do you want to know about the setting and the characters?

Strategy 2

Marking a Text

Marking up a text is a good way to make a book your own. You can respond to the author and characters, give yourself helpful reminders, collate information, and record your reactions to the unfolding of the plot. Here are some helpful hints on what you can do if you read with a pen or pencil that will add to your reading experience.

Book As Conversation

By definition, when you read a book, you're experiencing an author who has something to say. With pen in hand, you can speak back. Questions, comments, evaluations, and even arguments are fair game. Some comments you might want to use are:

- Yes/No
- !!!!! (as many as you need)
- TAT ("think about this")—for points that need pondering
- WM? ("what [does this] mean?")—for points that need clarification

Memory Aids

Are you reading for a class? You know that you will need to find things again. Underlining and marking marginal notes can help. Here are some ideas:

- Title untitled chapters with a name that will help you recall the contents.
- On the inside front cover or first page, make lists of items you need to find again: important quotations, appearance of symbols, page numbers of significant events.
- Invent a system of marginal notation to record the occurrence of repetition, symbols, connections, themes, and other important details such as key words or important quotations.

Links/Connections

As already indicated, noting places in which repetition ties one part of a book to another is important. But beyond that, sometimes a book will call up a link to another source—a reference or allusion will be known to you; a thought or quotation will connect to something someone else said or wrote in another book or medium. Write it in the margin. You may find the connection valuable later.

Writing a Paper?

When you're writing a paper, your marginal notes will be only part of what will be useful. Flags and self-stick removable notes can be really helpful. One thing you may wish to do is mark each page that begins a chapter with a numbered flag. This makes locating information much easier than thumbing through every time. You can also color-code your different topics to make your task easier.

1. If you own the book, use this opportunity to begin developing your own system of text marking. If you don't have the chance now, try it at the first opportunity you have.

Directions: Read the explanation; then begin work on the exercise. You will add to your answer as you continue to read.

Chapter 1

Vocabulary

assuaged: 3, eased
apothecary: 3, old-time pharmacist who prepared and sold medical drugs
piety: 3, devotion to religious duty
brethren: 3, members of a religious sect
thence: 4, from that place
strictures: 4, restrictions
dictum: 4, authoritative decree
chattels: 4, slaves; property
impotent: 4, helpless
taciturn: 4, silent; not inclined to talk
trot-lines: 4, long fishing lines attached to many, small, baited lines
spittoon: 4, receptacle for spit (as for those who chew tobacco)
unsullied: 4, new and in perfect condition
alleged: 5, accused but not proven
detention: 5, holding in custody
imprudent: 5, indiscreet; lacking in discretion
derived: 5, received; obtained
sweltering: 5, oppressively hot
ambled: 5, walked in a leisurely way
slat: 6, a wide, but thin strip of wood used in a bed frame to support a mattress
epic: 6, legendary; more than ordinary
entity: 6, being; creature
collard: 6, a smooth-leafed kale-like plant
revelation: 7, finding; discovery
eccentric: 8, odd or whimsical; out of the ordinary
quaint: 8, unusual in character or appearance; old-fashioned
repertoire: 8, list of pieces that can be performed
vapid: 8, lacking in liveliness; dull
jutted: 8, stuck out; projected
eaves: 8, the lower border of a roof that hangs over the outside wall
veranda: 8, roofed porch or balcony attached to the exterior of a building
malevolent: 8, vicious; evil
phantom: 8, ghost; apparition
morbid: 9, grisly; gruesome
nocturnal: 9, at nighttime
mutilated: 9, cut up; maimed; destroyed
culprit: 9, person guilty of a crime
eddy: 9, whirlpool
predilection: 9, preference
domiciled: 10, dwelling; living
flivver: 10, a small cheap automobile
beadle: 10, minor officer whose duties include keeping the peace
disorderly conduct: 10, less serious legal offenses including disturbing the peace and
    behaving inappropriately
disturbing the peace: 10, acting in defiance of law and order
assault and battery: 10, threat to use force on someone and carrying out the threat
abusive: 10, insulting or vulgar
profane: 10, irreverent; vulgar
scold: 11, (noun) one who is noisy and quarrelsome
asylum: 11, institution for the care of the insane
nebulous: 11, unclear
intimidation: 11, threats; bullying
cannas: 11, tropical plants with large leaves and irregular flowers
ramrod: 12, straight, metal rod for ramming home the charge in a muzzle loading gun
gouges: 14, digs
foray: 15, raid by an enemy

Journal and Discussion Topics

1. How old are Scout and Jem in Chapter 1?
2. When Scout says that Calpurnia's hand was "wide as a bed slat and twice as hard," what conclusion can you draw?
3. How does the first sentence describing Atticus's first case give a different impression than when you hear the rest of the story?
4. Describe Atticus's relation to Maycomb.
5. How did the sheriff make his decision about what to do with Boo? What were the results?
6. How and why were the Radleys set apart from the rest of Maycomb?
7. Begin a map to show Scout's neighborhood in Maycomb. Add to it as you get more information.
8. What distinguishing features do Scout, Jem, and Dill have, as revealed in this chapter?
9. What do you think it means to make "people into ghosts"? What ways do you think Atticus might have had in mind?
10. Do you think the children were imagining the movement in the Radleys' house? If so, how do you account for their thinking something moved? If not, what do you think caused the movement?
11. Why do you think Dill is so fascinated by the Radley place and Boo?

Summary

Scout, now an adult, introduces the story of the events leading up to the breaking of her older brother Jem's arm when he was thirteen. The argument between Scout and Jem over whether the Ewells started it or whether it began with trying to get Boo Radley to come out of his house, thrusts us into *medias res.*

Scout continues by placing the family in historical and social perspective with a brief history of her ancestor Simon Finch who established the family in Maycomb County. Then she tells about her father, Atticus, and his brother and sister and the beginning of her father's law practice.

Scout then turns to the town of Maycomb and describes the setting, and moves from there to her household at the time she was five and Jem was nine, when the story began. Calpurnia (the cook), Jem, Scout, and Atticus were the family she knew. Her mother had died of a heart attack when Scout was two.

With the sentence beginning, "When I was almost six and Jem was nearly ten," the narration shifts to a closer perspective and begins to focus on the children's immediate experience and activities at the time indicated. Dill (Charles Baker Harris) is discovered in his Aunt Rachel's yard next-door to the Finches' home, and becomes an instant friend. The three children act out stories together based on their favorite books, such as Tarzan and Tom Swift, until their repertoire is worn out by repeated productions. Then Dill has the idea of making Boo Radley come out.

Scout discloses, without distinction, the melange of truth and fiction that both adults and children of Maycomb believe about Boo. With the sentence, "My memory came alive to see . . . ," she begins recounting her own recollections. Then Dill dares Jem to go closer to the Radley house than the gate, and the rest of the chapter tells the events leading up to Jem's winning the bet, including an exchange between Dill and Jem about making a turtle come out of its shell. Accompanied by Dill and Scout to the gate, Jem runs up to the house and slaps it with his hand, and all three race back to the Finches' front porch. From there, they think they see a movement of one of the inside shutters.

Strategy 3

References and Allusions— Consulting Outside Sources

Directions: Read the explanation; then begin work on the exercise. You will add to your answer as you continue to read.

A **reference** is a mention of something outside the work you are currently reading. It could be a reference to a real or imaginary event, person, or place or to another literary work (often in a quotation), an aspect of culture, or a fact. References are often documented. Works of historical fiction (see Strategy 18: Historical Fiction/Autobiography, p. 90) characteristically are peppered with references.

An **allusion** is an *indirect* reference—one that you need to recognize as a reference without the author telling you that it is one. After you recognize the allusion, you need to figure out what it means in the context. Sometimes an author will include clues like quotation marks or introductory words (e.g., as the great philosopher once said...), or use a name. But sometimes, especially if recognizing and understanding it are not essential to the author's point or if the author assumes that virtually every reader will recognize the allusion, the author may not signal the allusion. The author may, instead, rely on readers sharing a common knowledge of literature, history, biography, science, and art that in most cases will help readers figure out meanings. Sometimes allusions can be like private jokes, inserted for those who can get them. Allusions help the reader see the work as part of a greater literary tradition.

An example of an allusion is "Maycomb County had recently been told that it had nothing to fear but fear itself" (p. 6). This is an allusion to a famous speech by Franklin Delano Roosevelt—his First Inaugural Address, delivered on March 4, 1933. If you recognize this phrase, taken directly from the speech, but given without quotation marks, it will serve as a stand-in for the entire text, which provides context for the action of the book and also give you an approximate date for the beginning of the book. Here is the first paragraph of Roosevelt's First Inaugural Address:

> I am certain that my fellow Americans expect that on my induction into the Presidency I will address them with a candor and a decision which the present situation of our Nation impels. This is preëminently the time to speak the truth, the whole truth, frankly and boldly. Nor need we shrink from honestly facing conditions in our country today. This great Nation will endure as it has endured, will revive and will prosper. So, first of all, let me assert my firm belief that the only thing we have to fear is fear itself—nameless, unreasoning, unjustified terror which paralyzes needed efforts to convert retreat into advance. In every dark hour of our national life, a leadership of frankness and vigor has met with that understanding and support of the people themselves which is essential to victory. I am convinced that you will again give that support to leadership in these critical days.

Many references and allusions support or reinforce the meaning in the text. But this is not their only possible purpose. References and allusions can provide contrasts as well as parallels.

Works of Literature Mentioned in *To Kill a Mockingbird*

If you want to understand Jem's, Scout's, and Dill's mindset, one thing you could do is read some of the books that they read and acted out.

Name	Book Title	Where Available?
Edgar Rice Burroughs	*Tarzan*	Bookstores/libraries
Oliver Optic (pseudonym for William Taylor Adams, author of 126 books and hundreds of stories)	*Hope & Have; Taken by the Enemy; Within the Enemy Lines; Stand by the Union*	Text of the books is available on-line at http://www.lostclassicsbooks.com/optic.htm
	Poor and Proud or *The Fortunes of Katy Redburn*	http://gutenberg.esoterica.pt/by-author/op1.html
Victor Appleton (pseudonym for Edward Stratemeyer and his daughter Harriet S. Adams)	Tom Swift books	Bookstores/libraries
	(Stratemeyer also authored the following series: The Rover Boys, The Bobbsey Twins, Nancy Drew, the Hardy Boys, the Dana Girls.)	The Rover Boys books are not currently in print. *The Rover Boys in Business* or *The Search for the Missing Bonds* is available online at http://www.blackmask.com/books21c/roverboy.htm
Seckatary Hawkins (pseudonym for Robert Schulkers)	*Stoner's Boy; The Gray Ghost*	Not currently available.
Sir Walter Scott	*Ivanhoe*	Bookstores/libraries
Daniel Defoe	*Robinson Crusoe*	Bookstores/libraries

Biblical References

There are several quotations from the Bible in *To Kill a Mockingbird*, for which you might need to use some outside sources. The following are sources that are good for you to get to know:

The Bible (available in many versions and many languages; the version may matter, depending on your purpose)

Cruden's Concordance of the Holy Scriptures (helps you locate passages in the Bible that have a particular word in them)

General Sources

Since this is a work of historical fiction (see Strategy 18: Historical Fiction/Autobiography, p. 90), you will find many references to real events, objects, brand names, and the like. Try *Britannica On-line* or *Encyclopædia Britannica* for general information about such topics. There are also at least two on-line web sites with pages specifically devoted to *To Kill a Mockingbird* references:

http://mockingbird.chebucto.org/references.html

http://www.lausd.k12.ca.us/Belmont_HS/tkm/allusions_all.html

If you look up *To Kill a Mockingbird* on one of the major search engines, you may find more sites with more information.

Note: Some sites were created by students and may have incomplete, misleading, or erroneous information. Be careful about your sources.

Criticism

Critics, in the course of their analysis, often pursue the references and/or allusions in a work. For example, Claudia Durst Johnson in *To Kill a Mockingbird: Threatening Boundaries* lists references (or at least parallels) that she has found to the Scottsboro Trial on pages 5–11. You might want to read some of the published criticism. If you read it before you read the work itself, it will likely spoil the ending and interfere with your ability to form your own judgments, so it is recommended that you not read criticism until you have finished the work. Look at the Bibliography your teacher supplies to get you started. Also check out

http://www.Amazon.com

http://www.barnesandnoble.com

for lists of criticism. Then check the bibliographies in the critical works you read.

1. As you read farther in the book, look for elements that resonate with Roosevelt's First Inaugural Address. Write a paragraph telling how recognizing this allusion adds to understanding in reading this book.

2. Keep a record of the research you do to understand other references and allusions you come across. You might want to use a chart like this:

Reference/Allusion	Source Where Located	Meaning/Definition/ Background Information

Strategy 4   Plot—The Design of a Story

There are exciting stories and dull stories. There are spy capers, mysteries, thrillers, jungle adventures, romances, horror stories, science fiction stories, and fantasies. There are stories with happy endings and stories with sad endings. These differences can make stories seem worlds apart. But there is a common set of characteristics that almost all stories have—whether they are long or short, for adults or young people—that make them stories.

Every story has a plot or sequence of actions, a setting or settings where the action takes place, a character or group of characters who take action, and a narrator who tells the story to the reader.

People who study literature have come up with several different ways of talking about plot. When people talk about stories with young children, they often refer to the beginning, the middle, and the end. This is not just a notion for little kids. These three parts are the way screenwriters and television writers arrange their scripts. Playwrights, on the other hand, traditionally worked with a five-act play. Each of the five acts represented an essential and sequential part of the play. Narrative is also sometimes presented in high school and college classes as having the following five-part structure:

1. **Exposition**—introduction of essential background information, as well as characters, situations, and conflicts. Exposition may be found throughout a story, as well as at the beginning.

2. **Complication**—the beginning of the central conflict in the story.

3. **Crisis**—(sometimes called the **turning point**) usually the point at which the main character's action or choice determines the outcome of the conflict. Also called climax—the high point of the action.

4. **Falling Action**—the time when all the pieces fall into place and the ending becomes inevitable.

5. **Resolution or Denouement**—the conflicts are resolved and the story is concluded.

So do we look at a story as having five parts or three parts? One way we can think about it is to see where the five parts fit into the beginning, middle, and end:

Beginning: Exposition
Middle: Complication, ends with the Crisis or Climax
End: Falling Action (the beginning of the end) and Resolution

Writers adapt the plot structure to a particular story. They decide how much exposition should be included and where, how many conflicts there are, what's told to the reader, and what is left for the reader to figure out. In *To Kill a Mockingbird*, you know from the beginning what the Crisis or Climax will be—it is the incident in which Jem's arm is so badly broken. But the implications and context of this incident are only revealed gradually, as the story unfolds.

In some stories, the conclusion is purposely not conclusive on one or more levels. This may be done for a variety of reasons, including to reflect reality, which seldom comes in neat, tidy packages.

1. As you read *To Kill a Mockingbird*, pause at the end of each chapter, and identify for yourself where it fits in the plot structure. Place it on a Freytag Pyramid of your own. The shape of your pyramid may not exactly match the model in the margin.

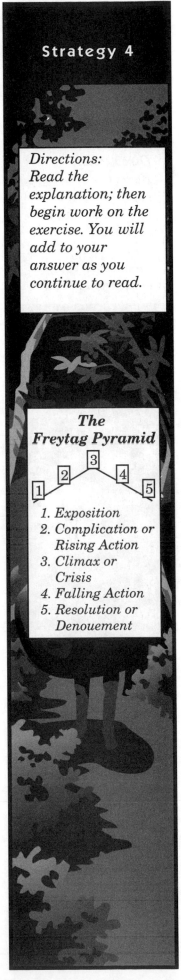

Directions: Read the explanation; then begin work on the exercise. You will add to your answer as you continue to read.

The Freytag Pyramid

1. Exposition
2. Complication or Rising Action
3. Climax or Crisis
4. Falling Action
5. Resolution or Denouement

Strategy 5 Forming Hypotheses

Directions: Read the explanation; then begin work on the exercises. You will add to your answer as you continue to read

Sometimes we make guesses about causes, results, and intentions. When we guess, we may rely on intuition or what we wish to be true more than anything else. A **hypothesis** is special in that it is an *educated* guess. Unlike a "regular" guess, it is a prediction based on evidence.

Some people associate the word *hypothesis* strictly with scientific investigation. But that is not the limit of its application. Readers are constantly making and testing hypotheses about story characters' reasons for acting and making choices, about what will happen next in the plot, about what is true in the world of the story, and about the author's intentions. Here are some criteria for a good hypothesis.

- **It should be of significance in the world of the story.** If we were reading a medical journal, which bone(s) in Jem's arm was/were broken would be of some significance, but it's not important here. The nature of the person called Boo Radley, on the other hand, is the subject of much speculation on the part of characters in the story and should hold some interest and focus for the reader. The stories about Boo are not descriptions that can be skipped over or ignored. It seems apparent that the author is carefully shaping the material to create suspense about the nature of this reclusive person.

- **It should be clearly stated and specific so that you can easily tell what it means, but it should reach beyond what you know for certain.** If you formed the hypothesis, *Maybe Boo Radley is important,* it would not do you any good. That Boo is significant in this story is something we have already established. A hypothesis is a statement about which you do not yet know the truth.

- **It should identify the motivation, result, or intention that you think you have identified.** For example, some of the description of Boo makes him sound like someone hideously evil and malicious. On the other hand, he is trapped in a house with and has the courage to attack the man whom reticent Calpurnia identifies as "the meanest man ever God blew breath into" (p. 12). Perhaps the man who was locked away in solitary confinement in a place that was likely to kill him and who has been made into a ghost as Atticus suggests (p. 11) has another side. Given the evidence, you might form the following hypothesis: *Maybe prejudice and bias prevent people from really seeing Boo Radley.* Once you form a hypothesis, you should look for further information to verify or disprove it.

1. Form a hypothesis about Boo Radley. Collect and record evidence from Chapter 1 that supports your hypothesis. Write your hypothesis and give the evidence that supports it. You may wish to arrange the evidence in the order of decreasing importance (most important point first) or increasing importance (most important point last). As you continue reading, after each chapter, add a paragraph to your paper with a revision of your hypothesis based on new information and insights.

Strategy 6   Rhetorical Figures

Directions: Read the explanation; then answer the question.

Rhetoric means either the art of persuasion or the techniques used by writers in their craft. It includes considerations of sentence structure such as **parallelism** (the repetition of grammatical structures), an example of which is shown in the description of life in Maycomb:

> There was no hurry, for there was nowhere to go, nothing to buy and no money to buy it with, nothing to see outside the boundaries of Maycomb County (p. 5).

Notice the repeated negative elements, separated by commas, to indicate the limitations of life during the Great Depression in Maycomb.

Rhetoric also includes the techniques called rhetorical figures or figures of speech. The rhetorical figures include the following:

- **Simile**—a comparison using words such as *like, as,* or *as if*: "Ladies . . . by nightfall were like soft teacakes with frostings of sweat and sweet talcum." (p. 5)
- **Metaphor**—a comparison in which two things, which are in fact different, are equated: "Mrs. Dubose was plain hell." (p. 6)
- **Personification**—attributing human characteristics to nonhuman (often inanimate) things. Sometimes the qualities of something living but not human are applied to something inanimate for a related effect: "Maycomb . . . was a tired old town" (p. 5) Sometimes its hard to tell if the attribution is personification or just animating the inanimate: "The courthouse sagged in the square" (p. 5)
- **Onomatopoeia**—the use of words that echo the meaning they represent: "shooed us between two rows of swishing collards" (p. 53)
- **Hyperbole**—overstatement: exaggeration for effect: "Jem gave a reasonable description of Boo: Boo was about six-and-a-half feet tall, judging from his tracks; he dined on raw squirrels and any cats he could catch, that's why his hands were bloodstained" (p. 13) Note that "reasonable" is ironic.
- **Understatement**—the opposite of hyperbole, this is actually a form of verbal irony when what is said is not what is meant (see Strategy 9: Irony, p. 42); understatement includes **euphemism**, the substitution of a neutral or inoffensive phrase for one that is strong or offensive: "disturbance between the North and the South" (p. 4) is a euphemism for the Civil War.
- **Alliteration**—the repetition, particularly of initial consonant sounds for effect and emphasis: *"flicked flies in the sweltering shade"* (p. 5)

Other rhetorical devices include **idioms**, expressions the meaning of which can't easily be figured out from the words themselves. "Simon made a pile" (p. 4) means that Simon made so much money it would have made a significant stack if piled up in one place.

1. Find one example each of parallelism, hyperbole, simile, personification, euphemism, and idiom in Chapter 1.

Chapter 2   Scout's First Day of School

Vocabulary

transaction: 15, deal
indigenous: 16, occurring naturally; native
seceded: 16, withdrew; became separate
catawba: 16, native American grape
literate: 17, able to read and write
wallowing: 17, luxuriating; delighting
illicitly: 17, unlawfully; against the rules
union suit: 17, an undergarment with shirt and pants in one piece
covey: 18, small flock; group; company
pronouncements: 18, authoritative announcements; formal declarations of opinion
impressionistic: 18, based on impression instead of fact
entailment: 20, restriction on how property can be inherited
vexations: 21, worries; troubles
mortgaged: 21, borrowed against and held as security until the loan is paid back
mortification: 21, embarrassment

Journal and Discussion Topics

1. What does Jem mean when he says "school's different"? What differences does Scout actually find?
2. What does Jem think of Miss Caroline? On what is his opinion based?
3. In what ways does Miss Caroline misjudge the first grade?
4. Why does Miss Caroline want Scout's home tuition in reading and writing to stop?
5. What is the Dewey Decimal System? What do you think Jem may have meant when he used the term?
6. What kind of student does Miss Caroline wish to discover in her classroom?
7. What information does Scout use to make her assessment of Miss Caroline?
8. What information does Scout use to understand Walter's behavior?
9. Summarize the effects of the Stock Market Crash on Maycomb.
10. Why does Miss Caroline bury her head in her arms when the class leaves?
11. What do you predict will happen when the class returns after lunch?

Summary

Looking forward to beginning school captures Scout's attention after the loss of Dill who returns home to Meridian. At Atticus's instigation, Scout is accompanied to school by Jem. Jem warns her that while things will be the same at home, at school they are to live separate lives. Scout already knows Miss Caroline, who boards at Miss Maudie's. When Miss Caroline identifies herself as being from Winston County, Scout immediately can place her because Winston County has a reputation.

Miss Caroline begins the day by reading the class a work of fiction obviously written for very young children with talking, personified cats. The class is uninterested, but Miss Caroline misses their reaction. She invited the class to identify the capital letters as "the alphabet," which they all can since, as Scout mentions, most of them are repeating first grade. After having Scout read the alphabet, the first grade primer, and the stock market report from the paper, Miss Caroline commands her to instruct her father not to read with her anymore since it will "interfere" with her reading. Scout attempts to explain how naturally reading came to her, but concludes that Miss Caroline thinks she is lying. Miss Caroline repeats her prohibition against Scout reading with Atticus, adding that she will try to "undo the damage." Reading suddenly takes on an importance to Scout because reading at home is forbidden. When Scout seeks comfort from Jem at recess, he explains that Miss Caroline is introducing the "Dewey Decimal System," a new way of teaching which, according to him, is more experiential.

After recess, Miss Caroline, without comment, holds up flashcards with words printed on them. Bored, Scout begins a handwritten letter to Dill. Miss Caroline discovers it and chastises Scout, saying that it is appropriate to print until third grade, the point at which one is *supposed* to learn handwriting. This, skill, we learn, is Calpurnia's "fault."

At time for lunch dismissal, Miss Caroline inspects the lunch pails of the students who do not go home. Walter Cunningham has no lunch. Unaware of the implications of Walter's not having a lunch, Miss Caroline presses him until he lies to her, saying he forgot it. She tries to lend him a quarter to buy lunch, but he refuses. Encouraged by the class, Scout tries to explain to Miss Caroline, telling her that Walter is "a Cunningham." While to the class, this is a complete and sufficient explanation, it means nothing to Miss Caroline. Scout wades in further and further, explaining as best she can that the Cunningham's land is entailed, and that they do not take charity and refuse any offer that they cannot pay back by barter. Frustrated with the situation, Miss Caroline takes out her anxiety on Scout by whipping her and sending her to stand in the corner, causing the class to burst out laughing. When Miss Caroline threatens the entire class, they break out again, and the sixth grade teacher comes in to quiet them.

The bell rings, and "Jean Louise" is let out of the corner, where she has stood in disgrace, to go home for lunch. As she leaves, she sees Miss Caroline bury her face on her arms, and remarks that she would have felt sorry for her, had Miss Caroline been kinder to her.

Strategy 7   Characterization

Directions: Read the explanation; then answer the questions.

A **character** in a story is someone or something whose actions, choices, thoughts, ideas, words, and influence are important in developing the plot. Characters are often people, but they also include other living creatures and sometimes even nonliving things. A force, such as good or evil, can operate as a character in a story.

Most stories have a single character or a small group of characters whose goal or problem is the core of the plot. This character or group of characters is called the **protagonist**. The protagonist does not have to be good, but a good protagonist may be referred to as the hero of the story. Readers usually identify with the protagonist and hope that the protagonist will succeed in attaining his or her goal. The character, group, or force that opposes the protagonist is called the **antagonist**. In certain stories, this character may be referred to as the villain.

Characters, whether human or not, have what we call personality—a set of characteristic traits and features by which we recognize them.

Characterization is the name for the techniques a writer uses to reveal the personality of characters to the reader. Characterization is achieved in a number of different ways:

- **Words**—comments by the narrator, dialogue by others about the character, as well as the character's own words; what is said, as well as how it is said—dialect, slang, tone—are important; what is *not* said can also be important
- **Thoughts**—what's going on in the character's mind, the character's motives and choices
- **Appearance**—the character's physical characteristics and clothing
- **Actions**—what the character does
- **Interactions**—how the character relates to others
- **Names**—often symbolic of a major character trait or role (see Strategy 14: Names and Characterizing Terms, p. 69)
- **Chosen Setting**—the items, furnishings, and the like with which the character chooses to surround him- or herself
- **Change/Development**—the occurrence of and direction of internal change or development a character undergoes

1. Think back to Chapter 1 and the focus there on the character of Boo Radley. In what ways could it be said that this is a book *about* characterization?

2. Analyze how the techniques mentioned here are used by people of Maycomb to interpret the character of each of the Radleys.

3. Atticus apparently allows his children to address him by his first name. What does this suggest about his character?

4. How does Jem interact with others?

5. How would you characterize Miss Caroline and her role in the story thus far?

6. What does the argument about the turtle reveal about Dill's and Jem's characters?

7. What methods have been used so far to build up a characterization of Atticus?

8. How is Miss Rachel characterized before we "meet" her?

Writer's Forum 1   Description

In a piece of descriptive writing, you let the readers know about the attributes of something so they can picture it in their mind's eye. You choose the features to mention based on what stands out among the physical properties and internal attributes of whatever you are describing, and these features will change depending on your topic. For example, if you were describing the Radleys' house, you might choose features such as "grounds" and "architecture." If, however, you were describing a character, Scout, for example, you would use different features: physical appearance, personality traits, actions, opinions, and habits.

Here are some questions you can use to help you formulate your description of a place or object:

- What is it?
- What are its attributes?
- How is it apprehended by the senses—how does it look, smell, taste, feel, sound?
- How does it relate to other things in its environment or context?
- How can it be described by the Five W's and How?

The way you organize the information in the description of a place or object can vary depending on what you are describing. Organization can help convey meaning. You can organize your description from

- top to bottom
- front to back
- side to side
- inside and outside
- around the perimeter
- from the beginning to the end of its cycle or process
- most important trait to least important (or vice versa)

When you are describing a person, you can use the elements that work together to create characterization:

- manner of verbal expression
- appearance
- interactions with others
- change/development
- thoughts, motives, choices, and feelings
- actions
- meaning of name, if important or symbolic

Source words that can help you express concepts of continuity and diversity in your description of a person, place, or thing include:

Continuity/Similarity

- also
- and
- as well as
- similarly
- besides
- furthermore
- likewise
- alike
- in addition
- too
- at the same time
- resemble

Diversity/Dissimilarity

- differ
- whereas
- however
- while
- but
- on the contrary
- conversely
- though
- on the other hand

1. Write a characterization of Dill. See how many of the techniques for characterization mentioned in Strategy 7: Characterization (p. 36) you can find and include.

Strategy 8

Plot—Conflict

Directions: Read the explanation; then answer the questions. You will need to read beyond this chapter to answer some questions.

Conflict is the core of a story's plot. Conflict is what makes us wonder if the protagonist will attain his or her goal. Conflict is what adds suspense and excitement to stories. Usually there is one overarching conflict that takes up much of a book. But each chapter or scene in the book usually also has conflict on a smaller scale.

The struggles that a protagonist undergoes in a story can be either internal or external. In an **internal conflict**, the protagonist undergoes an interior struggle. He or she might have conflicting desires, values, personality traits, and/or motives. People often have internal conflicts as they grow and develop from one stage in their lives to the next. An internal conflict takes place within the character's mind and heart.

In an **external conflict,** the protagonist struggles with something or someone outside of himself or herself. The conflict may be with another individual, with a task or problem, with society, with nature, with an idea, or with a force, such as good or evil.

1. Whom do you think of as the protagonist of this story? What leads you to this conclusion?

2. What does the overarching conflict in this story seem to be? Cite evidence to support your conclusion.

3. Make and fill in a chart like the following sample to show the main conflict for each chapter. Add to your chart as you continue to read.

Chapter No.	Conflict
1	
2	
3	
4	

Writer's Forum 2

Journal

In a journal entry, you record the important events of the day from your own point of view. Journals may also contain memories, linking the present to the past. They sometimes include hopes, dreams, or plans for the future.

Some parts of a journal might be rather objective—for example, straightforward descriptions of people, places, or occurrences. Other parts might be very personal and subjective. Journal writing is often informal—because people usually write journals for themselves, they don't always follow all the rules of grammar, punctuation, and usage. People may use words with private meanings, abbreviations, slang, and so on.

Journals are not necessarily all your own words. Some people choose to add quotations of others' words that they find helpful, interesting, or meaningful. Some people have a combination journal and scrapbook. Others draw in their journals. Since a journal is personal, it can take many forms.

1. Suppose that Scout spent part of her lunch time writing a journal entry about her first morning at school in order to deal with her frustration. Write an entry as the character of Scout. Include:

   • your expectations of what school would be like

   • what actually happened

   • your reactions

   • what you hope for now

   Feel free to embellish and elaborate the text, while staying "in character."

Chapter 3

**Walter Cunningham
and Burris Ewell**

Vocabulary

onslaught: 23, fierce attack

speculation: 23, meditating or pondering on something; reflection

dispensation: 23, giving out

irked: 23, annoyed; irritated

hain't: 23, slang for *haunt*; a ghost

pizened: 23, dialect for *poisoned*

Priss: 23, finicky; prim and precise; used as a derogatory name

expounding: 24, explaining in detail

erratic: 24, irregular; inconsistent

tranquility: 25, peace; a state of calmness

iniquities: 25, wicked acts; gross injustices

flinty: 25, stern; unyielding; hard

persevere: 25, to persist (in spite of obstacles)

furor: 26, flurry of activity; outburst of public excitement

wrought: 26, caused; created

verge: 27, border; edge

contemptuous: 27, expressing dislike or distaste; disdainful

truant: 27, child who fails to attend school as legally required by the state

contentious: 27, argumentative; likely to cause trouble; belligerent

diminutive: 27, small and short

slut: 28, prostitute—a person who accepts payment for sexual intercourse

dispersed: 28, sent out from a small group or clustering

fraught: 28, filled; supplied

fractious: 29, quarrelsome; irritable

amiable: 29, friendly; comfortable

judiciously: 31, wisely; discreetly; with sound judgment

misdemeanor: 31, crime less serious than a felony, carrying a punishment of a fine or local imprisonment

capital felony: 31, serious crime punishable by death

begrudges: 31, is displeased about allowing

compromise: 31, mutual agreement

concessions: 31, yieldings; sacrifices of something

disapprobation: 31, disapproval; condemnation

discernible: 32, apparent; understandable; detectable

aloft: 32, up

severed: 32, cut off

Journal and Discussion Topics

1. Why do you think Jem invited Walter to dinner?
2. What does it mean when Scout says, "By the time we reached our front steps Walter had forgotten he was a Cunningham"?
3. How do Scout's and Calpurnia's ideas of company differ?
4. What can you gather from Scout's approach to "fixing" Calpurnia by drowning herself?
5. Scout says Little Chuck Little was a gentleman. What does that term mean to you? What does it seem to mean to Scout?
6. What do you think Scout learned in her first day of school? What does Miss Caroline learn? What did you learn about Scout's schooling?
7. How is Atticus's response to how Scout should approach Miss Caroline similar to Dill's response to Jem about the turtle in Chapter 1?
8. Do you agree with Atticus that "Sometimes it's better to bend the law a little in special cases"? Under what principle could this be justified? Explain your response.

9. Atticus says that Miss Caroline learned "not to hand something to a Cunningham." He also says, "it's silly to force people like the Ewells into a new environment." We can presume that if Atticus says it, it's true. How can we know when it is useful to codify observations like this, and when doing so might lead to injustice through prejudice?

Summary

Scout catches Walter in the schoolyard and is in the process of beating him up, when Jem breaks up the fight. Listening to Scout's explanation, he responds to the situation by inviting Walter to come home to dinner. At first it seems as if Walter will refuse, but he finally follows along. Jem politely keeps the conversation going on the topic of Boo Radley.

When they reach the house, Scout and Jem are surprised to see that Atticus speaks to Walter as to an equal. Scout is also surprised to see Walter pour molasses over his entire plate of food, but when she comments, she is quickly summoned to the kitchen by Calpurnia who chastises her for her unseemly treatment of a guest.

Upon returning to school, Scout is recalled out of her reverie of dislike for Calpurnia by Miss Caroline's first view of a louse, spotted on the forehead of one Burris Ewell. Little Chuck Little helps her recover her composure, and, after amending her roll-book to include Burris's given name, she consults a reference and advises Burris how to get rid of the lice. Burris stands up, revealing himself to be the dirtiest human Scout had ever seen. He laughs in Miss Caroline's face and declares that he has only come to register his presence at the school on the first day, as he has for the past two years, and will not be returning. Miss Caroline tries to convince him to stay, making him angry, and Little Chuck Little intervenes, threatening Burris with his hand on his pocket. Burris leaves, but not before calling Miss Caroline a slut and reducing her to tears. The class rallies to her aid, even inviting her to read another story, and she obliges with the tale of a toadfrog.

At home, Scout is planning to run away: refraining from reading and writing is more than she can bear. Calpurnia is especially kind to Scout, which Scout takes as Calpurnia recognizing the error of her ways. But when Atticus invites her to read, Scout feels overwhelmed. She asks Atticus if she can get her schooling at home, as he did, but he refuses. He advises her that the way to understand another person is to "climb into his skin and walk around in it." He points out what she might have learned, had she tried this with Miss Caroline. Scout proposes Burris Ewell as a model and says that, like him, she'll just go the first day. But Atticus explains that the law is bent for the Ewells—in this and other areas—for a particular reason that doesn't apply to her. Scout thinks it's bad to allow some people to break the law, but Atticus points out the injustice that would result from a strict adherence to the law. He then proposes a compromise for Scout: she goes to school, but they continue to read—without Miss Caroline's knowledge.

Strategy 9

Irony

*Directions:
Read the
 explanation; then
begin work on the
exercise. You will
add to your
answer as you
continue to read.*

Irony comes from a Greek word meaning someone who hides under a false appearance. When irony is used, things appear to be different from, even the opposite of, what they really are: unexpected events happen; what people say is not what they mean. Authors use irony to create interest, surprise, or an understanding with their readers that the characters do not share. There are three types of irony.

Verbal irony is irony in the use of language. Verbal irony means that what is said is different from or the opposite of what is meant. A difference between tone of voice and the content of what is said is one kind of verbal irony. When Scout says, "Jem gave a reasonable description of Boo" (p. 13), and then we read Jem's description, it is revealed to be a fantastic conglomeration of horror movie characteristics and not a very likely description of the man. Understatement is another type of verbal irony, as mentioned in Strategy 6: Rhetorical Figures (p. 33). Calling the Civil War the "disturbance between the North and the South" (p. 4) is an example.

In **dramatic irony**, there is knowledge that the narrator makes available to the reader, but the characters are unaware of it. For example, readers understand that Dill is reluctant to speak about his father because of some personal problem, but Scout doesn't catch on to this (p. 8). In this story, Lee uses foreshadowing—hints in the text that suggests things to the readers without saying them directly—as one means of creating dramatic irony. You'll see an example in Chapter 4.

Situational irony can occur either from the point of view of a character or the reader. It describes a situation when something that is expected with a great deal of certainty doesn't happen (this can be from either the reader's or the character's point of view) or when something that is intended fails to materialize (this is only possible from a character's point of view, except in Choose-Your-Own Adventures or other books in which the reader participates by making a choice). For example, it is ironic that with all Scout's interest in learning, aptitude for reading and writing, and longing to go to school, she is chastised for her talent, made to promise that she will not try to advance her understanding, and is thoroughly bored.

1. Keep a record of other examples of irony in this story as you continue to read.

Strategy 10

Point of View

Directions: Read the explanation; then answer the questions.

A story is always told by someone. This person is called the narrator. The narrator may be someone who participates in the action of the story or someone outside the action of the story. The narrator may have a limited range of knowledge or may know everything there is to know about the story. The narrator may be reliable or unreliable. All these factors go into what is called the story's **point of view.**

Stories can be told in the **first-person point of view.** In this case, the narrator is usually someone who was present or involved in the action of the story, and this person tells the story using the pronoun *I* to indicate personal involvement.

Stories can also be told in the **second-person point of view,** which is distinguished by the fact that the narrator speaks to the reader as *you* and addresses the reader directly, as if they were speaking together.

The **third-person point of view** is that of a narrator who is separate from the action and tells it from a greater distance than a first-person narrator would.

A third-person narrator can be **omniscient**, knowing all the action of the story even including what is going on in all the character's minds and knowing what will happen in the end before it happens, or **limited** to knowledge of only the perspective of one character. When an author chooses a limited point of view, she or he is more likely to use devices like irony to allow readers to know more than the character from whose point of view the story is told.

This story has an additional twist: a first-person narrator tells the story, but Scout did not write the book as a five- to nine-year-old child, her age at the time of the action of the story, but as an adult. So the narration provides two levels of viewpoint—the view of Scout the child and the view of Scout the adult after years of rethinking and rehashing with Jem, and with the insight of an adult.

It is an essential point that the reader cannot assume that the narrator of a story is the author. Usually the narrator of a work of fiction is a persona created by the author for the purpose of conveying the story. Thus, when quoting from this book, we should not say or write, Lee says, "Mrs. DuBose was plain hell" (p. 6) (a) because the narrator, not Lee, says it and (b) because at this point the narrator seems to be recording her thoughts as a five year old, not the thoughts of the mature persona of narrator, let alone the thoughts of Lee.

1. When do you first have evidence that Scout, the narrator, is a girl?

2. Find three passages that show the narrator reporting her feelings as a five year old. Find one passage that shows her reporting her adult understanding.

3. Does the narrator report anyone else's inner thoughts and feelings besides her own?

Writer's Forum 3

Compare and Contrast Essay

Comparing and **contrasting** puts two or more subjects side by side in order to draw insights from their similarities and differences. In a compare and contrast essay, you show the similarities and differences between two people, things, ideas, approaches, or other subject, and draw some conclusion based on this examination. You choose the categories to compare and contrast based on your purpose, and these categories will change depending on your topic. For example, if you were comparing and contrasting Mr. Ewell and Mr. Cunningham, you might choose categories such as "responsibility to children," "economic status," and "relationship to society." If, however, you were contrasting Miss Caroline's teaching methods with Calpurnia's, you would use different categories, such as "techniques," "effectiveness," and "fairness." A Venn diagram or a chart can help you organize the information you will use. A Venn diagram shows visually what two or more subjects have in common and what characteristics they have independently that they do not share.

Here is an example:

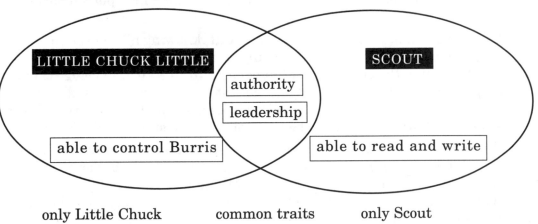

LITTLE CHUCK LITTLE

SCOUT

authority

leadership

able to control Burris

able to read and write

only Little Chuck   common traits   only Scout

Source words that can help you express concepts of similarity and difference include:

Similarity

- also
- and
- as well as
- similarly

- besides
- furthermore
- likewise
- alike

- in addition
- too
- at the same time
- resemble

Difference

- differ
- whereas
- however

- while
- but
- on the contrary

- conversely
- though
- on the other hand

1. Make a list of the categories you would use to compare and contrast your own town or city with Maycomb.

2. Write an essay comparing and contrasting Burris Ewell and Walter Cunningham.

Chapter 4

Gum in the Oak Tree

Vocabulary

auspicious: 32, favorable
legislature: 32, branch of government that makes laws
scuppernongs: 35, plum-flavored, yellowish green grapes
ethical: 35, having to do with what is good and bad and moral duty
arbitrated: 37, made a decision between disagreeing parties
I declare if I will: 38, slang for *I won't*
phenomena: 39, occurrences
Gothic: 39, mysterious and violent
evasion: 40, avoidance of a direct answer
quelling: 41, subduing; calming

Journal and Discussion Questions

1. How does the narration change from the end of Chapter 3 to the beginning of Chapter 4?
2. Recall the hypotheses you formed as the interaction of the children with the items in the tree unfolded. What explanations did you think made sense?
3. Describe Jem's and Scout's "ethical culture" in your own words. Is it the same as or different from what you believe? Explain.
4. Scout reports that Calpurnia, their Black cook, calls the legend about Hot Steams "nigger-talk." Assuming that Scout reported Calpurnia's words accurately, what do you think Calpurnia meant? Do you consider this to show racial bias? Why or why not?
5. What factors lead to the invention of the new drama, "Boo Radley"?
6. Why doesn't Scout want to play "Boo Radley"? Why do the boys think she doesn't want to play?
7. "One Man's Family" was a Sunday evening radio serial that began in April of 1932. The longest running serial drama in the history of American radio, it unfolded the story of the family of Henry Barbour until 1959. How does this information add to your understanding of what the children were doing?
8. Do you think Atticus knows what the children are doing? Explain.

Summary

From her adult perspective, Scout reflects on the ineffectiveness of the schooling she was exposed to. Returning to her five-year-old understanding, she recounts running by the Radleys' on the way home from school and being stopped by the sight of what turned out to be two pieces of gum in the knot-hole of a tree in front of the Radleys' house with only their silver inner wrapping still on. After thoroughly checking the gum, she chews it and does not die. Jem, upon coming home a half hour later when the older class is dismissed and hearing the story, makes her spit out the gum, utters dire predictions, and orders Scout to gargle.

On the last day of school, all classes are dismissed early, so Jem and Scout return home together. So they are both there to spot a tiny package left in the same knot-hole in which Scout found the gum. They take the package home and open it to discover two carefully shined Indian-head pennies. Together they consider whether they have inadvertently found someone's secret hiding place and decide to ask people when they get back to school. Jem points to how carefully polished they are, and the fact that they are not just regular pennies, but special, good-luck Indian-heads, and asserts that they must belong to someone.

But, knowing that chewing gum doesn't last, they can't figure out why someone would store it in a tree. And Jem seems to be spending a lot of time trying to figure out the mystery.

Two days later, Dill arrives, claiming to have seen a set of Siamese twins on the train. He also says he's seen his father, who is president of a railway, and asserts that he got to help the engineer on the train. Jem tells him to "hush."

The three children try to figure out what to play. Rover Boys are suggested and dismissed, and Jem doesn't feel like making up something out of his head. Dill claims to be able to smell when somebody's dying, and the subject of Hot Steams—souls who can't get to heaven and suck people's breath if they can catch them—comes up. Jem gives Dill a long explanation, which Scout dismisses with Calpurnia's judgment that it's all "nigger-talk." Scout doesn't realize how angry Jem is until they are playing at rolling in the tire (at her suggestion), and he gives her a particularly hard shove which lands the tire and Scout on the Radleys' front walk, inside their gate. Scout is dizzy and nauseous, so it takes her a moment to regain her equilibrium. Jem shouts to her to get up and come back quickly, and bring the tire. Scout gets up, stares at the house paralyzed, and when she can move, runs back to the boys without the tire. Jem berates her, she dares him, and Jem gets the tire himself. Scout comments cryptically, "There was more to it than he knew, but I decided not to tell him."

At that instant, Calpurnia calls them for their regular midmorning lemonade break, and as they are drinking, Jem invents the game of "Boo Radley." Scout is reluctant to play, but Dill accuses her of being scared, and Jem insists that Boo is probably dead. Reluctantly, Scout joins in the game, which grows and expands and becomes a play drawing upon all the gossip and legend they've heard from the townsfolk. Dill plays Mr. Radley, Jem plays Boo, and Scout plays various parts, including Mrs. Radley and the probate judge. The only dangerous parts of the play are stealing Calpurnia's scissors to enact Boo's stabbing of his father and escaping the neighbors' notice. Atticus, however, catches them one day with the scissors and asks them if their play has anything to do with the Radleys. Jem denies it. Scout thinks Atticus knows, but Jem says that if he did, he'd tell them straight out. This gives Scout a second reason to avoid playing this game, and now she reveals the first. The thing that paralyzed her in front of the Radleys was the sound of someone inside the house laughing.

Strategy 11

Setting and Mood

Setting refers to both the world in which the story takes place and the changing scenery that serves as the backdrop for each scene or chapter. Setting includes what the characters see, hear, smell, and can touch in their environment. Sights include:

- time of day
- season of the year
- plants and animals
- natural features

- weather
- landscape
- buildings or other structures

Directions: Read the explanation; then begin work on the exercise. You will add to your answer as you continue to read.

Settings can serve different functions in different stories and at different times in the same story. Setting may be a mere backdrop to the story, or it may have a more integral part. The setting may be symbolic and be a source of information about the inhabitants of the area. The setting may create conflicts for the characters of the story; help or hinder the characters in achieving their goal; provide materials or resources that help the characters solve problems; or create physical hardships or challenges that are difficult to overcome.

Although a novel like *To Kill a Mockingbird* is classified as a narrative—a type of writing that tells a story—sections of a novel that deal with the setting are usually passages of description. You may be aware of the shift back and forth from narrative to description as you read.

The setting of a story affects how we and the characters feel about their surroundings. This feeling is called **mood**. The setting can make things seem pleasant or create an air of foreboding that hints that something bad is about to happen. The description of the Radleys' house (p. 8) is a good example of creating mood. Notice that, except for the town of Maycomb and the Radley place, so far Lee has spent a lot more words on people and situations than on setting.

In historical fiction (see Strategy 18: Historical Fiction/Autobiography, p. 90), setting helps provide the background that evokes the time and place in history. All these aspects of setting give readers a "flavor" of the real time and place and add to the realistic "feel" of the book.

- **Physical setting** includes the region, location (city/town/etc.), climate, buildings, and so forth. *To Kill a Mockingbird* is set in the South, in Maycomb, Alabama. The climate and architecture is described initially in Chapter 1 (pp. 5–6).
- **Historical setting** is the date(s) (day, month, and year) in history and the occurrences and events that took place during that time. The reference to Roosevelt's inaugural address (p. 6), which was delivered on March 4, 1933, can lead us to infer that the story begins in the late spring of 1933.
- **Cultural setting** includes situations, events, and ideas that shape thought and behavior, as well as entertainment, religion, art, and other aspects of culture. The reference to "One Man's Family" is an example of the way Lee incorporates cultural setting.
- **Social setting** reveals the people (and peoples) who are there and how they treat each other. Maycomb is a community of two races: Black and white. The community has many different religious affiliations, all of them Protestant Christian.

As you notice the setting, try to figure out what the writer is trying to convey. Pay attention to the possibilities and problems created by the setting and to the mood the setting creates for you in order to take advantage of hints the writer is giving about what might happen next.

1. Extend the following chart to create a record of *To Kill a Mockingbird* settings and their function(s). Begin with Chapter 1.

Page No.	Setting Description	Function(s) in Story

Strategy 12

Foreshadowing and Flashback

Directions: Read the explanation; then answer the questions. You may need to read beyond this chapter to answer some questions.

Writers do not always tell plot events in chronological order. For one thing, they may hint at events before they occur or at information before it is revealed. This is called **foreshadowing**, and it lets readers know beforehand something about what is going to happen or what they're going to find out later. This technique helps create suspense and irony and keeps the reader involved in the unfolding plot.

Foreshadowing may come from a character, from the setting, or from the narrator. (In this book, it may be difficult, sometimes, to distinguish the narrator from the character of Scout.) In Chapter 4, for example, when the narrator says, "Until it happened I did not realize that Jem was offended by my contradicting him" (p. 37), we are warned that Jem is going to try to get even with Scout in some way.

Writers may also go back to material that happened prior to the beginning of the story or earlier in the plot sequence. This is called **flashback**. Flashbacks give the reader necessary background material to understand the story or reiterate important material. Flashbacks may come from the narrator or the characters. When the narrator reviews the history of the Radley family, saying "My memory came alive to see" (p. 11), this material is flashback.

1. Find another example of a character having a flashback. What information does it contain?

2. Find other instances of foreshadowing in Chapter 4.

3. As you continue reading, find as many examples as you can of foreshadowing and flashback. Are they from characters, the setting, or the narrator? Did you realize that the foreshadowings were hints of what was to come when you read them, or only later, in retrospect?

Chapter 5

Vocabulary

benign: 42, harmless

tacit: 42, unspoken; wordless

magisterial: 42, authoritative

Old Testament pestilence: 42, punishment sent by God, such as the plagues inflicted on the Egyptians to encourage them to free the Israelites

cordiality: 43, affection; friendship

benevolence: 43, generosity

communion: 44, a sacrament of Christian churches in which bread and wine are believed to represent, or to really be in their essence, the body and blood of Jesus

baptistry: 44, the particular beliefs of the sects of Baptists

raveling: 46, to undo weaving by pulling a thread

placidly: 46, calmly

scuttled: 47, scurried

clapper: 48, the part of the bell that strikes the side to produce a tone

inquisitive: 49, curious

barged: 49, entered in a rude way, without invitation

asinine: 49, done without exercise of good judgment

edification: 49, instruction and improvement (used ironically)

Journal and Discussion Topics

1. Since early Christianity, there has been a discussion of the difference between the "letter" of the law and the "spirit" of the law (it's in the New Testament in 2 Corinthians 3:6: "a new covenant, not of letter but of spirit; for the letter brings death, but the Spirit gives life"). Following the letter of the law is following literally the exact wording of the law. Following the spirit, is going beyond and behind the words, when applicable, to try to grasp the deeper reality that the words are based on, which may demand more than the words are able to convey. Apply this distinction to Jem's and Scout's dialogue after Atticus's arrival in Chapter 4 and to the first paragraph of Chapter 5.

2. What do you think Scout means by calling Miss Maudie a "chameleon lady" (p. 42)?

3. "Old Testament pestilence" refers to Chapters 7 through 11 of the Book of Exodus in the Hebrew Scriptures or Old Testament of the Christian Bible. Look this up and also find out about the Second Battle of Marne and explain what rhetorical figure Lee is using in discussing Miss Maudie's reaction to nut grass.

4. Why do you think seeing Miss Maudie's bridgework was what "cemented" her friendship with Scout?

5. According to Scout's understanding, Atticus thinks God is "loving folks like you love yourself" (p. 45). How do you think this works in practical realities?

6. What do you think Miss Maudie means by "The Bible in the hand of one man is worse than a whiskey bottle in the hand of . . ."? Explain in your own words.

7. Miss Maudie says of the legends about Boo Radley that Scout recounts to her, "That is three-fourths colored folks and one-fourth Stephanie Crawford." What does she mean? Do you consider it to show racial bias? Explain.

8. Scout compares and contrasts Miss Maudie and Stephanie Crawford. What criteria does Scout use for evaluating people?

9. What insight do you think Scout gains from speaking to Miss Maudie about "Mr. Arthur"?
10. Why does Dill want Boo to come out? Give as many reasons as you think are applicable.
11. How do you think Scout would have ended the sentence "Okay, okay, but I don't wanta watch. Jem, somebody was—" if Jem hadn't interrupted her (p. 47)?
12. Why do you think Jem doesn't take Scout's suggestion to use the front door (p. 48)?
13. Why do you think Lee chose not to put Atticus's lecture in direct address?
14. What was the lawyer's trick that Jem fell into?
15. What sense do you make of Jem waiting until Atticus could no longer hear him and then yelling after him?

Summary

On account of Scout's nagging, Jem finally agrees to stop the Boo Radley game temporarily, while continuing to insist that technically Atticus hadn't forbidden it and with a back-up plan to go ahead playing the game with the names changed if Atticus should ever explicitly forbid it. Dill agrees with Jem, and as the two boys grow closer, Scout turns to Miss Maudie for company.

Scout tells of Miss Maudie's double life, dressed in men's clothes in the garden during the day, and beautifully bedecked on her porch in the evening; her war on nut grass; her bridgework; her ability to bake cakes. She recounts the conversation about Mr. Arthur (Boo), during the course of which Scout considers Jack Finch, the different denominations of Baptists, the relative merits of Stephanie Crawford and Miss Maudie, and the difference between private and public lives, especially the fact that Atticus is the same in private as in public.

The following day, Dill and Jem concoct a plan to get a note to Boo inviting him to come out and have ice cream with them. Scout tries to dissuade them. Dill stands by the light-pole with a dinner-bell to ring in case someone comes, Scout stands guard on the sidewalk, and Jem tries to use a fishing pole to put the note on a window sill. Then Atticus comes. Reluctantly, Jem tells him what they were doing. Atticus tells them to stay away from the house and to stop the game they've been playing and not make fun of anyone. Jem, interrupting to deny that they were making fun of Boo, inadvertently admits that they were acting out his life. He realizes how he was tricked, and after Atticus is out of earshot, shouts that he wanted to be a lawyer, but now he isn't sure he does anymore.

Strategy 13 Dialogue

Directions: Read the explanation, then answer the questions.

Dialogue is the conversation that takes place in narrative. Even one person speaking is characteristically referred to as dialogue, even though dialogue usually means a conversation between or among two or more people. There are several important aspects to reading dialogue.

WHO IS SPEAKING?

Sometimes dialogue is attributed. Sometimes it isn't. In those cases, there are a few clues that can help you figure out who is speaking.

Two People

- **Alternating dialogue.** Dialogue goes back and forth, by nature. It is an exchange of ideas, views, thoughts, and the like. So every *other* line (1, 3, 5, 7, 9 or 2, 4, 6, 8, 10, if they were numbered) is spoken by the same character.

Three or More People

First, decide whether it's important to know who said what. When the students are comforting Miss Caroline after Burris Ewell leaves (p. 28), their dialogue is run together, and this is a sign from Lee that identifying the speaker of each phrase or sentence is not important in this case.

When knowing who is speaking *is* important, in addition to the alternating nature of dialogue, look for the following signs:

- **Vocatives.** A vocative is a word that shows who is being addressed in a sentence. When Atticus says, "Son," he means Jem. When Jem says, "Miss Priss," he means Scout. Almost always, the next person to speak after a sentence with a vocative is the person addressed. Sometimes, a vocative can help you identify the person who spoke in the preceding sentence if the sentence is an answer or a response to what came immediately before (don't look now, but you'll find an example when you get to p. 54).

- **Speech characteristics.** Just as people have certain habits of movement, they have certain habits of speech, characteristic expressions, and responses that can help you to recognize them, even when you have very little else to help you recognize who is talking. In this book, Lee is careful to provide enough clues that you don't need to rely on speech characteristics to figure out who is speaking.

DIALECT AND IDIOMS

Lee uses spelling and apostrophes to indicate the characters' pronunciations that differ from standard English. Sometimes you can figure out the words that are meant just by looking at them in context or saying them out loud. The on-line sites mentioned in Strategy 3: References and Allusion— Consulting Outside Sources (p. 29) are also useful for identifying instances of dialect. A number of idioms will be found in any standard collegiate dictionary. Try *Merriam Webster's Collegiate Dictionary, Tenth Edition,* or *The American Heritage Dictionary of the English Language.*

What Isn't Said

Sometimes one character interrupts another. And sometimes a character chooses not to complete a thought. Pay attention to the unsaid in dialogue. Try to imagine what the speaker had intended to say.

Language Shifts

People speak differently in different settings—they adapt their speech to the people and social context. Watch for the ways in which people vary and do not vary their language to meet the social situation.

1. Choose four passages with unattributed dialogue. For each one, explain what strategies you used to figure out who was speaking.

2. Choose five examples of dialect and idiomatic speech. Use sources to find the meaning. Use the chart below to record your research.

Dialect or Idiom	Source	Meaning

3. Give an example of a character adapting language to a given situation and audience.

4. Scout points out that Dill hasn't said anything about his father (p. 8). What do you gather from what Dill hasn't said?

Writer's Forum 4 Dialogue

Dialogue is a particularly powerful way to reveal a character's personality, thoughts, taste, and culture. The language that each character uses should reflect such important characteristics as age, education, and background. The level of formality the character uses should reflect his or her personality and approach to life as well as the social situation in which the speech takes place.

Dialogue can also reveal relationships. How two (or more) people speak to each other shows a lot about their feelings for each other. Do they give each other a turn to speak? What tones of voice do they use? Do they ask questions when they don't understand? Do they use polite phrases, slang phrases that they both know, more than one language?

In terms of text organization, dialogue can help to break up narrative passages, and can be more interesting than reported speech.

Punctuating dialogue shows which words are the exact words that the speaker said. Follow these rules:

- Put quotation marks around the words each speaker said.
- If the tag line that identifies the speaker comes before the quotation, put a comma after it, before the quotation marks.
- If the tag line follows the quotation, put a comma inside the final quotation mark if the quotation ends with a period. If the quotation ends with a question mark or exclamation mark, skip the comma.
- If you place the tag line in the middle of the quotation, place a comma before it inside the quotation marks and after it, before the quotation marks.
- Start a new paragraph each time there is a new speaker, or if a speaker speaking for a long time switches topics.

1. How does Atticus's speech differ from Scout's and Jem's? How about Calpurnia's speech?

2. Write a dialogue that you imagine might have occurred when Dill told Jem and Scout about going up in the mail plane, visiting Nova Scotia, or seeing an elephant. Pay attention both to each character's speech characteristics and to the dynamics between and among the participants.

Vocabulary

Look at each group of words. Tell why it is important in the story.

1. unknown entity, malevolent phantom, ghost_____

   _____

2. apothecary, piety, stinginess _____

   _____

3. revelation, cowlick, pocket Merlin, eccentric_____

   _____

4. truant, contentious, contemptuous, "slut"_____

   _____

5. chameleon, benign, magisterial, benevolence, cordiality, poundcake_____

   _____

   _____

Essay Topics

1. Look back at the predictions you made about the book for Strategy 1. Record what you think of your earlier predictions based on what you know now. Make new predictions for the rest of the book.

2. What's your favorite moment in the story so far? Explain your choice.

3. Which character do you think is the most interesting so far? Why?

4. If you were in the situation Atticus faces in this novel, what would your priorities be? Explain your thinking.

5. How do you think the relationships between and among Jem, Scout, and Dill will develop over time?

6. What do you think prevents Boo from coming out? Consider the suggestions made in the text.

7. Miss Maudie's praise of Atticus in Chapter 5 rests on a valuation of consistency or *integrity,* which literally means entire or undivided. From what you've read so far, give three examples of a character's behavior that shows a lack of integrity. Give three examples of behavior that demonstrates integrity.

8. Do you think Boo will come out in the course of the book? Explain what you think might happen.

Chapter 6

Jem Loses His Pants...
and Recovers Them

Vocabulary

ensuing: 51, following
prowess: 51, skill; ability
Kingdom coming: 51, the return of Christ heralding the end of the world
ramshackle: 52, on the verge of collapse; rickety
eerily: 52, weirdly; strangely
dismemberment: 55, having one's limbs torn off (used figuratively)
malignant: 55, aggressively malicious
waning: 56, decreasing
desolate: 57, gloomy

Journal and Discussion Topics

1. Despite her skepticism and fear, Scout joins Dill and Jem in their attempt to look through the Radleys' window. Why? Explain in detail.
2. Do you think that the sentence, "The back of the Radley house was less inviting than the front" was intended to be ironic? Explain why you think as you do.
3. What image from this chapter is clearest in your mind? Either explain in detail or draw a picture.
4. What does the clause "Jem fielded Dill's fly with his eyes shut" mean?
5. What does it mean to Jem that Atticus has never whipped him?
6. Explain how Jem and Scout parted company, as Scout sees it.
7. Remember Scout's phrase, "it was not time to worry yet." When you understand what its significance is, write your answer here.
8. What did you expect to happen to Jem when he said he was going back for his pants? For example, did you think Mr. Radley would shoot him?
9. Tell what you think happened to Jem when he got to the Radleys.

Summary

After receiving permission from Atticus to sit with Dill in Miss Rachel's yard, Jem and Scout go with him for a walk, even though Scout is suspicious that there is a plot being hatched. When the boys reveal that they have decided to have a look through the Radleys' window, Scout tries to talk them out of it and only agrees to go with when Jem accuses her of being "like a girl."

They go through the back garden and into the backyard, avoiding the large leaves of the collards that would make a loud swishing sound if brushed, and lubricating the rusty gate with spit so it won't creak. In the yard, trying to avoid the chicken droppings, they approach the house, and Dill is lifted to the window where he sees only curtains and a small light in the distance.

Deciding to explore further, Jem climbs the steps of the back porch to look in a window there, and the shadow of a man falls across first one, then another of the children. When the shadow moves around the side of the house, they flee, going straight through the collards, hitting the ground as a shotgun fires. Jem catches his pants in the fence and leaves them, and they run all the way home, by which time all the adults in the neighborhood are out in front of the Radleys' house listening to Nathan Radley's story of shooting at a nigger in his garden. The children join the group and are able to excuse their absence, but Stephanie Crawford notices Jem's lack of pants. Dill and Jem invent a cover story on the spot of a game of strip poker (played with matches, not cards), and Jem is sent by Atticus to retrieve his pants from Dill. Atticus calms Miss Rachel, as the children are leaving, so Dill does not have to ex-

pect trouble. But Jem needs to have pants by morning. Rising in the night from a sleepless bed, he whispers to Scout that he is going to the Radleys' to try to recover them. She tries to talk him out of it, threatens to wake Atticus, to come with him, anything to stop him. He insists on going and won't take her along. Scout sees a parting of the ways between herself and Jem in his insistence that he will risk his life (as they think) in order to avoid Atticus finding out, or in Jem's saying that they shouldn't have done what they did. At any rate, he goes out, and Scout waits, saying to herself a phrase that will turn out to be one of Atticus's most repeated lines in the book: "it was not time to worry yet." Finally, Jem reappears, silently holds up his pants, and goes to bed without a word.

Writer's Forum 5   Persuasion

Persuasive discourse attempts to change what the audience thinks, feels, believes, or values, or to move the audience to take action. In most persuasive discourse, the writer or speaker states a position and then provides evidence or reasons that attempt to convince the audience to embrace that position. Look back at the paragraph beginning, "Jem thought about it for three days" (p. 13) and following. This is an example of persuasion.

Writers and speakers use a variety of techniques to make their communications persuasive. Some of these techniques are logical and reasonable and accepted in our culture as examples of convincing argument. Other techniques that appeal to the audience's prejudices or to instincts that most people would consider base (like greed) may be used but are often seen as inappropriate. **Appealing to the audience's emotions** may or may not be considered acceptable depending on the context and exactly what you say, and must be used carefully. **Name calling,** which attacks an opponent's character, is never considered appropriate. Both techniques are known as arguments **ad hominem**—appeals to the emotions or feelings rather than to the intellect. **Threats** would also fall into this category.

Here are some examples of valid techniques for persuasion:

- **Follow the standards for discourse in your community.** Make sure that your approach is courteous and presented in an appropriate forum. Use the forms of address accepted in your community.
- **Tell the truth.** If you cannot find convincing evidence, consider changing your point of view.
- **Appeal to reason.** If something makes good sense, that in itself can be convincing. Telling your audience what benefits they would derive from following your advice can be helpful.
- **Appeal to authority.** Use this technique as a way to substantiate your claims. Make sure that the authority you cite is well respected. Usually when we talk about appealing to authority we mean a well-respected person or authoritative book. The authority of experience also carries a great deal of weight.
- **Appeal to a principle, belief, or ideal that you and your audience share.** Finding common ground is helpful in persuading others.
- **Use specific details.** This includes statistics and other numerical data. If you use numbers or other facts, verify them carefully. You have a responsibility to present accurate information.
- **Address the other person's point of view.** Ask yourself, have I ever been in a similar situation? How would I feel if...? If you feel that the other person has drawn an erroneous conclusion, carefully explain how you see the situation.
- **Make your point in several different ways.** This will help to ensure that you have communicated clearly and may help to reinforce your point.

Organization can be important in persuasion. Think carefully about the order in which you will present your evidence or arguments. Writers are often urged to put the most important reason first (or last), and then to organize the other reasons in descending (or ascending) order of importance.

Knowing your audience is particularly important in persuasion. Knowing how their views differ from yours will show you what points you need to address. If you can anticipate their counterarguments, you can forestall them by showing why they either don't apply or are not valid for some other reason.

1. In each of the following passages, analyze the elements of persuasion you find.
   a. " 'Please don't send me back, please sir' " (Scout to Atticus, p. 29).
   b. " 'Ain't no snot-nosed slut of a schoolteacher ever born c'n make me do nothin'!' "(Burris to Miss Caroline, p. 28).
   c. "How would we like it if Atticus barged in on us without knocking, when we were in our rooms at night?" (Scout's report of Atticus's words to her and Jem, p. 49).
   d. "I'm goin' after 'em," he said. . . . 'You do an' I'll wake up Atticus.' 'You do and I'll kill you' " (Jem and Scout, p. 56).
   e. " 'Come on home to dinner with us, Walter,' he said. 'We'd be glad to have you . . . Our daddy's a friend of your daddy's' " (Jem to Walter Cunningham, p. 23).
   f. "Mr. Bob Ewell, Burris's father, was permitted to hunt and trap out of season. 'Atticus, that's bad,' I said . . . 'It's against the law, all right,' said my father, 'and it's certainly bad... but he'll never change his ways. Are you going to take out your disapproval on his children?' " (Atticus and Scout, p. 31).
   g. " 'If I hear another sound from this room I'll burn up everybody in it' " (Miss Blount to the first grade, p. 22).
   h. " 'You weren't born reading the *Mobile Register*.' 'Jem says I was' " (Scout and Miss Caroline, p. 17).
   i. " 'Arthur Radley just stays in the house, that's all,' said Miss Maudie. 'Wouldn't you stay in the house if you didn't want to come out?' " (Miss Maudie to Scout, p. 44).
   j. " 'You never went to school and you do all right, so I'll just stay home too. You can teach me like Granddaddy taught you 'n' Uncle Jack' " (Scout to Atticus, p. 29).
   k. " 'We're askin' him real politely to come out sometimes, and tell us what he does in there—we said we wouldn't hurt him and we'd buy him an ice cream' " (Dill to Scout about persuasion directed at Boo Radley, p. 47).

2. In the persona of the character suggested, write one of the following pieces of persuasion as you imagine the character might speak it under the circumstances.
   a. Atticus convincing Miss Rachel not to punish Dill for playing "strip poker."
   b. Jem attempting to convince Scout to mail a letter to Boo at the post office.
   c. Scout trying to persuade Miss Caroline to let her read Tom Swift in school while the other students are working on the First Grade Reader.
   d. The truant lady trying to convince the Ewells to go to school.

Chapter 7

Soap Figures; Thank You; Filling the Knot-hole

Vocabulary

perpetual: 59, lasting forever
embalming: 59, treatment of a dead body in order to preserve it
hoo-dooing: 59, dialect for *voodoo*; Scout is referring to the practice of attempting to change reality by making images and doing things to the images
tarnished: 60, dulled by exposure to air
ascertaining: 61, checking
cleaved: 61, stuck firmly
palate: 61, roof of the mouth
rendered: 61, caused to become; made
vigil: 62, period of watchfulness
meditative: 62, thoughtful

Journal and Discussion Topics

1. How does Scout respond to Jem's silence?
2. Why does the recovery of his pants worry Jem?
3. Whom do you think fixed Jem's pants? What motivation do you think was involved? What evidence points to your conclusions?
4. What does Atticus mean when he says of Jem's recounting of Egyptian history "delete the adjectives" and Scout would then have the facts?
5. Whom do you think is placing items in the tree? Do you think they were intended for Jem and Scout? What evidence supports your conclusions?
6. What do you think Jem is considering telling Atticus but decides not to tell yet?
7. What do you think was Mr. Radley's motivation for filling up the knot-hole?
8. Why does Jem cry?

Summary

School starts, but still Jem has not told Scout what happened when he went back for his pants. Scout finds second grade worse than first. She still is not allowed to read and write. Finally, after a week, Jem speaks. He tells Scout that he left his pants twisted in the fence, but when he went back they were mended where he'd torn them, folded, and hung on the fence for him to find. Jem is spooked by somebody knowing what he was going to do (return for his pants in the night). Scout comforts him that only those who are close to him can really know him, and not even they can know everything. As they are speaking, they pass "their" tree and discover a ball of gray twine in the knot-hole. They try again to figure out why somebody is leaving things there, conclude that it must be a hiding place, and leave the twine. But when it is still there on the third day, they take it, and from then on they consider items left there to belong to them.

Items begin to show up more often. In October, they find two soap carvings of a boy and girl whom they recognize as themselves. Shortly thereafter, they find a whole pack of chewing gum; the next week, a tarnished medal from a local spelling bee appears; and four days later they find a broken watch on a chain with a knife attached, which Atticus says would be worth $10 if new. Jem does not put this last item in his trunk, but tries to fix it to use. Now the children evolve the idea of writing a thank-you note to the gift giver who, after a little argument, they agree is a man, as yet unnamed. Jem seems to be on the verge of telling Scout and/or Atticus something, but he doesn't. The next day, on the way to school, they find that the knot-hole has been filled in with cement. That day and the next, Jem waits on the porch after dinner for Mr. Radley to pass by. When he does, Jem asks him about the tree, and Mr. Radley says it's dying. Without preface, Jem asks Atticus if the tree is dying, and Atticus tells him that the tree is as healthy as he (Jem) is. But when Jem tells him that Mr. Nathan Radley said it was dying, Atticus backs off, saying the Mr. Radley must be trusted for more intimate knowledge of his own tree than they have. Scout follows Atticus into the house, but Jem stays out on the porch until nightfall. When he comes in, Scout sees that he has been crying.

Writer's Forum 6 Thank-you Note

A **thank-you note** is a piece of writing that can range from very informal to extremely formal. It might be as simple as "Thanks for the lift on Wednesday!" followed by initials. In general, the more significant the gift or deed or assistance for which you're thanking someone, the longer, more serious, and more formal your thank-you will be.

Personal thank-you's are generally printed or handwritten, partly because they're often informal, and partly because they're personal. Typing is used for more formal thanks, or for thank-you's within the context of a business relationship. Like Jem's and Scout's note to Boo, most of your thank-you's at this time in your life will probably be in the form of personal letters.

Personal letters are informal. They differ from business letters in the following ways:

- They include only the date, not the return address in the **heading**.
- They do not include an **inside address**.
- The **salutation** ends with a comma, rather than a colon.
- Each paragraph of the **body** is indented, not put in block form.
- The **closing** is friendly and personal and followed by a comma.
- They are usually handwritten rather than typed.

_____	Date
____,	Salutation followed by comma
_____	Body with indented paragraphs
____,	Closing followed by comma
	Handwritten signature

Words often used to express thanks include:

- thank you (very much)
- appreciate
- gratitude
- your kindness
- your thoughtfulness
- pleased

1. Write the letter you imagine Scout and Jem were trying to get to Boo. Include the elements Scout mentions, and any others you think are appropriate. Remember to stay in character.

Chapter 8

Snow and Fire

Vocabulary

unfathomable: 63, not possible to comprehend
aberrations: 63, deviations from the norm
touchous: 64, slang for *touchy*; irritable
bade: 64, ordered
accosted: 65, challenged
meteorological: 65, science of weather and weather forecasting
perpetrated: 67, committed
libel: 67, defamation of character; harming someone's reputation using writing or
representation so that the injured person is identifiable and a third party knows of it.
Libel must be intentionally malicious.
caricatures: 67, comic imitations; exaggerated distortions
morphodite: 68, Scout's misunderstanding of Miss Maudie's word, *hermaphrodite*, which
refers to a person with both male and female sexual characteristics; Miss Maudie
perceives that the snowman is a cross between a man (Mr. Avery) in shape and a woman
(herself) in accessories.
tousled: 68, rumpled
squaw-fashion: 71, thought to imitate Native American women
perplexity: 73, confusion; bewilderment

Journal and Discussion Topics

1. How do you interpret the phrase "to our disappointment," which Scout uses to describe hers and Jem's reactions on hearing that Mrs. Radley died of natural causes?
2. Why is Eula May important in Maycomb?
3. Scout says she "reflected that if this was our reward, there was something to say for sin." What does she mean?
4. Why did Jem place the worms aside?
5. Why does "a stick of stovewood" complete the picture of Mr. Avery?
6. How do Jem's goals for the snowman differ from Atticus's goals?
7. When Atticus says, "See which way the wind's blowing?" what conclusion does Jem draw?
8. What does Jem's phrase "it ain't time to worry yet" echo?
9. How is Mr. Avery's girth important in this chapter?
10. How does Jem show his trust of Atticus in this chapter?
11. Explain the exchange between Jem and Atticus after Atticus sends Jem for the wrapping paper. Why does Scout think that Atticus didn't understand what Jem said? Do you think Atticus understood? Explain.
12. How would you describe Miss Maudie's state of mind the morning after the fire?
13. What two alternatives does Jem suggest to Miss Maudie to keep her from getting her hands dirty with yardwork? What conclusions can you draw?
14. What did Miss Maudie find so funny that she "whooped"?

Summary

Winter comes, and Mrs. Radley dies. Jem and Scout figure that Boo killed her and are disappointed to learn that she died of natural causes. Jem expresses a suspicion that Atticus knows that they were not playing strip poker with Dill that summer night, but it's only a suspicion.

The following day, Scout thinks the world is ending when she looks out her window and sees snow for the first time. It is the first snow since 1885. Atticus reassures her, and when school is cancelled, Jem and Scout set out to make a

snowman. Jem has the ingenious idea of making a foundation of mud and applying the scanty snow like veneer to create the outside layer. As he builds, it becomes evident that he is making Mr. Avery. Upon coming home for lunch, Atticus, after a few moments, sees the resemblance and insists that Jem alter the image so that it won't be offensive. Jem responds by borrowing Miss Maudie's sun hat and hedge clippers, leading to Miss Maudie's remark (misunderstood by Scout) that the snowman is a hermaphrodite.

That night, Atticus wakens his children, bundles them up, and sends them down to stand by the Radleys' house: Miss Maudie's house, directly across the street from the Finches', is on fire. Many men and three fire trucks come out to help. They remove what they can from Maudie's house and try to protect the neighbors' homes. Jem and Scout watch, agonizing over Mr. Avery who gets stuck in Maudie's upstairs window, and wondering if their own house is safe. Finally, the fire is quelled by the tin roof, and the house caves in. The fire is quenched.

At home, Atticus makes cocoa for the children, but Scout notices him looking at her, first in curiosity and then with disapproval. He reminds the children that he told them to stay put, and they assure him that they did not move from in front of the Radleys' house, but they cannot tell where the blanket around Scout's shoulders came from. Jem blurts out that Mr. Nathan was at the fire, and Atticus tells Jem to go get wrapping paper so they can return it, but Jem realizes the implications and blurts out to Atticus the whole story of the knot-hole and his pants. Atticus, understanding Jem's implications, agrees that they will not return the blanket and suggests that someday, perhaps, they will be able to thank him. Scout thinks that Atticus doesn't understand what Jem said, and she doesn't understand what Atticus says, for she asks him, "Thank who?" Atticus explains to her that it was Boo who put the blanket around her.

Atticus permits them to sleep in, reasoning that they would not benefit from going to school without sleep. When they rise, they clean the front yard, and go to Miss Maudie's to return her hat and clippers. They are surprised to find her cheerful and looking forward to a smaller house and a larger and more beautiful garden. She shows them her hands, dirty from yardwork, and Jem tells her that she should hire a colored man or that he and Scout would help her. But Miss Maudie points out that they have their own work to do in their yard. Scout says they can clean up the "morphodite" in a jiffy, and after mouthing the word to herself, Miss Maudie realizes that this is Scout's interpretation of "hermaphrodite," and bursts into laughter. Neither Jem nor Scout understand why she is laughing.

Writer's Forum 7

A **parody** imitates something in an exaggerated way to create humor or to mock the original or its author. Jem means the "morphodite" to be a portrait—a faithful and acceptable rendering of Mr. Avery. But because of the medium and, perhaps, the skill of the artist, Atticus thinks that Mr. Avery might not find it flattering. And so it is considered a caricature—as we call a parody of a person rendered in two or three dimensions.

A parody focuses on the stylistic peculiarities and propensities of the original, and calls attention to them, often by overuse. When the original work is pompous, offensive, overly serious or sentimental, makes much of something trivial, or is just plain obtuse, parody can function as criticism as well as humor.

It is important that a parody be similar enough to the original that the audience can recognize what is being parodied. A parody of a poem, for example, might imitate the original meter and some of the wording, but change the subject. Or it might keep the subject and treat it humorously. Sometimes parodies focus on a single piece of writing, and sometimes they make fun of the whole body of an artist's work. Song parodies are easy to recognize because they use the original melody.

1. Write a parody of a poem or song that you find problematic or bothersome in some way. See if your classmates can guess the work you based your parody on.

Chapter 9 — Atticus Accepts the Robinson Case; Scout Fights Francis

Vocabulary

defended: 74, represented the defendant in a court of law

gastric: 75, stomach

ringworm: 75, contagious fungal disease

still: 75, equipment for distilling alcohol

come to trial: 75, be scheduled for a hearing by a judge and jury

postponement: 75, delay granted in hearing a court case

licked: 76, beaten

inordinately: 76, in a way that exceeds reason

lineaments: 77, features

induce: 77, persuade

ingenuous: 77, innocent; childlike

diversions: 77, pastimes; games

changelings: 77, infants secretly exchanged for others by fairies

analogous: 77, comparable

hookah: 78, water pipe

relativity: 78, state of one thing being dependent on another

cussing: 78, dialect for *cursing*; swearing

innate: 78, inherent; natural

provocation: 79, purposeful stirring up; incitement

inevitable: 79, unavoidable

bluff: 79, cliff; high steep bank

jetty: 79, a landing wharf

bales: 79, large bundles (of cotton, hay, etc.)

guilelessness: 80, innocence (used ironically)

trousseau: 80, the complete wardrobe that a bride assembles for her marriage

gravitated: 80, moved toward

fanatical: 81, excessively enthusiastic

deportment: 81, behavior, particularly manners

mishaps: 81, unfortunate accidents

ambrosia: 82, dessert made of oranges and shredded coconut

constituted: 82, made up; were part of

runt: 82, unusually small

subdued: 84, conquered; brought under control

crooned: 84, said in a quiet murmuring manner

impaired: 84, damaged; injured

tarried: 84, lingered; waited

obstreperous: 85, unruly and aggressive noisiness

romped on: 87, raged at

tenterhooks: 87, sharp hooked nails; the expression "on tenterhooks" means in a state of suspense or uneasiness

invective: 87, insulting or abusive language

evidence: 88, material or testimony legally submitted to a tribunal and accepted as part of a court's inquiry into the truth of some matter

jury: 88, group of people summoned and held under oath to decide on the facts at issue in a trial

Journal and Discussion Topics

1. What does Scout mean by "a rather thin time for Jem and me" (p. 74)?
2. Atticus says that Scout is "far too old and too big for such childish things" as fighting. How old is Scout? What conclusions can you draw about Atticus's views on fighting?
3. Explain the odd spelling in the line, "Do all lawyers defend n-Negroes, Atticus?" (p. 75)?
4. What do you think of the court case Atticus is involved in? What predictions do you have?

5. Atticus says, "this time . . . we're fighting our friends." What do you think he means? If you fight people, how can they still be your friends?
6. What foreshadowing do you find in this chapter?
7. What do you think Scout meant when she said Uncle Jack "never behaved like a doctor"?
8. Uncle Jack's story about Rose Aylmer is the second instance of a story about someone eating a finger. Compare and contrast the stories.
9. What's ironic about Scout asking Uncle Jack to pass the "damn ham, please"?
10. Uncle Jack suggests that Scout wants to grow up to be a lady, and she says she doesn't. What do you think each means by the word *lady*?
11. Scout lied by saying to Francis that she thought his presents were nice. Was this a good thing to do? Explain.
12. What do you make of the particular circumstances under which Atticus spoke sharply? What does this reveal about him?
13. What do you think of Atticus's explanation of Aunt Alexandra's behavior—that she didn't understand girls much because she'd never had one?
14. What is Scout thinking when she says she is "reflecting on relativity" (p. 85)?
15. "Let this cup pass from me" is a quotation from the New Testament. Jesus says these words in his prayer in the Garden of Gethsemane, the night before his Crucifixion. He continues, "nevertheless, let it be as you, not I, would have it" (Matthew 26:39). Why do you think Uncle Jack quotes these words?
16. Why did Atticus want Scout to overhear his conversation with Uncle Jack?
17. How do Cecil Jacobs and Francis use the word *nigger* differently than Calpurnia uses it?

Summary

The chapter opens with Scout in the midst of a fight with Cecil Jacobs who has called Atticus a "nigger-lover." Scout asks Atticus about the accusation, and he gives her minimal information about an upcoming court case: He is defending a Negro named Tom Robinson. Calpurnia knows him from church. Some people in town think Atticus shouldn't defend Tom. The judge has given them a postponement. Atticus explains to Scout that if he didn't defend Tom, he would lose his integrity, and warns her that she will hear more ugly talk, but asks her not to fight, no matter what. Scout asks if they will win the case. Atticus says no, and it will be harder than other cases because their opponents are friends this time. Remembering this conversation, Scout walks away from a fight for the first time. Then, the narrator tells us (foreshadowing a fight from which Scout does not hold back), "Christmas came and disaster struck."

Christmas brought Scout together with Uncle Jack, Atticus's brother, as well as his sister Alexandra and her family: Uncle Jimmy, who has only spoken to Scout once in her life to tell her to get off a fence, and their grandson, Francis, who is a year older than Scout. Uncle Jack is the most tolerable doctor Scout knows—respectful toward his patients, honest about how much something will hurt, and able to catch her off guard with humor in an approach to medicine that he calls "relativity."

As Atticus, Jem, and Scout meet Jack at the train station on Christmas Eve, we discover that Scout has begun cursing earlier in the week, and Atticus advises ignoring her. But when she curses again at dinner, Jack intervenes and says he doesn't want to hear cursing while he's visiting for the week unless there's "extreme provocation."

Christmas morning, Jem and Scout discover that Atticus has had Jack bring them air rifles. Jack, says Atticus, will also have to be the one to teach them to shoot. They are warned not to misstep, or their rifles will be confiscated. Atticus insists that they set out for Finch's Landing and Alexandra's house. In describing the house, the narrator reveals more about Simon Finch, notably, his distrust of his daughters, the staircase to whose bedroom began in their parents' bedroom, so that their comings and goings were always known.

The initial conversation between Scout and Francis shows Scout on her best behavior, telling a social lie to smooth the conversation, and Francis, provoking Scout by disparaging Jem's chemistry set for no reason. The narrator reflects on talking to Francis and on Alexandra and her criticisms of Scout's attire and behavior. Atticus tells Scout pretty much to ignore Alexandra's criticisms. But Alexandra seems to take out her displeasure on Scout by having her sit apart from the rest of them at dinner, as if at seven she cannot behave well enough to sit at the adult table as eight-year-old Francis does.

Dinner is wonderful, and afterward Scout and Francis discuss cooking, which leads to consideration of Dill and marriage for Scout. Francis says disparaging things about Dill, some of which are probably true. But he excuses Scout for her ignorance because, he says, it's obviously due to Atticus's poor parenting. On that subject he adds that Atticus is a nigger-lover and is shaming the family so that they won't be able to walk openly in Maycomb. Scout is too angry to follow Atticus's request not to fight, and though she has to chase Francis several times, and gets a warning from Alexandra, she finally catches him and splits her knuckles on his teeth. She is going in again when Uncle Jack catches her. Jack tells her that he warned her and that she's in trouble. Atticus won't comfort her, but says it's time to leave, and Scout goes without saying goodbye. At home she goes to her room, ignoring Jem's attempt to be nice.

Jack comes to her door, and her first response is to send him away. When he says she'll be in trouble again if she speaks that way, she allows him in, but turns her back on him. He doesn't understand why she's holding a grudge against him. When he finally gives her a chance, she explains that he never got her side of the story, that she was "provocated" by Francis. Jack not only agrees but is ready to go back out to Finch's Landing on the spot to make sure Francis doesn't get away with his criticisms of Atticus. But Scout begs him not to on account of her promise to Atticus—she doesn't want Atticus to know that she was fighting to defend him. Jack agrees to silence, and peace is restored between them as he bandages her hand. But when she asks him to explain the term she called Francis (a "whore-lady"), he talks about something else.

Later, Jack and Atticus talk, and Scout happens to overhear as she is getting a drink of water. Jack expresses his remorse at his treatment of Scout, but without telling why, much to her relief. Jack also tells about avoiding Scout's question, and Atticus tells him to always answer a child's questions. He reveals that he's not as worried about Scout's bad language as her ability to keep her head because of what's coming up in their lives. Atticus has never "laid a hand on" Scout, but gives her credit for trying, even when she doesn't succeed completely. Jack asks how bad things will get, and Atticus explains the fundamental problem in winning the case: Tom, a Black man, will have to pit his word against the Ewells, who are white. It is a foregone conclusion that the jury will side with the white man. Jack asks what he will do. Atticus says that he will jar the jury a bit, and that he thinks there is a chance when the case is appealed, but that he has this case because it was given him. Jack quotes Jesus' words in the Garden of Gethsemane, "Let this cup pass from me." Atticus says that Jack knows what will happen and that he hopes he can get Scout and Jem through it, and that they trust him rather than what they hear in town. Here he interrupts himself to call to Scout and tell her to go to bed. She doesn't understand how he knew she was listening. The adult narrator says that it wasn't until much later that she realized that he wanted her to overhear.

Strategy 14

Names and Characterizing Terms

Directions:
Read the explanation; then answer the questions. You may need to read beyond this chapter to answer some questions.

Character names (and place names) can be symbolic or descriptive. Names can also have a meaning based on the literal meaning of the word in the original language from which the name comes or connected to a real person who had that name.

Nicknames, like Jem, Scout, and Dill, are more widely used than pet names. Jem and Scout are called by their nicknames outside of their home.

Pet names are very personal terms of affection that are used only by those in very close relationships. *Honey* and *Dear* are common in some parts of our country. Pet names may also include such dubious terms of affection as "Little Three-Eyes," which Jem calls Scout (p. 55).

Pejorative terms belittle or disparage someone or something. Substituting a pejorative term for someone's name is a particular form of verbal abuse. Jem calling Scout "Miss Priss," is an example. Jem also uses *girl* as a pejorative word. *Nigger* is used as a pejorative term also.

1. The best way to see if this sort of meaning applies is to test a few names and see if the connections add meaning. As you continue reading, note evidence that supports or undercuts a symbolic interpretation of the following names:

   - **Atticus**—"Attica" refers to the Greek city-state of Athens; strongly identified with Solon (known as "the wise"), the lawgiver who reformed the government in 594 B.C. with his law code known for its humaneness. Particular attention is focused on this name because Jem and Scout use it, instead of *Father, Daddy,* and the like.
   - **Calpurnia**—This was the name of Julius Caesar's wife, who warned him not to go to the Senate on the day of his assassination, showing that she is trustworthy and has foresight.
   - **Scout**—A scout is a dependable, forward-looking person who may guide others.
   - **Jean Louise**—Both names are feminine versions of masculine names, *Jean* of *John* and *Louise* of *Louis*. These two names could be related to Scout's closer ties to the world of boys than that of girls. *Louise* has a meaning similar to *Scout*: protector of the people.
   - **Ewell**—According to the *Oxford English Dictionary, ewelle* is an old spelling of the word *evil*.
   - **Finch**—A finch is a songbird, like the mockingbird of the title.
   - **Alexandra**—This name is a feminine form of *Alexander*, which means defender of men and connects to Alexander the Great who conquered much of the known world in Eurasia in his time.
   - **Arthur**—This name means strong as a bear; noble; exalted.

2. How are femininity, being a girl, and being a lady characterized in the book? Follow the use of the words *girl* and *lady* in the book. What do you think of how the feminine is portrayed?

3. Keep track of other pejorative terms that are used in the rest of the book.

Chapter 10

Mad Dog

Vocabulary

rudiments: 90, basics; fundamentals
mausoleum: 90, large tomb
Jew's Harp: 91, a small musical instrument held between the teeth and struck with a finger
breastworks: 91, temporary fortifications
foliage: 95, leaves, flowers, and/or branches
alist: 95, leaning to one side
vehemently: 95, with forceful energy; impassioned
articulate: 97, able to speak; able to express himself
jubilantly: 99, joyfully

Journal and Discussion Topics

1. Which of Atticus's skills does Miss Maudie hold up for Scout's admiration? What qualities do you discern from them? Why don't Scout and Jem find these skills worthy of honor?
2. The title of the book suggests that any statement about mockingbirds in the book deserves particular attention. Extrapolating from what Atticus says about it being a sin *to kill a mockingbird*, make a generalization about what you think is Atticus's principle for determining what is sinful.
3. What is the significance of the fact that it's February?
4. Why does Jem say it doesn't make a difference that Calpurnia violated the rule that Blacks are supposed to use the back door of the house when she goes to warn the Radleys?
5. Why is Tim Johnson's behavior so frightening to Scout?
6. What is the significance of what happens to Atticus's glasses?
7. Explain the meaning of Miss Maudie's pronouncement that "People in their right minds never take pride in their talents." Do you agree or not? Why?
8. In what ways do Jem and Scout misjudge Atticus? What do you think leads to their misapprehensions?
9. What has Jem found to admire in Atticus by the end of the chapter?
10. What does this chapter reveal about the Maycomb community?
11. Why do you think Atticus didn't teach Jem and Scout to shoot, since he obviously could have?

Summary

Scout gives her and Jem's review of Atticus and the many areas in which they find him lacking. He is and does nothing that gives them bragging rights. He wouldn't teach them to shoot, merely instructing them not to shoot mockingbirds because they do no harm and only sing for people's enjoyment. It is the only thing that Scout has ever heard Atticus refer to as sin. Miss Maudie goes on to list Atticus's skills: making an airtight will, playing checkers, playing a Jew's Harp.

Scout goes home when the builders come to put up Miss Maudie's new home, and constructs a bulwark from behind which she can aim at a likely target, Miss Maudie's rear end. Catching her in action when he comes home, Atticus warns her never to point her gun at anyone again. Scout then consults Calpurnia who says that Atticus can do many things, but she is unconvincing because she can't give even one as an example. Jem and Scout are further embarrassed at the Baptist-Methodist football game, when Cecil Jacob's father

scores often for the Baptists, and Atticus doesn't even play for the Methodists, but stands on the sidelines.

One Saturday, Jem and Scout go out hunting south of the Radleys' property, and Jem spots Tim Johnson, a liver-colored dog, acting funny. Jem insists that they go home, and nags Calpurnia until she comes out to look and confirms what he suspected—that despite all conventional wisdom (that mad dogs come out in August, that they foam at the mouth, that they are rabid and vicious), this quiet, moseying dog in February is mad and dangerous. Calpurnia quickly calls Atticus, has the operator, Eula May call Miss Stephanie and Miss Rachel and everyone else on the street, and herself runs down to warn the Radleys, going to the front door, despite the demand of social custom that as a Black woman going to a white family's house, she use the back door. Jem says, "Don't make any difference now."

Atticus arrives home with Heck Tate, the sheriff. They spot Tim Johnson, confirm that he's mad, and quietly debate their course of action. Heck prepares to shoot the dog, but at the last moment, Heck defers to Atticus and insists that he take the shot. Despite his bad eye, Atticus finally accepts the gun and, breaking his glasses in the process, fires one shot that kills it. Jem is paralyzed and amazed. Miss Maudie says that she forgot to tell them that Atticus used to be called "One-Shot Finch." The children can't understand why Atticus never said anything about his ability and doesn't use a gun. Miss Maudie suggests that he gave up shooting because he felt it gave him an unfair advantage over other creatures. Scout protests that he should be proud of it, but Miss Maudie responds that "People in their right minds never take pride in their talents." Scout wants to tell everyone at school, but Jem dissuades her. He realizes that there is something to the fact that Atticus never told them of his ability. He suddenly has great pride in his father and says he no longer cares about measurable accomplishments because he understands that his father is a man of character: " 'Atticus is a gentleman, just like me!' "

Strategy 15

*Directions:
Read the
explanation;
then answer the
questions. You
may need to read
beyond this
chapter to answer
some questions.*

We often speak of **character traits** as absolutes—that is, characters either have them or not. So we might describe a character as shy and reclusive. This is useful for a start. But even a character that we recognize as shy and reclusive in general can be more or less retiring and act more or less timidly, depending on the situation. Considering the variations in character traits can be the first step in taking a more realistic view of the complex thing we call character. We can consider character traits as existing on a continuum, a scale with opposite traits at the ends and a whole range of possible points in between. For example:

daredevil _____ courageous

Think about Jem. He is presented initially as a boy who is able to overcome his fear to win a dare or do something exciting, and we might call him bold or adventurous or a daredevil. But when he goes back to the Radleys' alone at night to get his pants in order to preserve his relationship with his father, he exhibits a different, more substantial, and deeper quality that we might call courage. You can see that Jem's traits are responsive to circumstances. It may be, given his age, that Jem is on the way to developing the mental and moral virtue that we call courage out of the daredevilry of a young boy who likes a thrill.

1. For each continuum, collect information as you read so that when you are done reading you can write a paragraph telling how the character(s) indicated move(s) along it during the course of the book.

   daredevil _____ courageous
   (Jem)

   insensitive _____ compassionate
   (Scout/Dill)

   shy _____ intrepid
   (Boo)

   obtuse _____ discerning
   (Atticus/Scout)

2. Choose a single character and write a full-page description of his or her character traits. Explain how his or her behavior varies along each continuum that you identify. Use the information you have acquired so far, and add to your description as you finish the book.

Chapter 11

Mrs. Dubose

Vocabulary

passé: 99, outmoded
CSA: 99, abbreviation for Confederate States of America
apoplectic: 100, with symptoms similar to those of a stroke
livid: 100, discolored (with anger); enraged
bedecked: 100, decorated
obscurely: 101, mysteriously
arbor: 101, latticework covered with climbing vines
camisole: 101, a short sleeveless undershirt for girls
lawing: 101, slang for *practicing law*
philippic: 102, speech of condemnation
degeneration: 102, decline; deterioration
umbrage: 102, offense
mental hygiene: 102, sanity
acquisition: 102, purchase
rectitude: 102, trying to be correct in judgment and behavior; righteousness
guff: 102, nonsense
tranquil: 102, calm
disposition: 102, temperament
interdict: 102, prohibition
skulked: 103, hid out of fear or cowardice
palliation: 103, something that eases or makes better
reconnaissance: 105, survey
'druthers: 105, dialect from contraction of *would rather*; free choices
ear syringe: 106, a device to remove fluid from the ear
tirade: 106, lecture, often marked by harsh language
undulate: 107, to move in waves
viscous: 107, thick, semi-liquid
propensities: 108, leanings; inclinations
infuriated: 108, angered
devoid: 110, empty; without
escapade: 111, adventurous act that breaks some convention or rule
cantankerous: 111, irritating
beholden: 112, obligated; indebted

Journal and Discussion Topics

1. What do you think is wrong with Mrs. Dubose?
2. Why do Jem and Scout hate Mrs. Dubose?
3. What makes Scout think Atticus was the bravest man who ever lived? In what sense is this ironic?
4. What is objectionable in what Mrs. Dubose says to Jem and Scout? Do you think Atticus is showing good sense in his treatment of her and in demanding that his children behave toward her as he suggests?
5. What's the significance of Jem telling Scout "just hold your head high and be a gentleman"?
6. Why do the biscuit and butter taste "like cotton"?
7. Do you agree with Atticus that people are entitled to respect for their opinions, even when they're racist and biased and nasty? Explain.
8. Atticus says, "The one thing that doesn't abide by majority rule is a person's conscience." What does he mean?
9. Were you surprised that Scout went to Mrs. Dubose's house with Jem? Why or why not?
10. Do you agree with Atticus that name-calling doesn't hurt a person? Explain.

11. What's the difference between what Jem means when he says "well," in response to hearing that Mrs. Dubose is dead, and what Atticus means when he repeats, "well"?
12. What do you think Atticus's definition of "lady" is now?
13. Compare and contrast the courage of Atticus in Chapter 10 and Mrs. Dubose in Chapter 11.
14. How is this chapter parallel to Chapter 9?

Summary

As they grow older and the center of town holds more interest for them, Scout's and Jem's activities move from the south of their house where the Radleys live to the north. And there, between the Finches' house and town, lay the house of Mrs. Dubose, a woman whom Jem and Scout hate. She finds fault with their speech, Atticus's parenting, and Scout's clothes; makes false accusations; and threatens them with dire punishments.

And then one day when the children are going to town so that Jem can buy himself a steam engine and Scout a baton, Mrs. Dubose says, "Your father's no better than the niggers and trash he works for," and follows this by comments on the family's mental health. They continue to town, purchase the items, and return. As they reach the Dubose property, Jem takes the baton, runs through Mrs. Dubose's yard decapitating her camellias, and breaks the baton over his knee. Then he pulls Scout's hair and kicks her.

They do not meet Atticus coming home, and when he comes in with a camellia and asks Jem if he is responsible, Jem admits his guilt and, in answer to Atticus, explains that he did it because of remarks about Atticus. Atticus responds that what Jem did to a sick old lady is inexcusable and sends him to Mrs. Dubose to have a talk. Scout is afraid that Mrs. Dubose will shoot Jem, since she is known for keeping a Confederate pistol, but Atticus assures her that Jem is safe, using the phrase we have heard from both Scout and Jem: "It's not time to worry yet." He explains that in the summer there will be even more provocation, but that he couldn't pray to God if he didn't defend Tom Robinson. Scout thinks Atticus must be wrong since so many people think he is, but he says that a person's conscience is not run by majority rule.

Jem returns, saying that he apologized even though he wasn't sorry and that Mrs. Dubose wants him to read to her two hours, six days a week for a month. Atticus replies that there's no point in saying something that isn't true, and that he will indeed have to read to her. Scout accompanies Jem to read, and she notices that after a short time of berating Jem and correcting his reading of *Ivanhoe,* Mrs. Dubose goes "away from" them. Then her alarm clock rings, and Jessie, her Black cook, sends the children home.

Scout asks Atticus what "nigger-lover" means, and he says it is a meaningless term like "snot-nose," used by people who are afraid that Blacks are being favored above themselves. Questioned further, he says that he is a "nigger-lover," since he tries to love everyone. He tells Scout that it's never an insult to be called a name, since it simply reveals the poverty of the person who uses it.

Unnoticed by Scout, Mrs. Dubose has been staying lucid for longer and longer periods while Jem reads. Jem's reading period is extended an additional week by Atticus despite his protests, after Mrs. Dubose says, "Only a week longer, I think . . . just to make sure." Finally she dismisses Jem, warning him that the next time he attacks her flowers, he should pull them up by the roots. A short time later, Atticus is called out one night and returns to tell the children that Mrs. Dubose is dead. He explains that she was a morphine addict who had become addicted accidentally after using it as a pain-killer, and that the reading sessions were a technique to help her break the habit before she died. Atticus says that a person as ill as Mrs. Dubose would be justified in taking anything to make it easier, but she held herself to a higher standard. Jem asks if she "died free," and Atticus is able to confirm that she did. Then he gives Jem a candy box with a perfect camellia that Mrs. Dubose sent to him. At first Jem is livid, but sheltered in Atticus's arms, he is told by Atticus that Mrs. Dubose was trying to tell him that everything's all right. He adds, "You know, she was a great lady," and Jem cannot understand how Atticus can call her a "lady." But Atticus insists she was. He explains that he did not want the children to think, from his shooting of the mad dog, that courage was to be found in a man with a gun. Courage, says Atticus, is to take on a battle that is lost before its begun, and to see it through to the end, and occasionally, you do win. Mrs. Dubose did, according to Atticus. Scout goes to bed, leaving Atticus reading the paper and Jem fingering the camellia.

Writer's Forum 8   Definition

A **definition** is a complete, succinct explication of a concept, term, or idea. A definition attempts to get at the essential nature of the thing being defined, either by direct statement or by showing the thing in a revealing context. A good definition is clear, exact, and complete. It is helpful in letting people know if they are really talking about the same thing.

Definitions answer the following questions, as appropriate:

- What is the name of the thing being defined? How are you going to consistently refer to it?
- What categories or groups can it be placed in? or What kind of thing is it?
- What are its essential attributes?
- How does it work?
- How did/does it originate or arise?
- What does it do/accomplish?
- What are its functions?
- What are examples of it?
- What are some things that might be mistaken for it, but are not really it, and how can they be distinguished from the real thing?
- What is its value or usefulness?

Some words that you might incorporate include:

- for example
- e.g.
- specifically
- for instance
- as
- such as
- like
- consists of

1. Write a definition of courage as you understand it now. When you are close to the end of the book, you will re-evaluate your definition and have the opportunity to revise it, incorporating any new understandings you have gained from finishing *To Kill a Mockingbird*.

Vocabulary

Look at each group of words. Tell why it is important in the story.

1. cussing, provocation, obstreperous, romped on _____

_____

2. perpetrated, libel, caricatures, morphodite _____

_____

3. apoplectic, livid, philippic, moral degeneration, mental hygiene, cantankerous_____

_____

Essay Topics

1. Is it important to do the right thing even when you're sure it won't lead to justice? If you agree with Atticus, expand on his arguments. If you disagree, offer a rebuttal.

2. In Chapter 8, Scout thinks the snow is hot, but Jem explains that it is actually so cold that it feels as if it's burning. Explain why it does or does not make sense to interpret this symbolically.

3. Why is it ironic that Atticus sends Jem and Scout to the Radley place during the fire?

4. Part of growing up is learning how to be courteous in all kinds of situations. Scout commits some social blunders in the novel. Identify five examples and tell what she might have done instead.

5. According to Francis, Alexandra said that since Atticus has become a "nigger-lover we'll never be able to walk the streets of Maycomb agin" (p. 83). Compare and contrast this with what Atticus says about the trial in the beginning of Chapter 9.

6. Think about the placement of Chapter 10 in the book. Why do you think Lee waited so long to reveal something about Atticus of which his children could be proud?

7. How does Chapter 11 provide a culmination for the important ideas (themes) presented in the ten chapters that preceded it?

8. Now whom do you think is the protagonist in this book? Explain your view.

9. If you were writing this story, what would happen next? Explain how you would develop the plot.

Part Two
Chapter 12 Calpurnia's Church

Vocabulary

altercation: 115, noisy dispute

boded well: 115, foretold good things ahead

diligently: 116, earnestly and steadily

frivolous: 116, not serious

Shadrach: 117, one of the three men who were placed in a fiery furnace by King Nebuchadnezzar and survived because of their faith in God—from Daniel 3 in the Hebrew Scriptures or Christian Old Testament

castile: 117, a hard soap made of olive oil, originally from Castile, Spain

habiliments: 117, clothes

Mardi-Gras: 118, "Fat Tuesday" from the French: a yearly Christian celebration, often with feasting and parades, before the forty days of fasting called Lent begin on the following day—Ash Wednesday; now often secularized

First Purchase African M. E. Church: 118, M. E. stands for Methodist Episcopal

asafoetida: 118, a yellow-brown bitter resin from plant roots

Brown's Mule: 118, a brand of chewing tobacco

unceiled: 120, having no ceiling

rotogravure: 120, a print made from an engraved plate using photographic methods

ecclesiastical: 120, having to do with the church

impedimenta: 120, equipment

dispelled: 120, driven away

garish: 120, gaudy; tastelessly showy

Garden of Gethsemane: 120, the site where Jesus was praying when he was identified by Judas and taken away to be crucified

ethics: 120, morals

qualms: 120, concerns; scruples

artillery: 121, mounted firearms, such as cannons

Deity's: 121, God's

denunciation: 122, condemnation

austere: 122, morally strict

bootleggers: 122, illegal producers of alcohol

voile: 123, a sheer fabric used for dress-making

tedious: 124, lengthy

Blackstone's _Commentaries_: 125, important book on British law

enarmored or enamored: 126, covered with armor (here used figuratively); _enamored_ seems to be a misprint, appearing in only certain editions

Journal and Discussion Topics

1. What is the significance of Calpurnia referring to Jem as "Mister Jem"?
2. What suddenly makes being a girl attractive to Scout?
3. What conclusions did you draw about Scout from the sentence "I stayed miserable for two days" (p. 116)?
4. Explain the figure of speech: "scrape a few barnacles off the ship of state" (p. 116).
5. Who was Shadrach (p. 117)? What's the connection with Eunice Ann?
6. Were you surprised that Calpurnia refers to Jem and Scout as "my children" (p. 118)? Explain.
7. Why is it ironic that Jem is "color-blind" (p. 118)?
8. Why does Calpurnia change her language when speaking to different groups? Look back at her explanation of speaking two different ways. Describe two situations in your life in which you speak differently and the changes you make in your use of language to fit each situation.
9. Summarize the role of the church in Cal's community.
10. The word used to describe Aunt Alexandra as she sits on the porch is "enarmored" in the edition we are using for our main resource, but "enamored" in the hard cover. What do you think is meant?

Summary

Jem, now twelve, suddenly exhibits mysterious changes, which Atticus and Calpurnia interpret for Scout as being related to growing up. Dill is absent, and Atticus is away at an emergency session of the state legislature, when Calpurnia decides to take Scout and Jem to church with her, so they won't get into trouble by themselves.

After careful preparation, Calpurnia takes them to First Purchase, and they are greeted respectfully, except by Lula. The rest of the congregation drives Lula away, and they are given seats of honor in the front pew. Reverend Sykes introduces the service, and Zeebo, Calpurnia's son and the local garbage man, leads the lining of the hymn in his role as music superintendent. After the intercessory prayers, Reverend Sykes gives a homily and takes up a collection for Helen Robinson. When he doesn't receive the ten dollars he hopes for, he admonishes his congregation until the amount is donated. As Calpurnia guides Jem and Scout out, Reverend Sykes says, "This church has no better friend than your daddy," revealing the reason behind their treatment.

Scout innocently asks the Reverend about the collection for Helen, and in the conversation that ensues, it is revealed that people are reluctant to hire her because of the nature of the crime of which Tom is accused. When Scout learns that the Ewells made the accusation against Tom, she considers what Atticus has said about them and her own knowledge, concludes that they are the parties likely to be in the wrong, and assumes that others who know about the Ewells will draw the same conclusion. She asks Calpurnia what rape is and is directed to consult Atticus.

Jem asks about the method of singing the hymn and suggests that they save money for hymnbooks, but Calpurnia explains that it would be useless since Cal is one of only four members of the congregation who read. A discussion of how Cal taught Zeebo, her oldest son, to read, leads Jem to consider the differences in Calpurnia's language in the Finches' home and at church. The question is posed in terms of the language of white's being "right." Calpurnia, without using the term, explains the notion of "social registers": of adapting one's language to the social situation one is in, considering such factors as level of formality and intimacy, occasion, and the like. Scout, whose interest in Cal's other life is apparently piqued by this conversation, asks if she can visit Calpurnia at home, to which Calpurnia quickly agrees. It is only later when Aunt Alexandria prohibits Scout from visiting Calpurnia that the irony of the juxtaposition of this conversation with the appearance of Aunt Alexandra on the Finches' porch as if she owned it becomes clear.

Strategy 16

Prior Knowledge

*Directions:
Read the
explanation;
then answer the
questions.*

Prior knowledge is the information and understandings you have before you read and bring to bear as you interpret. Authors make assumptions about readers' prior knowledge. They guess what will be familiar and not require explanation. They estimate how much each unfamiliar topic needs to be explained, knowing that, as you read, the parts of the book that you have finished also become prior knowledge that you apply to reading the latter portions of the book. So now, in addition to everything you knew before you began, the information in Part One of this book has become your prior knowledge for Part Two.

In *To Kill a Mockingbird*, prior knowledge is a subject of the book itself. What, if anything, is actually known about Boo Radley, is a subject dealt with early on. The question of prior knowledge continues to be relevant to the plot as the trial of Tom Robinson unfolds. In Chapter 12, we learned that Tom is accused of raping a Ewell. Scout's prior knowledge about the Ewells—her own experience and Atticus's comments—leads her to certain conclusions about how Helen would be treated that we may judge to be unrealistic. We know that there is prejudice in Maycomb, and that it will play a role in peoples' decisions.

The trial will bring together the jury, with their prior knowledge and views and perhaps prejudices, and the facts presented as evidence in court. Even though jurors are supposed to leave their preconceptions behind, this does not always happen. We will see whether they can judge the evidence on its merits.

1. How does Scout's and Jem's prior knowledge about Calpurnia affect their view of her behavior at her church?

2. How does Scout's prior knowledge about church services affect her interpretation of the service at Calpurnia's church?

3. How does Miss Caroline treat Scout's prior knowledge of reading?

4. What prior knowledge do you have about the trial from Part One and Chapter 12?

Chapter 13

Vocabulary

Lord's Day: 128, Sunday, the Christian Sabbath on which the resurrection of Jesus from the dead is celebrated every week

corset: 128, close-fitting undergarment for women, often made of bone

formidable: 128, awe-inspiring

in the affirmative: 128, with a "yes"

Amanuensis: 129, secretary

prerogative: 129, special rights or privileges

hereditary: 129, inherited; passed on genetically

incestuous: 130, sexual relations between persons so closely related that they are prohibited from marrying by law and moral code

obliquely: 130, indirectly

myopic: 130, near-sighted

caste system: 131, division of society based on wealth, social class, and occupation

dicta: 131, plural of *dictum*; observations intended to be treated as authoritative

discreet: 131, quietly secretive

mandrake roots: 132, herb resembling the human body and thought to have magical powers

warily: 132, cautiously

inflection: 133, tone that gives personal quality to the voice

Journal and Discussion Topics

1. What first impression did Aunt Alexandra create for you in this chapter?
2. If Scout *had* said, "Cal's a girl," what do you think Aunt Alexandra would have replied?
3. What do you think of what Scout says about lying (p. 128)?
4. What does Atticus mean by "the summer's going to be a hot one"?
5. Explain Aunt Alexandra's theory about people and how they behave.
6. The narrator says, "It was a sad thing that my father had neglected to tell me about the Finch Family, or to install any pride into his children." Explain whose point of view is being conveyed and how you know.
7. Discuss identity as conceived of in the following quotation: "She wants to talk to you about the family and what it's meant to Maycomb County through the years, so you'll have some idea of who you are, so you might be moved to behave accordingly."
8. What change did Atticus undergo during the conversation with Jem and Scout?
9. What is the meaning of the last paragraph of this chapter: "I know now what he was trying to do, but Atticus was only a man. It takes a woman to do that kind of work"?

Summary

From her first words to Calpurnia, it is clear that Aunt Alexandra is to be obeyed as a senior member of the household, not received as a guest. Since Atticus has not explained her arrival, she explains it to Scout and Jem, presenting it as a joint decision that has to do with Jem's and Scout's growing up. When Atticus arrives later from legislative duty in Montgomery, he adds the reason, cryptic to Scout, that "the summer's going to be a hot one." Aunt Alexandra both fits into and, to a certain degree, takes over Maycomb Society.

The narrator explains Aunt Alexandra's theory of heredity and the heredity of Maycomb, leading up to Aunt Alexandra's attempt to impress Jem and Scout with the spiritual wisdom of their cousin Joshua St. Clair. She does not reckon with Atticus's account of Cousin Joshua's history, which included his attempt, apparently while insane, to murder the president of the local

university. Aunt Alexandra apparently speaks her mind to Atticus, who comes to Jem's room, and with great discomposure tries to convey to Jem and Scout his support of Alexandra's attempts to teach them family respect and gentility. This makes all three of them extremely uncomfortable. Finally he relents and tells them to "forget it." The narrator concludes that from her adult perspective she understands what Atticus was trying to do, but that "it takes a woman to do that kind of work."

Strategy 17

Distinguishing Fact and Opinion

Directions: Read the explanation; then answer the questions.

The characterizations of Maycomb families sound prejudiced and smack of stereotyping. They are the kind of personal, idiosyncratic approach that we might easily label "opinion." But it's easy to group all the comments in the chapter and not distinguish. Let's look more carefully.

Scout says that "Aunt Alexandra was of the opinion . . . that the longer a family had been squatting on one patch of land the finer it was" (p. 130). This is an opinion because what constitutes a "fine" family is a judgment of value that cannot be proven true or false. But much of what is said about people in the chapter is not, in fact, the kind of personal judgment that is beyond argument, that is, it is *not* opinion. If we recall that a fact is a statement that can be proven true or false, we can see that comments such as "All Bufords walk like that" are testable. We can observe the world and see if they are true or false. And, according to Scout, these simplistic-sounding characterizations are true.

It's also important to distinguish between fact and opinion carefully when dealing with matters of personal taste. When Atticus asks if Scout would like to have Aunt Alexandra live with them and she tells us, "I said I would like it very much" (p. 128), the statement, "I would like it very much," is a factual statement about Scout's preferences. And, as Scout tells us, it is a false statement—a lie. It is *not* a statement of opinion. This is different than when Scout told Miss Maudie, "You're the best lady I know" (p. 45). Since the word *best* tells us that an evaluation has taken place, and we categorize statements of value as opinion, Scout's assessment is an opinion. In the same way, "I like chocolate ice cream," whether true or false, is a statement of fact about my preferences. "Chocolate ice cream is better than strawberry ice cream," is a statement of opinion based on my personal taste, which no one can dispute, but which no one else has to accept, either.

Not all values, however, are matters of personal taste. When we speak from a philosophical or religious basis, we may express the belief in values that we hold to be objectively true. Our country and our government, our court system and the rights we enjoy in America reflect a set of values that we hold to be objectively true. We esteem justice and liberty, for example. We may argue about exactly what they mean or how to obtain them. But it is rare to hear someone question their worth. Likewise, when Atticus tells his children, "it's a sin to kill a mockingbird" (p. 90), the word *sin* lets us know that he is not talking about a matter of private preference. Nor is he speaking solely about a particular species of bird. He is saying that it is Wrong with a capital *W* to injure a harmless creature. Which brings us to the next point.

We also take a different approach to labeling statements as fact and opinion in more poetic or figurative writing or conversation. When the narrator, in describing Maycomb, says, "Ladies . . . were like soft teacakes with frostings of sweat and sweet talcum" (p. 5), we don't analyze the statement as a fact and declare it false. Rather we try to follow her simile and understand the meaning of what she's trying to convey; we try to see the picture.

Note: Watch out for sarcasm and irony, which sometimes involve saying the opposite of what is meant. It wouldn't be useful to analyze such statements as false facts.

Decide whether the following statements are true facts, false facts, figurative language, irony/sarcasm, or opinions. Look at the context of each statement. Explain your reasoning.

1. " 'Mrs. Dubose . . . was the bravest person I ever knew' " (p. 112, Chapter 11).

2. " 'Turtles can't feel, stupid' " (p. 14, Chapter 1).

3. " 'That makes the Ewells fine folks, then' " (p. 130, Chapter 13).

4. "The Governor was eager to scrape a few barnacles off the ship of state" (p. 116, Chapter 12).

5. " 'People in their right minds never take pride in their talents' " (p. 98, Chapter 10).

6. " 'Atticus, you are a devil from hell' " (p. 91, Chapter 10).

7. " 'Uncle Jack . . . you don't understand children much' " (p. 85, Chapter 9; see page 87 as well).

8. " 'It's lovely, Jem' " (said of the morphodite; p. 67, Chapter 8).

Chapter 14

Dill Runs Away

Vocabulary

enema bags: 135, method for delivering liquid to the anus

rape: 135, in this book it refers to a particular sex act: forced heterosexual intercourse by a man with a woman, involving penetration of the vagina by the penis—today *rape* has a wider meaning, including other kinds of sexual assault with force and without consent and the wording of the laws in many states has been changed to be gender neutral

carnal knowledge: 135, sexual intercourse (literally, "knowing someone through the body"), defined as in the definition of *rape*

pensive: 135, thoughtful

penitentiary: 136, prison

revived: 137, used figuratively: brought back to life

taut: 137, tight

antagonize: 137, provoke the hostility of

rankling: 137, causing irritation or bitterness

Jee crawling hova: 138, Jehova is the name of God; the interjection of "crawling" indicates that it is being used as a curse

reverent: 139, respectful, as one would be toward God

ventilator: 140, a grate through which air can pass into or out of a room

manacles: 140, handcuffs

infallible: 140, perfect; unerring

fortitude: 142, strength of mind; courage

bestowed: 142, given as a gift

Journal and Discussion Topics

1. Why are Jem and Scout getting public attention?
2. Does Atticus follow the rule he gave Jack about answering a child's question when Scout asks him about rape? Explain why you think as you do.
3. Do you think Atticus would have let Scout visit Calpurnia? Why or why not?
4. What does Jem mean when he says, "They've been fussing"?
5. Why did Scout get so angry with Jem in this chapter?
6. Why does Scout say Dill was "home" when he'd just run away from home?
7. What code did Jem break? When did he break it earlier in the story?
8. Dill and Scout have reasons for running away that seem almost opposite. Explain this paradox in your own words.
9. Why do you think the chapter ends where it does?

Summary

When Scout hears the word *rape* as she and Jem are going to town on Saturday as usual, she remembers that she wants to ask Atticus what it means. He gives her a legal definition, and Scout wants to know why Calpurnia wouldn't tell her. With this opening, the story of Jem and Scout accompanying Calpurnia to church comes out, to Atticus's amusement and Aunt Alexandra's dismay. Following up, Scout asks Atticus's permission to visit Calpurnia at home, and Aunt Alexandra interrupts, saying, "You may *not*." Scout points out that she didn't ask her aunt, but her father, which brings her into direct conflict with him. First, he makes her apologize. Then he explains that her aunt is to be obeyed while she is in the house. Scout escapes by going to the bathroom.

She returns to find Alexandra and Atticus arguing over whether Calpurnia is still needed at the Finches' home. When they speak about Scout, she feels that her life is being too closely controlled, and considers running away. Atticus gives a series of reasons for Calpurnia staying until she wishes to leave: He couldn't have gotten along without her; she's a faithful member of

the family; there's too much work for Alexandra to do it all; Calpurnia brought up the children, and didn't let them get away with anything; the children love her.

Jem tells Scout privately not to antagonize Aunt Alexandra and is so condescending that Scout starts a fight with him, not satisfied until he is fighting back, at which she concludes that they are still equals. Atticus and Alexandra arrive to stop the fight, and Atticus says that Scout only has to mind Jem if he can make her. Alexandra is complaining about their behavior as the adults walk away, which unites Jem and Scout again.

As Scout goes to bed, she steps on something rubbery on the floor under her bed. She calls to Jem, who brings a broom to pull it out from under the bed, when suddenly, Dill pops out. After some milk and corn bread to revive him, in response to Scout's question how he got there, Dill tells his usual fantastic story about his adventures. When he's done, Jem repeats the question, and Dill tells the truth. The narrator concludes, "He was worn out, dirty beyond belief, and home." Jem earns Scout's and Dill's disdain by telling Atticus that Dill is there. Dill gets to stay the night, and Jem is forgiven. Dill goes to sleep in Jem's room but comes into Scout's room to join her several hours later. At her request, he explains why he ran off, but Scout can't fathom what it would be like to not be needed. Dill begins talking about babies, and Scout asks him why he figures Boo Radley never ran away. Dill suggests that maybe Boo doesn't have anywhere to run to.

Chapter 15

Friends in the Yard; Mob at the Jail

Vocabulary

defendant: 144, one charged with a crime; the accused; the person against whom a criminal proceeding is begun; to be distinguished from *criminal*, which refers to a person who has been convicted of a violation of the criminal law

trial: 145, the procedure by which a judge or jury makes a finding of fact concerning a lawsuit

change of venue: 145, change of the location in which a trial is to be held; often requested when the defendant is considered to be in danger

inaudible: 145, unable to be heard

shinnied up: 145, drunk

chair: 145, the electric chair by means of which capital punishment (death sentence) was carried out in Alabama at that time

ominous: 146, threatening

Ku Klux: 147, Ku Klux Klan; a secret society advocating the supremacy of the Caucasian race

seen the light: 147, experienced a conversion in which one accepts Jesus as Savior and God

linotype: 147, typesetting machine

venerable: 150, honored

Gothic: 150, an architectural style of western Europe in the late Middle Ages/early Renaissance; features of the style include battlements and flying buttresses (different meaning than earlier use on p. 39)

façade: 150, front wall

detractors: 150, those who criticize

Victorian: 150, from the period of Queen Victoria of England (reigned 1837–1901)

privy: 150, outhouse; toilet

oblivious: 151, unaware

snipe hunt: 151, idiom: a fruitless search; a wild goose chase

succinct: 151, concise

acquiescence: 152, acceptance

mutual defiance: 152, resisting each other

justification: 153, good reason

futility: 153, ineffectiveness

aggregation: 154, group

uncouth: 154, uncultivated in appearance or manners

impassive: 154, giving no sign of feeling or emotion

encumbered: 155, burdened

Journal and Discussion Topics

1. What was the effect on your expectations of each of the following sentences: "A nightmare was upon us"; "In Maycomb, grown men stood outside in the front yard for only two reasons: death and politics"?

2. What does Link mean when he says Atticus has everything to lose? What does Atticus mean when he says, "Do you really think so?"?

3. What kind of irony do you find in Atticus's statement, "Link, that boy might go to the chair, but he's not going till the truth's told. . . . And you know what the truth is"?

4. Why does the "Fine Folks" criteria not preserve Sam Levy from having the Klan parade by his house?

5. What does the following snippet of conversation suggest about the trial? ". . . in favor of Southern womanhood as much as anybody, but not for preserving polite fiction at the expense of human life."

6. Why do you think Atticus likes to sit by himself in church?

7. Heredity as a way of predicting behavior has been emphasized. How do Jem and Scout make predictions about Atticus?

8. Why is it ironic that the men speak in whispers?

9. What impact did the clause "Its owner was a shadow" (p. 152) have?

10. How do Scout's inaccurate judgments contribute to the scene at the jail and after?
11. What do you think made Mr. Cunningham decide to leave?

Summary

Dill finally receives permission to stay in Maycomb, but after one peaceful week, the turmoil that Atticus had predicted ("the summer's going to be a hot one") arrives. It begins with the appearance of the sheriff and a group of men in the Finches' front yard on the Saturday night before the Monday on which the trial is to take place. Telling his children to stay inside, Atticus goes out to them. They have come to warn Atticus about possible trouble from the "Old Sarum bunch," a group of fellow citizens who can be uncivil when they drink and, it is feared, may attack Tom when he is brought to the Maycomb jail the following day. They also question Atticus's decision to defend Tom. Atticus makes it clear that he has no intention of doing anything but what he's set out to do: The truth will be told. Jem and Scout, watching from the darkened living room are frightened, thinking that the group is a gang. Atticus explains that the men were friends. After Scout returns from walking Dill home, Jem tells her that he's concerned that someone might hurt Atticus.

On Sunday, another group shows up to speak to Atticus in the churchyard between services, including the sheriff and Mr. Underwood, the owner of *The Maycomb Tribune*. The afternoon is quiet, but after supper, Atticus takes a long extension cord with a light bulb at the end, announces to Jem and Scout that he won't be back till after they're in bed, and goes out, taking the car, which he virtually never drives except for business trips. The children's curiosity is piqued. Scout eventually heads for bed, but hearing Jem making unusual noises, she asks what he's doing. He announces that he's going downtown. Scout retorts that she's going with him, and adds that Dill will want to join them. They sneak out of the house, whistle for Dill, and head for Atticus's office, based on an unnameable feeling of Jem's that something is up. But Atticus's office is dark. As they walk up the street, they see a light outside the jail, which doesn't have an outside light. Coming closer they see the extension cord Atticus had taken and Atticus sitting in an office chair, leaning against the front door of the jail and reading the newspaper. Jem, satisfied that Atticus is all right, prevents Scout from running to him and makes ready to leave and go home.

As the three children are cutting across the town square, four cars pull up and stop in front of the jail. Atticus puts down his paper and waits for them. The children run back to the door of the hardware store, from which they can see what's happening. The men get out of the cars and gather around Atticus. They ascertain that Tom is in the jail and tell Atticus to move away from the door. Atticus tells them that the sheriff is around somewhere, but they counter that they've sent him off on a wild goose chase (snipe hunt). Scout, not understanding the situation, runs to Atticus, eluding Jem's attempts to catch her. But as she breaks into the circle, she discovers that these are not the same men she had seen gathered around her father the night before—they are strangers. Atticus commands Jem to take Scout and Dill home, but uncharacteristically, he refuses and continues to refuse as Atticus continues to press him and as a man in the crowd threatens Atticus that he'd better make them go.

While Atticus and Jem are engaged in their standoff, Scout looks around the group and recognizes Walter Cunningham, Sr., whom she greets. She strikes up a one-sided conversation about his entailment and his son. He finally acknowledges with a slight nod that Scout's classmate Walter is his son, and she continues to talk until she realizes that the whole group is looking at her. She becomes embarrassed. After an uncomfortable silence, Mr. Cunningham bends down, takes her by the shoulders, and promises that he'll greet Walter for her. Then, standing up, he beckons to the other men to leave. Following his lead, they return to the cars. Scout goes up to Atticus, who is leaning against the jail overcome with emotion, and asks if they can go home. Tom Robinson calls down from his cell, and Atticus assures him that he can sleep—the men are gone and won't disturb him. Mr. Underwood unexpectedly chimes in, telling Atticus that he'd had him covered with his double-barreled shotgun the whole time. Dill offers to carry Atticus's chair, and he and Scout trail Atticus and Jem home. Scout expects Jem to get a scolding, but instead she sees Atticus stroking Jem's hair affectionately.

Strategy 18

Historical Fiction/ Autobiography

Directions:
Read the explanation. Begin work on the exercise you have chosen now or when you reach the point at which you can do so.

Historical fiction is a work of the imagination that is set in and uses to a high degree an actual location at an actual time in history. Historical fiction may contain mentions of or references or allusions to actual historical and cultural events, people, publications, circumstances, attitudes, values, ways of life, and so on. Even the made-up part of the story is presented in a realistic way to make it fit as seamlessly as possible with the factual elements.

Sometimes certain kinds of historical elements are fictionalized in such works. Lee did this with both her own life (autobiographical events) and events in the larger community. For example, *To Kill a Mockingbird* is set in Maycomb, a town modeled on Monroeville, Alabama, where Lee grew up. Lee based the character of Dill on her childhood friend, author Truman Capote. The mob outside the Finches' house and the pageant and its aftermath at the end of the book both draw on details from a Halloween party that Capote held at his Aunt Jenny's house in Monroeville. Monroeville's main street has been held to be the model for the street the Finches live on in Maycomb. And a careful analysis reveals parallels between the trial of Tom Robinson, about which you will read beginning in Chapter 17, and the historical so-called Scottsboro Trials.

Do one of the following two activities.

1. Choose seven items from the following categories, look them up, and— when you've read the chapter they appear in—explain their significance in the book.

Inventions	**People**	**Organizations**
Dewey Decimal System, p. 18	Dixie Howell, p. 103	Ku Klux, p. 147
	William Jennings Bryan, p. 160	CSA, p. 99

Documents	**Things**	**Food**
Rosetta Stone, p. 63	Prohibition ticket, p. 159	scuppernongs, p. 35
Missouri Compromise, p. 76		
Indian-head pennies, p. 34		

Events	**Places**
Second Battle of the Marne, p. 42	Appomattox, p. 65
Spanish American War, p. 257	Bellingraths, p. 73
Creek Indian Wars, p. 258	

2. When you are done reading *To Kill a Mockingbird*, read the following passages from the book *A Bridge of Childhood: Truman Capote's Southern Years* (Henry Holt Company, 1989), a biography of Truman Capote by Marianne M. Moates. The book is based on the recollections of Jennings Faulk Carter, Truman's cousin, who made up the trio of playmates along with Harper Lee and Capote, on which the trio of Jem, Scout, and Dill is based. Write an essay explaining how Lee adapted one of the passages to create material in her novel.

a. "The Boular house sat on the corner next to the school yard, about half a block from the Lee and Faulk houses. . . . The Boulars didn't seem to want anybody in—or out . . . . Sonny [Boular] was . . . a tall, thin young man with a face so pale he looked almost ghostly, leading some of our friends to develop a legend about him: Sonny's dangerous and if he ever gets out of his yard, he'll kill you with a butcher knife" (p. 54).

b. Aunt Jenny to the sheriff: "the last time that worthless bunch of no-'count Klansmen raised Cain in Monroeville, it was all over nothing. And you know it was. They had all that trouble with the colored boy and were threatening to hang him. Why all they had to do was ask that little white hussy he was accused of molesting. . . . You know how loose that girl is. The colored boy should have known better. All he did was talk to her. Just talk. The Klan got all excited and wanted to hang him" (p. 57).

You may wish to encourage interested students to read the whole section of the book on "Miss Jenny's Halloween Party" (pp. 51–64).

Vocabulary
Look at the group of words. Tell why it is important in the story.

1. heredity, caste system, dicta _____

_____

2. Gothic, façade, Victorian_____

_____

3. denunciation, austere, bootleggers, tedious_____

_____

Essay Topics
1. Think about Calpurnia calling Jem and Scout "her children." What makes us belong to each other?

2. Compare and contrast the group in the Finches' front yard and the group outside the jail.

3. Evaluate Scout's theory of humanity. What are its values and its flaws?

4. Describe the role of the church in the Black community in Maycomb.

5. What's the significance of the practice of "lining"?

6. So far, how is Part Two of *To Kill a Mockingbird* different from Part One?

Chapter 16

The Courtroom

Vocabulary

fey: 156, strange
christened: 156, named at baptism
lurched: 158, swayed
straight . . . ticket: 159, to vote by party rather than by individual candidate
Prohibition: 159, forbidding by law of manufacture, transportation, and sale of alcohol except for medical and sacramental church use
ablaze: 159, as if on fire
akimbo: 159, with hands on hips, elbows pointing outwards
cometh/departeth: 159, outdated verb forms, still popular in some translations of the Bible, for *comes / goes away*
countenance: 159, facial expression
Roman carnival: 159, the celebration in Rome of the season called "carnival" (i.e., the time of merrymaking and feasting preceding the fasting and austerity of Lent)
subpoena: 160, legal document requiring one's appearance in court
elucidate: 160, explain; clarify
picking the jury: 160, the process of deciding which community members will hear a particular case; both the lawyer for the defense and the prosecuting attorney have a role in the selection
gala: 160, (adjective) festive
affluent: 160, rich; wealthy
chillun: 161, dialect for *children*
reminiscent of: 162, able to call to mind
vista: 162, view
sundry: 162, various
solicitor: 163, the chief law officer of a municipality
circuit clerk: 163, clerk for the circuit court—the circuits are judicial divisions of a state
probate: 163, the court whose main business is wills and estates
unobtrusive: 163, inconspicuous; unnoticeable
circuit solicitor: 164, the representative of the state; the prosecutor
champertous: 165, as in a proceeding in which someone not party to a lawsuit bargains to carry on the pursuit of the case in exchange for a share of the profits
connivance: 165, consent to wrongdoing
litigants: 165, the parties engaged in a lawsuit
indulge: 165, take part

Journal and Discussion Topics

1. Why did Scout start crying?
2. If Mr. Underwood "despises Negroes" (p. 156), why would he guard Tom?
3. What's your reaction to Aunt Alexandra's statement, "Don't talk like that in front of them" (p. 156)?
4. Do you agree with Atticus that Mr. Cunningham is a friend? Why or why not?
5. What do you know about Mr. Dolphus Raymond that is true? How can you tell?
6. How is Miss Maudie's comparison of the day's activities to a Roman carnival apt?
7. What's your reaction to the discussion of mixed races?
8. What's the significance of the conversation among the members of the Idlers' Club?
9. What's the significance of Jem, Scout, and Dill being given seats?

Summary

Jem comes to get Scout, who is crying in her room, takes her into bed with him, and tries to comfort her, saying, "It'll all be over after tomorrow, maybe" (p. 156). They had come in quietly from the jail so as not to wake Aunt Alexandra,

and suddenly Scout realized the significance of what had happened, connecting it to the rabid dog incident.

At breakfast the next day, Alexandra criticizes the children for sneaking out, and Atticus counters that he's glad they did. Alexandra infers that their appearance was unnecessary, since Mr. Underwood had the situation well in hand. While Calpurnia is serving coffee, Atticus makes the comment that Mr. Underwood despises Negroes, and as soon as Calpurnia returns to the kitchen, Alexandra, tells him not to "talk like that in front of them" (p. 156). Atticus defends himself and Calpurnia.

Scout is confused by Atticus's having called Mr. Cunningham a friend, considering the events of the previous night. Atticus explains that Mr. Cunningham is basically a good man, and that a mob is always made up of people. He concludes that Jem and Scout made Walter Cunningham "stand in my shoes for a minute," recalling the advice he gave Scout earlier (p. 30). Scout promises to lay in wait for Walter when school starts again, and Atticus warns her not to fight or even hold a grudge, no matter what. Alexandra starts in saying, "I told you so," and Atticus excuses himself, warning Jem as he leaves that he doesn't want either of his children downtown on this day.

Dill arrives, and Alexandra warns the children to stay in the yard. From the front yard they watch people pass, and Jem's commentary to Dill on people's backgrounds and histories provides the reader with a portrait gallery: Mr. Dolphus Raymond, a group of Mennonites, Mr. X Billups, Mr. Tensaw Jones, Miss Emily Davis, Mr. Byron Waller, Mr. Jake Slade, and a wagon-load of foot-washing Baptists who square off with Miss Maudie. Miss Maudie, when questioned, says she has no business downtown, and immediately a foil is set by Stephanie Crawford who claims that she is going to the Jitney Jungle, but when pressed by Maudie, admits that she "might" stop by the courthouse.

At noon, Atticus comes home for dinner and reports that they've picked the jury. Jem and Scout stop by for Dill and head to town, where they find Maycomb's citizenry all turned out for the event. Again they see Mr. Dolphus Raymond, and a discussion of his life, his drunkenness, and his mixed race children follows. Jem, Scout, and Dill try to make sense of attitudes toward race, but they can't.

On the way into the courthouse, being careful to avoid being seen by Atticus, Scout hears the Idlers' Club tell that Atticus was *appointed* to defend Tom, but, they go on, what upsets people is that Atticus intends to *actually* defend him. This puzzles Scout. While she is hanging back to listen, the three children lose their chance of getting the seats Jem wanted. Reverend Sykes appears, confirms that there are no seats downstairs, and asks if it would be all right for them to come to the balcony with him. When Jem says yes, they go to the colored balcony and are given front row seats by four people who then have to stand. This gives them a great vantage point, and as Scout looks around she notices that a couple of members of the jury look like "dressed-up Cunninghams." The chapter ends with a description and brief biography of Judge Taylor, the presiding official, and the fact that the sheriff is already on the witness stand.

Chapter 17

Heck Tate and Robert E. Lee Ewell Testify

Vocabulary

testifyin': 166, dialect for *testifying*; giving sworn testimony in a law court

witness chair: 166, the place reserved for the witness to occupy during testimony; it is placed on the witness stand

convened: 166, assembled to begin official business

scrutiny: 166, examination

witnesses: 166, ones who are called upon to testify in court; eye-witnesses made personal observations at the time an event took place

objection: 167, opposition to a question or line of questioning by the opposing counsel; there are rules governing the criteria for finding a question objectionable; the judge may sustain (admit) or overrule (reject) the objection

took advantage of her: 167, raped her (see definition of *rape*, p. 85 of this guide)

court reporter: 168, court official in charge of recording court proceedings

turbulent: 169, agitated; tempestuous

opposing counsel: 169, the lawyers for the defense and prosecution respectively

title dispute: 169, disagreement over the legal ownership of some property

corroborating evidence: 169, evidence that supports a claim

bantam cock: 169, person of small stature and combative nature

crepey: 170, crinkled; puckered

so help me God: 170, part of the oath taken by witnesses in which they swear to "tell the truth, the whole truth, and nothing but the truth, so help me God"; the form of the oath includes placing the left hand on a Bible and raising the right hand

fluctuations: 170, changes; shifts

congenital: 170, passed on genetically by inheritance

corrugated: 170, shaped into ridges or grooves

varmints: 170, animals classified as vermin (mice, rats, etc.)

snaggle-toothed: 170, with bent and/or broken teeth

deigned: 171, condescended

recess: 171, official break in court proceedings as ordered by the presiding court officer

acrimonious: 171, harsh

obscene: 172, morally repulsive

o'kindlin': 172, dialect for *of kindling*; wood to start a fire

distangled: 173, dialect for *untangled*; disentangled

ruttin': 173, dialect for *rutting*, a term for sexual intercourse that is usually reserved for animals, specifically male deer

gavel: 173, judge's mallet, used to command attention in the courtroom

picknickers: 173, people having picnics

contempt charges: 174, charged with open disrespect for or disobedience to the authority of a court of law

sexual intercourse: 174, see definition of *rape* (p. 85 of this guide)

testimony: 176, evidence given under oath in a court of law

on the stand: 176, giving his testimony (while standing on the "witness stand" in the courtroom)

irrelevant 'n' immaterial: 176, inapplicable and of no substantial importance (to a particular situation)

overruled: 177, the judge's rejection of the objection raised by a counsel to the opposing counsel's question or line of questioning

cross-examination: 177, requestioning of a witness by the opposing counsel on matters discussed in the *direct examination* carried on by the lawyer who called the witness in the first place

tenet: 177, principle

ambidextrous: 178, able to use both hands with equal ease

Journal and Discussion Topics

1. Social gaffes is a repeated plot element in *To Kill a Mockingbird*. Ewell commits many in the courtroom. List them. What do they reveal?
2. What do you think was "made plain to" Heck (p. 168)?

3. During Atticus's cross-examination of Heck Tate, the sheriff says, "Yes sir, she had a small throat, anybody could'a reached around it with—" (p. 169) at which point Atticus interrupts him. What was Heck going to say? Why did Atticus stop him?
4. How does Scout judge the excitement at the trial?
5. Scout predicts, "everything would come out all right." Is this believable? Why or why not?
6. The geraniums might be considered a symbol. What do you think they represent?
7. What does Scout's description of the Ewells and their neighbors suggest?
8. The narrator directly addresses her readers about the trauma of the courtroom. What do you make of this?
9. Why does Judge Taylor say that Bob Ewell's comment is obscene (p. 172)?
10. What do you think of Reverend Sykes's suggestion to send Scout home?
11. Make a case for the following phrases being ironic:
    a. "surveying his handiwork" (p. 173)
    b. "devaluin' my property" (p. 175)
    c. "I can use one hand good as the other" (p. 178)
12. What do you think made Judge Taylor look at Bob Ewell as if he were a "fragrant gardenia"?
13. Explain the following expressions:
    a. "gone frog-sticking without a light" (p. 177)
    b. "counting his chickens" (p. 178)
14. What proof has been offered by the prosecution that a rape actually took place?

Summary

Sheriff Heck Tate, dressed for court, is on the witness stand being questioned by Mr. Gilmer, the prosecuting attorney. With a few clarifying questions from Mr. Gilmer, Heck tells that on the night of November 21, just as he was about to leave his office, Bob Ewell came in and said that "some nigger'd raped his girl." Heck drove to their house, and found Mayella still lying on the floor in the front room, "pretty well beat up," but able to stand with his assistance. When he asked who hurt her, she said Tom Robinson; so Heck arrested Tom.

Atticus then questions Heck. First he asks about a doctor being called. Heck says, "It wasn't necessary," because Mayella was so beaten that it was "obvious" that something had happened. Heck describes Mayella's injuries. He says she was beaten around the head and arms and, after some thought, declares that her right eye was blacked. This makes him realize something, and he looks at Tom Robinson. He goes on to describe finger marks on her throat, but Atticus interrupts his description.

The narrator then describes how the calm and order of the courtroom dispelled the terror that had made Scout cry the previous night.

Mr. Robert E. Lee Ewell is called to the stand, and after a brief description of his appearance, the narrator gives us some background on the Ewells, their filthy living conditions, and their disregard for education. She compares them, implicitly, with the Black settlement down the road, and then says explicitly that Bob is only "better" than his neighbors because under the filth, his skin is white.

Ewell's testimony is characterized by lack of knowledge of courtroom etiquette, by incivility, and by crudity. When he describes seeing Tom "ruttin' on my Mayella," the courtroom erupts and Reverend Sykes suggests that the children leave. Jem counters that Scout can't understand and that Atticus can't see them, avoiding the Reverend's question about whether they have permission to be there. Judge Taylor threatens the spectators with contempt charges and quells Ewell, and Mr. Gilmer returns to questioning his witness. Ewell completes his testimony with a verbal attack on the nearby Black settlement, which he claims is "devaluin' " his property. He leaves the stand, only to run into Atticus, who is ready to cross examine him.

Atticus begins by asking Ewell if he had gotten a doctor. He says no, it would have cost five dollars, emphasizing again the lack of corroborating evidence that a rape occurred. Atticus then asks if Ewell agrees with the sheriff's description of Mayella's injuries, and after some consideration, he says he does. Atticus asks if Ewell can read and write, and though Mr. Gilmer objects that this is immaterial, Judge Taylor allows Atticus to go on. When Atticus asks Ewell to sign his name, and he signs with his left hand, Judge Taylor's interest and Jem's jubilant exclamation, "We've got him," point strongly to the inference that it was Ewell who beat Mayella. But, as Scout points out in the last paragraph, Tom Robinson might also be left-handed.

Strategy 19

Sensory Language

Directions:
Read the
explanation;
then answer the
questions.

Sensory language engages the senses of sight, hearing, smell, taste, and touch, by images that appeal to the senses. Sight is the sense most often invoked, and taste usually the least. Sensory language helps readers imagine the scene in the "movie" in their minds. It helps bring the black and white of the printed book to life.

Sometimes a writer will concentrate emphasis on one particular sense. In the courtroom, where voices and being heard are supremely important, Lee has chosen to emphasize the sense of hearing. There is a special category of words having to do with sound of which you should be aware. **Onomatopoetic** words are words that sound like the sound they name. *Buzzzzz* sounds like the droning of a bee. *Plunk* sounds like a drop of water dripping. Keep an eye (or ear) out for such sounds as you read.

1. Make a list of sounds in Chapter 17 that evoke your sense of hearing.

2. Now find at least three words in Chapter 17 for each of these senses: touch, sight, and smell.

Chapter 18

Mayella Ewell Testifies

Vocabulary

strenuous: 179, arduous; requiring hard work
lavations: 179, baths; washings
mollified: 180, soothed (in temper)
chiffarobe: 180, combination of a wardrobe and chest of drawers
brash: 181, tactless; arrogant
state: 181, the party initiating a criminal suit; same as the prosecutor
sass: 182, disrespectful speech
evoked: 182, caused an emotional response of...
let the record show: 182, a request to the clerk to enter something into the record outside of the counsel's questions and witness's responses
tollable: 183, dialect for *tolerable*: acceptable
riled: 184, angry; agitated
arid: 185, extremely dry; without emotion
wrathfully: 185, angrily; vengefully
browbeating: 186, intimidating; overpowering
rested: 188, finished its case
distilled: 189, extracted the important parts of; concentrated
reversed: 189, found a judge's decision to be erroneous and changed a not guilty finding to a guilty finding or vice versa
exodus: 189, departure
intriguing: 189, fascinating; worthy of note
vibrations: 189, small regular movements (in structures, furniture, etc.) created by sound

Journal and Discussion Topics

1. How does the initial description of Mayella emphasize opposing traits?
2. How could someone mistake courtesy for mockery?
3. What do you make of Mayella's failure to understand the words *friends* and *love*?
4. Explain the irony of this interchange:
   "You want me to say something that didn't happen?"
   "No ma'am, I want you to say something that did happen."
5. What's the significance of Atticus calling Mayella "child" (p. 187)?
6. What's the effect of the word *real* in "burst into real tears" (p. 188)?
7. Scout says, "Atticus had hit her hard in a way that was not clear to me" (p. 188). Explain how Atticus "hit her."
8. Why do you think Mr. Gilmer was "prosecuting almost reluctantly" (p. 189)?

Summary

Mayella Ewell is called to the witness stand. When she doesn't respond to Mr. Gilmer's request to tell what happened in her own words, he begins to lead her through the story when she suddenly bursts into tears, claiming that she's afraid of Atticus. Mollified by Judge Taylor's reassurances, she tells that her father had gone to the woods, leaving her with the task of chopping up an old chiffarobe. Not feeling up to the task and seeing Tom Robinson passing, she says that she offered him a nickel to do the job. She tells that he entered the yard, but when she went into the house to get the nickel, he ran after her, grabbed her around the neck, hit her repeatedly, and "took advantage" of her. Her next recollection is of her father standing over her, and then of Sheriff Tate helping her up.

Atticus begins his cross-examination, but Mayella refuses to answer him because she claims he is mocking her by addressing her with a title of respect and calling her "ma'am." The judge again intervenes, explaining that Atticus is

simply being polite. Atticus begins again, bringing out the facts that Mayella's mother is dead, but she doesn't know for how long; that she went to school for a couple of years, but she's not sure how many; that she has seven siblings; and that they live in dire poverty. When Atticus asks her about friends and whether she loves her father, she doesn't understand either concept.

Having established this background, Atticus surprises Mayella by asking if she had ever asked Tom to do chores before. She says no and then claims to be unable to remember. He then focuses on her injuries, first the choking and then particularly the blows to her face, which at first she says she can't recollect, and then says she can. He then asks her to certainly identify the man who raped her (the first use of the word *rape* in the trial). She identifies Tom Robinson, who stands at Atticus's request, revealing that his left arm and hand are useless. Atticus asks Mayella to explain how Tom was able to rape her, choke her, and beat her while she was fighting back. Mayella, realizing suddenly the flaws in her story, changes her testimony to account for Tom's inability to use his left arm. He asks her why her siblings didn't come when she screamed, or whether perhaps she hadn't screamed until her father came, and whether it wasn't her father, rather than Tom, who beat her. Mayella doesn't answer but finally accuses the court, jury, and lawyers of being cowards if they won't do something about the "nigger" who took advantage of her.

After a ten-minute recess, Judge Taylor suggests that they try to wind up before the end of the day and instructs Atticus to call his witness.

Strategy 20   Imaging

Directions: Read the explanation; then begin work on the exercise. You will add to your answer as you continue to read.

The meaning of a work of literature is not captured first and foremost in the words we use to speak or write about it. It is felt in our experience as we read and enter into the story. In the act of reading, the words of a book are translated into experience by the reader, experience that for many readers can (and should if possible) include images and feelings.

Writing instructor Janet Burroway explains that "Fiction tries to reproduce the emotional impact of experience. And this is a more difficult task, because written words are symbols representing sounds, and the sounds themselves are symbols representing things, actions, qualities, spatial relationships, and so on. Written words are thus at two removes from experience. Unlike the images of film and drama, which directly strike the eye and ear, they are transmitted first to the mind, where they must be translated into images [by the reader]" (*Writing Fiction: A Guide to Narrative Craft*, sixth edition, New York: Longman, 2002, p. 54)

Different texts foster different amounts and different kinds of imagery and feeling (also called "affect"). This can result from the author's use of more or less description and more or less sensory language, the author's focus on abstractions as opposed to concrete things, a very complex writing style, or academic diction, and so on. So your **imaging** won't always be exactly the same. Even when your imaging is at its most vivid, it is likely that it will not be as specific as a photograph or movie is, for example. The visual images we create in our minds are characteristically not sharp and finely focused, a quality that literary critic Wolfgang Iser calls "optical poverty." This is an important point because you shouldn't expect these images to be something they're not or force them into a mold. Just let them come into your head, watch them, and take note.

1. To keep track of your imaging, it is useful to write about or draw what you've seen. You might want to record the most striking image(s) that you recollect from each chapter. Don't worry about your drawing ability; just do the best you can in whatever medium is most comfortable for you or best conveys what you want to communicate or recollect about your experience. Create a record for Chapters 1 through 18 now, and add to it each time you complete another chapter. Feel free to look back through the chapters to help your recall.

Chapter 19 Tom Robinson Testifies

Vocabulary

convicted: 190, found guilty

serve: 190, complete an assigned jail sentence after being found guilty

fine: 190, amount assigned as restitution upon being found guilty

volition: 192, will

subtlety: 195, delicacy

predicament: 195, trying situation

under oath: 195, having sworn in court on a Bible to "tell the truth, the whole truth, and nothing but the truth," with God's help

ex cathedra: 195, Latin phrase meaning, literally, from the chair; by virtue of one's office or position

expunge: 196, delete; strike out

told the jury to disregard: 196, in a court proceeding, the jury's finding must be based on the evidence and testimony that has been presented in the case; anything outside this system (whether true or false) is not to be part of the jury's considerations in reaching their verdict

impudent: 198, insolent; disrespectful

thin-hided: 199, thin-skinned; overly sensitive

Journal and Discussion Topics

1. What is the effect of the first paragraph of description of Tom?
2. How is Mayella's treatment of Tom revealed to be ironic?
3. What's your reaction to the statement about Tom, "If he had been whole, he would have been a fine specimen of a man"?
4. Tom reports that Mayella told him "what her papa do to her don't count." What did she mean?
5. How would you characterize Mr. Gilmer's treatment of Tom in cross-examination? Give examples to support your evaluation.
6. Explain the nuances of meaning in Mr. Gilmer's two different pronunciations (shown by italics) of the sentence "You felt sorry for her" (p. 197).
7. Compare and contrast Dill's and Scout's views of Mr. Gilmer's cross-examination of Tom.

Summary

Tom's attempt to keep his left hand on the Bible while he takes his oath demonstrates how useless his left arm is. Tom is twenty-five years old, married with three children, and once served thirty days for disorderly conduct. He does fieldwork and yard work for Mr. Link Deas for a living. Tom reports that the previous spring Mayella had asked him to chop up a chiffarobe and offered him a nickel, which he declined. This was, he says, the first of many times that Mayella asked him to do chores, for which he was never paid. Each time, he was watched by Mayella's brothers and sisters. Tom says he never went on the Ewell's property except at Mayella's express request. He tells the court that as he was going home on November 21, Mayella called to him to help her fix a door inside the house. Coming up to the house and examining the door, Tom discovered nothing wrong with it, but Mayella closed it. Tom asked where the children were and she said that by saving for a year she has been able to gather enough money to treat them to ice cream in town. Tom prepared to leave, but Mayella asked him to step on a chair and get a box from on top of a chiffarobe in the room. As he did, Mayella grabbed him, causing him to hop down and turn over the chair. Then she hugged him and kissed him on the cheek, saying that what her father did to her didn't count, and told Tom to kiss her back. He tried to escape her embrace and get away without hurting her in any way, when Bob

Ewell appeared at the window and threatened to kill Mayella. Tom managed to escape from the house and run away. Tom claims that not only did he not rape Mayella, but that he was the one resisting *her* advances. As Atticus returns to his seat, Link Deas, Tom's employer, rises and yells out that he's never had any trouble with Tom, and Judge Taylor threatens him with contempt charges.

Mr. Gilmer begins his cross-examination by emphasizing Tom's prior conviction. He suggests that Tom had been planning to assault Mayella for a long time and that he had ulterior motives in doing chores for her. Tom, in trying to explain his motives, makes the mistake of saying that he "felt sorry" for Mayella, and Mr. Gilmer makes a great deal of the impudence of a poor Black man saying he feels sorry for a white woman. Then Mr. Gilmer takes Tom through the events of November 21 as Mayella recounted them. At every turn, Tom in refuting Mayella's lies, says that she was "mistaken in her mind." Mr. Gilmer implies that Tom ran away because he was guilty, but Tom claims he ran in an attempt to avoid being charged with a crime he didn't commit, as has in fact happened.

The account of the cross-examination ends abruptly because Jem insists that Scout take Dill, who has unaccountably begun to cry, outside. Dill says he couldn't stand how Mr. Gilmer was treating Tom, and Scout's explanation that Mr. Gilmer was just doing his job and that Tom is "just a Negro" do not solace him. From behind them a voice agrees with Dill, and the voice turns out to belong to Mr. Dolphus Raymond.

Chapter 20

Dill and Mr. Dolphus Raymond Meet; Atticus's Closing Speech

Vocabulary

fraud: 201, deception; twisting of the truth

capital charge: 202, a charge for which one can receive the death penalty if found guilty; same as *capital felony*

thunderer: 202, speaker with a loud voice

stark: 202, absolutely; totally

aridity: 203, lack of feeling

iota: 203, bit; very small amount

persevering: 204, persistent

swore out a warrant: 204, obtained, by making a charge under oath, a document from a judge allowing an officer to search, seize, or arrest

unmitigated: 204, inexcusable

temerity: 204, audacity

cynical: 204, contemptuous

caliber: 204, ability

distaff: 205, literally, a staff that holds unspun wool; here used as a metonymy to refer to women, meaning the First Lady

inferiority: 205, not being as good as others

idealist: 205, believer in living by ideals

integrity: 205, commitment to moral principles

Journal and Discussion Topics

1. Discuss Dill's and Scout's conversation with Mr. Dolphus Raymond in terms of (a) individual and community and (b) appearance and reality.
2. Compare and contrast the attitudes behind these two statements:
   a. ". . . after all he's just a Negro." (Chapter 19, p. 199)
   b. "Cry about the hell white people give colored folks without ever stopping to think that they're people, too." (Chapter 20, p. 201)
3. Why is Atticus's statement, "This case is as simple as black and white," ironic?
4. According to Atticus, of what is Mayella guilty? Do you think she or her father is responsible for her being in court? Explain.
5. How, according to Atticus, is the theory that heredity and race are determining factors of personality at issue in this case?
6. What does the phrase "distaff side of the executive branch" mean?
7. What is your reaction to Atticus's statement about equality (p. 205)?
8. What do you think of Atticus's criticism of public education?
9. Evaluate Atticus's closing argument. Do you think it is effective for the situation? What, if anything, could Atticus have done differently to make it more effective, in your opinion?

Summary

Mr. Dolphus Raymond claims to have something to settle Dill's stomach, and sipping from the concoction Mr. Raymond keeps in his paper bag, Dill discovers that it's Coca-Cola. Scout awkwardly refers to the fact that Mr. Raymond acts drunk, and Mr. Raymond explains that it's an attempt to help people who don't like the way he lives understand him, by giving them a reason to explain his choice of lifestyle. He decries the "hell" that white people give "colored folks."

Dill and Scout return to the courthouse and discover Atticus already well into his speech to the jury, pointing out that there is no corroborating evidence to support the charge of rape. Jem is sure of victory because the evidence is so clear.

With Judge Taylor's permission, Atticus uncharacteristically loosens his collar and tie and unbuttons his vest. He says that there is no medical evidence that the crime took place, and the only support for the charge is from two witnesses whose evidence is questionable. He says he pities Mayella, but not to the extent of excusing her choice to lie in order to cover up her own violation of the code that separates Blacks and whites. He suggests that Mayella's beating was given by Bob Ewell. Atticus reminds the jury that there is no characteristic true of all members of a given race, and that every person in the courtroom has told a lie and done something immoral at one time or another. He sites Thomas Jefferson's comment that "all men are created equal" and suggests that although this phrase has been misinterpreted, its proper meaning is clear: all are equal before the law, not as an ideal, but as a living reality. He concludes by asking the jury, "in the name of God," to do their duty and believe Tom Robinson.

As he finishes and turns around, Calpurnia walks into the courtroom.

Strategy 21 Revising Hypotheses

*Directions:
Read the
explanation;
then answer the
questions. You
may need to read
beyond this
chapter to answer
some questions.*

On page 32 of this book (Strategy 5: Forming Hypotheses), we suggested the hypothesis, "Maybe prejudice and bias prevent people from really seeing Boo Radley." Since then, we've seen that forming hypotheses about motivation and behavior are an integral topic of the story itself. A large portion of Part One treats hypotheses about how we understand, not only the one character Boo Radley, but human nature in general. And the second part, so far, has been devoted to unfolding Atticus's hypothesis about what really happened at the Ewells' on the November evening in question.

Now that it's become clear that the book has a wider focus, if we want a hypothesis about the broad meaning of the book, the hypothesis about Boo Radley needs to be expanded. As you work to revise your hypothesis to make it reflect Part Two as well as Part One, consider the relationship between Part One and Part Two—what ties them together? Don't forget the title of the book as you're thinking.

1. List situations in the book in which prejudice and bias block people's judgment.

2. Find and record important statements about prejudice made by characters in the book.

3. Make a new hypothesis that takes all this evidence into account.

Chapter 21

The Jury Decides

Vocabulary

verdict: 207, opinion of a jury on a question of fact
acquit: 207, bring a finding of not guilty
give (someone) down the country: 207, administer a scolding
remorse: 207, feelings of guilt caused by past wrongs
vengeance: 208, to an excessive degree
charged the jury: 208, entrusted the jury with their responsibility by giving them
    instructions concerning the guidelines they should apply as they seek a verdict
jury box: 209, location in a courtroom reserved for jury members during the trial
foreman: 211, the chairperson and spokesperson for a jury
polling the jury: 211, asking the jury, one by one, to verify their individual findings in the
    case that led to the joint verdict presented by the foreman

Journal and Discussion Topics

1. The following statements are on the topic of what's fit to say in front of others. Compare and contrast them by analyzing the attitudes behind them.
   a. " 'Don't talk like that in front of them' " (Aunt Alexandra, Chapter 16, p. 156).
   b. " 'Anything fit to say at the table's fit to say in front of Calpurnia' " (Atticus, Chapter 16, p. 157).
   c. " 'This ain't fit for Miss Jean Louise or you boys either' " (Reverend Sykes, Chapter 17, p. 173).
   d. " 'Ain't fittin' for children to hear' " (Calpurnia, Chapter 21, p. 207).
   e. " 'Mr. Jem, . . . this ain't a polite thing for little ladies to hear' " (Reverend Sykes, Chapter 21, p. 209).
2. What are the two different world views that prompt Jem's and Reverend Sykes's different predictions for the jury's findings?
3. Why does Lee compare the courtroom to a church (p. 209)?
4. What event in February led to the feelings that Scout experiences just before Heck returns? What does it mean in this setting?
5. What do the following statements have to do with each other?
   a. " 'Simply because we were licked a hundred years before we started is no reason for us not to try to win' " (Atticus, Chapter 9, p. 76).
   b. " 'courage is . . . when you know you're licked before you begin but you begin anyway and you see it through no matter what' " (Atticus, Chapter 11, p. 112).
   c. "it was like watching Atticus walk into the street, raise a rifle to his shoulder and pull the trigger, but watching all the time knowing that the gun was empty" (Narrator, Chapter 21, p. 211).
6. List the foreshadowings of the verdict in this chapter.
7. Why does Reverend Sykes insist that Scout rise?

Summary

Calpurnia gets Judge Taylor's attention and asks to give Atticus a message unrelated to the trial—his children are missing. Mr. Underwood, who spotted them in Chapter 18, tells Atticus that they're in the "colored balcony." The children go downstairs, and Jem shares his elation over his certainty that Atticus has won, but Atticus does not join in. He orders them to go home to supper and stay home; however, after Jem's pleading, Atticus considers that they've already seen the rest and gives permission for their return. They return home accompanied by Calpurnia's scolding remarks. Aunt Alexandra is shocked to learn where

they've been, and seems further dismayed by the news that Atticus has given permission for their return after supper.

They come back to find that Reverend Sykes has saved their places and the jury has been out thirty minutes. Jem and Reverend Sykes disagree on the likely outcome: Jem basing his ideas on the evidence, and Reverend Sykes basing his on history and human psychology. The waiting goes on till past eleven, and Dill and Scout fall asleep. Scout wakens and is overcome with a premonition that mirrors the feeling of waiting for the mad dog. Mr. Tate calls the court to order, and the jury returns. Scout notices that none of them look at Tom, and one by one they answer "guilty" to the poll. Atticus speaks to Tom briefly and walks quickly out of court. As Scout is just noticing that all the Blacks were rising to their feet at once, Reverend Sykes calls to her and tells her, "stand up. Your father's passin'."

Writer's Forum 9   News Article

A **news article** gives an objective report of an event that is important to the people who read that particular paper. The event can be local, national, or international, but it must have some impact on or hold some interest for the readership.

The headline of a news article both catches the reader's attention and declares the main topic of the article. Sports or feature articles may have a cryptic headline or one that includes wordplay to get the reader interested, but news headlines are usually straightforward.

The first paragraph of a news article gives the reader a quick summary of the important details, usually by telling the Five W's (Who, What, Where, When, and Why) and How. Following paragraphs give additional details that fill out the story.

News stories often include material gathered from interviews. This material may be stated indirectly or directly as quotations. If direct quotations are used, proper capitalization and punctuation should accompany it. Use care to make sure that you write the person's exact words.

Punctuating quotations properly shows which words are the exact words that the speaker said. Follow these rules:

- Put quotation marks around the words each speaker said.
- If the tag line that identifies the speaker comes before the quotation, put a comma after the tag line but before the quotation marks.
- If the tag line follows the quotation, put a comma inside the final quotation mark if the quotation ends with a period. If the quotation ends with a question mark or exclamation mark, skip the comma.
- If you place the tag line in the middle of the quotation, place a comma before the tag line inside the quotation marks and after it before the quotation marks.
- Start a new paragraph each time there is a new speaker, or if a speaker speaking for a long time switches topics.

1. Write a news story telling the world about the trial and verdict. You may choose to write it in the persona of Mr. Underwood, or you may pretend to be a reporter from another paper. If necessary, you may make up supporting information to add details to the story if your new material is in keeping with Lee's novel. You may also decide when the story was released. The story should include an interview with at least one individual who was at the trial.

   You may decide the readership of your paper. This will help shape how you choose to tell the story. Decide the name of the newspaper you are writing for. Give yourself a byline, and make your story look like a news article. You may include an illustration with a caption if you wish.

Vocabulary

Look at each group of words. Tell why it is important in the story.

1. Roman carnival, gala _____

_____

2. bantam cock, crepey, obscene speculations _____

_____

3. unmitigated temerity, distaff, idealist, integrity _____

_____

Essay Topics

1. Use these quotations to reflect on the appropriate relationship of the individual to the community.

   a. " 'He spends his time doin' things that wouldn't get done if nobody did 'em' " (p. 116).

   b. "A mob's always made up of people, no matter what" (p. 157).

   c. "He's half white. They're real sad. . . . They don't belong anywhere. Colored folks won't have 'em because they're half white; white folks won't have 'em 'cause they're colored, so they're just in-betweens, don't belong anywhere" (p. 161).

   d. "Every town the size of Maycomb has families like the Ewells. No economic fluctuations changed their status—people like the Ewells lived as guests of the county in prosperity as well as in the depths of a depression. No truant officers could keep their numerous offspring in school; no public health officer could free them from congenital defects, various worms, and the diseases indigenous to filthy surroundings. . . . Nobody was quite sure how many children were on the place . . . . Nobody had occasion to pass by except at Christmas, when the churches delivered baskets" (pp. 170–171).

   e. "Reverend Sykes leaned across Dill and me, pulling at Jem's elbow. . . . 'Mr. Finch know you all are here? This ain't fit for Miss Jean Louise or you boys either' " (p. 173).

   f. "Mayella Ewell must have been the loneliest person in the world. . . . white people wouldn't have anything to do with her because she lived among pigs; Negroes wouldn't have anything to do with her because she was white. She couldn't live like Mr. Dolphus Raymond, who preferred the company of Negroes, because she didn't own a riverbank and she wasn't from a fine old family. Nobody said, 'That's just their way,' about the Ewells. Maycomb gave them Christmas baskets, welfare money, and the back of its hand. Tom Robinson was probably the only person who was ever decent to her" (pp. 191–192).

   g. " 'Some folks don't—like the way I live. Now I could say the hell with 'em, I don't care if they don't like it. I do say I don't care if they don't like it, right enough—but I don't say the hell with 'em, see? . . . I try to give 'em a reason, you see. It helps folks if they can latch onto a reason. . . . It ain't honest but it's mighty helpful to folks' " (p. 200).

   h. "A court is only as sound as its jury, and a jury is only as sound as the men who make it up" (p. 205)

2. Compare Scout's crying (pp. 155–156) and Dill's crying (pp. 198–201) with Mayella's crying (pp. 179–180, 188).

3. Jem details the rape law in Alabama. Atticus says in his summation that it is a "capital crime," that is, it can be punished with the death penalty. Compare and contrast the information Jem and Atticus provide with the current sexual assault law in Alabama (see following excerpts from Code of Alabama, 1975). What is the crime that Tom would have been charged with under current law based on Mayella's testimony? What punishment might he have been given? What does the fact of the change in the law mean to you? What crime might Mayella have been charged with, if Tom had brought suit against her? What would the sentence be today?

Note: This is not an exercise in getting a verified legal opinion. Just apply common sense to facts as described in the text of the book and see how they seem to fit the law. Be aware that masculine pronouns are used sometimes in the code without regard to gender.

Excerpts from the Code of Alabama, 1975

Definitions

Sexual intercourse. Such term has its ordinary meaning and occurs upon any penetration, however slight, emission is not required.

Sexual contact. Any touching of the sexual or other intimate parts of a person not married to the actor, done for the purpose of gratifying the sexual desire of either party.

Forcible compulsion. Physical force that overcomes earnest resistance or a threat, express or implied, that places a person in fear of immediate death or serious physical injury to himself or another person.

Restrain. To intentionally or knowingly restrict a person's movements unlawfully and without consent, so as to interfere substantially with his liberty by moving him from one place to another, or by confining him either in the place where the restriction commences or in a place to which he has been moved. Restraint is "without consent" if it is accomplished by
a. physical force, intimidation, or deception, or
b. Any means, including acquiescence of the victim, if he is a child less than 16 years old or an incompetent person and the parent, guardian or other person or institution having lawful control or custody of him has not acquiesced in the movement or confinement.

Relative. A parent or stepparent, ancestor, sibling, uncle or aunt or other lawful custodian, including an adoptive relative of the same degree through marriage or adoption.

Crimes

Rape in the first degree A person commits the crime of rape in the first degree if:
1. He or she engages in sexual intercourse with a member of the opposite sex by forcible compulsion . . .

Rape in the first degree is a Class A felony.

Rape in the second degree A person commits the crime of rape in the second degree if:
1. Being 16 years old or older, he or she engages in sexual intercourse with a member of the opposite sex less than 16 and more than 12 years old; provided, however, the actor is at least two years older than the member of the opposite sex.
2. He or she engages in sexual intercourse with a member of the opposite sex who is incapable of consent by reason of being mentally defective.

Rape in the second degree is a Class B felony.

Sexual misconduct. A person commits the crime of sexual misconduct if:
1. Being male, he engages in sexual intercourse with a female without her consent, under circumstances other than those covered [under rape above]; or with her consent where consent was obtained by the use of any fraud or artifice; or
2. Being a female, she engages in sexual intercourse with a male without his consent. . . .

Sexual misconduct is a Class A misdemeanor.

Sexual abuse in the first degree. A person commits the crime of sexual abuse in the first degree if:
1. He subjects another person to sexual contact by forcible compulsion. . . .

Sexual abuse in the first degree is a Class C felony.

Criminal coercion. A person commits the crime of criminal coercion if, without legal authority, he threatens to confine, restrain or to cause physical injury to the threatened person or another, or to damage the property or reputation of the threatened person or another with intent thereby to induce the threatened person or another against his will to do an unlawful act or refrain from doing a lawful act.

Criminal coercion is a Class A misdemeanor.

Unlawful imprisonment in the first degree. A person commits the crime of unlawful imprisonment in the first degree if he restrains another person under circumstances which expose the latter to a risk of serious physical injury.

Unlawful imprisonment in the first degree is a Class A misdemeanor.

Unlawful imprisonment in the second degree. A person commits the crime of unlawful imprisonment in the second degree if he restrains another person.

A person does not commit a crime under this section if:
The person restrained is a child less than 18 years old, and
The actor is a relative of the child, and
The actor's sole purpose is to assume lawful control of the child. . . .

Unlawful imprisonment in the second degree is a Class C misdemeanor.

Sentencing Guidelines

Sentences of imprisonment for misdemeanors. Sentences for misdemeanors shall be a definite term of imprisonment in the county jail or to hard labor for the county, within the following limitations:

1. For a Class A misdemeanor, not more than one year.
2. For a Class B misdemeanor, not more than six months.
3. For a Class C misdemeanor, not more than three months.

Sentences of imprisonment for felonies. Sentences for felonies shall be for a definite period of imprisonment, which imprisonment includes hard labor, within the following limitations:

1. For a Class A felony, for life or not more than 99 years or less than 10 years.
2. For a Class B felony, not more than 20 years or less than 2 years.
3. For a Class C felony, not more than 10 years or less than 1 year and 1 day. . . .

4. Read Genesis 39-41 from the Hebrew Scriptures or Old Testament. Compare and contrast the story of the false accusation of rape made against a Hebrew slave by an Egyptian woman with the comparable part of *To Kill a Mockingbird*.

5. "Had he been less of a gentleman, [Atticus's] cross-examination of Mayella Ewell may have been more effective in revealing, for example, the father-daughter incest," says Claudia Johnson (*To Kill a Mockingbird: Threatening Boundaries,* p. 26) in explaining literary critic Tom Shaffer's evaluation of Atticus's handling of the case. Do you agree or disagree? Explain.

6. The narrator says of Dill, "After many telephone calls, much pleading on behalf of the *defendant* [italics added], and a long forgiving letter from his mother, it was decided that Dill could stay" (p. 144). What significance do you attribute to this placing of Dill in the same position as Tom Robinson?

Chapter 22

Reactions to the Verdict; Bob Ewell Threatens Atticus

Vocabulary

appeal: 213, request for a new hearing of a case by a higher court (which reviews the lower court decision) in hopes that the higher court may reverse the lower court's decision or call for a new trial

feral: 214, savage; wild and animal-like

diction: 214, style of speaking and word choice

fatalistic: 215, attitude of powerlessness

court-appointed defenses: 215, attorneys appointed by the court because the plaintiff is too poor to hire one

Journal and Discussion Topics

1. The evidence seems conclusive that Tom Robinson was innocent. Explain how you think it came about that the jury found him guilty.
2. What causes Jem to misjudge the outcome of the trial?
3. Two more characters cry in Chapter 22—Jem and Atticus. Why does each cry? What separates the characters who cry—Scout, Dill, Jem, Atticus, and Mayella—from the characters who don't?
4. Why does Atticus use the first person plural pronoun when he says about the outcome of the trial, "We've made it this way for them, they might as well learn to cope with it" (p. 212)?
5. Why does Atticus say about the Robinson case, "It's not time to worry yet" (p. 213)?
6. Aunt Alexandra accuses Dill of being cynical. Is he? Explain.
7. What does Miss Maudie mean when she says, "We're so rarely called on to be Christians, but when we are, we've got men like Atticus to go for us" (p. 215)?
8. What do you think Jem intended to say at the end of the unfinished sentence, "Soon's I get grown—"? Explain why you think so.
9. What's your reaction to Bob Ewell's threat?

Summary

Jem cries angrily as the children go to where Atticus is awaiting them and walk home. Aunt Alexandra expresses her sympathy, calling Atticus, "brother," for the first time in the children's memory. Atticus goes to bed, asking not to be awakened if he doesn't rise. But in the morning he is up as usual and reassures Jem that there will be an appeal. He interrupts himself to exclaim over the breakfast—chicken supplied by Tom Robinson's father and rolls made by another member of the Black community. Ushering Atticus to the kitchen, Calpurnia shows him the kitchen table loaded with gifts of food in gratitude for Atticus's service to Tom. Atticus, his eyes filled with tears, asks Calpurnia to convey his thanks and his wish that the givers not repeat their generosity, since times are so hard.

Atticus leaves for work, and Dill arrives. Jem chides him for going off the previous day without telling Miss Rachel, and Dill responds that he told her over and over—she was just too drunk to remember. Aunt Alexandra accuses him of being cynical, and he claims he's only being truthful. The children go out, and Miss Maudie calls them over to have some cake, an occasion worthy of note because for the first time Jem gets a slice of the "adult" cake, instead of his own little cake and because of the conversation between Jem and Maudie. Miss Maudie tells Jem that Atticus does the community's unpleasant jobs for it, and Jem reveals the essential issue for him: He had thought Maycomb folks "were the best folks in the world." Miss Maudie tries to make him see that there is support that he hasn't seen: that Judge Taylor didn't appoint Atticus by accident; that the jury was out for hours not minutes. Jem begins a sentence "Soon's I get grown—" inferring that he plans to leave Maycomb. Dill responds that when he's grown, he'll be a clown and (unlike most clowns who are sad) he's going to stand in the ring and laugh at folks. As they leave, they see Miss Stephanie and Miss Rachel waving, and the ladies announce that earlier in the day Bob Ewell had spat in Atticus's face and threatened to "get him."

Chapter 23

Picking the Jury in Retrospect; Folks

Vocabulary

threatened: 217, declared an intention to inflict damage or injury to another by a wrongful act

put . . . under a peace bond: 218, a bond imposed by a judge (on a person who has threatened to breach the peace) to guarantee the person's good behavior for a period of time

credibility: 218, believability; trustworthiness

furtive: 218, secretive; stealthy

commutes: 219, alters; reduces

acquittal: 219, a finding of not guilty; setting free from the charge of an offense

statute: 219, law

circumstantial: 219, evidence that proves a fact, not directly, as in an eye-witness account, but by inference

eye-witnesses: 219, those who see and report their observations pertaining to the matter at hand

reasonable doubt: 219, the technical term guiding jurors in the degree of uncertainty about a defendant's guilt that they must have in order to vote for acquittal

adamant: 220, unshakable

stolidly: 220, without showing much emotion

indignant: 221, angered by injustice

sordid: 221, morally impure

excuses: 221, relieves him from his civic duty of serving on a jury in this particular case following set criteria

strike him: 222, remove a prospective juror that counsel thinks may have an unfavorable view or bias in the case

droned: 223, murmured

infantile: 226, childish; immature

pot liquor: 226, liquid left in a pot after cooking something

Journal and Discussion Topics

1. In this chapter, how does Atticus demonstrate the truth of Miss Maudie's statement about him—"Atticus Finch is the same in his house as he is on the public streets." (p. 46)?

2. Do you think Aunt Alexandra is correct in her assessment of Bob Ewell? Do you think Atticus is? Why do Jem and Scout cease to be afraid?

3. What do you think of the circumstantial evidence argument?

4. The narrator says, "perhaps our forefathers were wise" in not putting women on juries. What's your reaction?

5. How does Atticus define trash (p. 220)? How does Aunt Alexandra (p. 225)? How does Scout (p. 226)? How does Mrs. DuBose (p. 102)? How does Dill (p. 161)? Do you think there's a purpose to having any of these classifications of people, whatever word is used to name them?

6. React to Scout's conclusion: "I think there's just one kind of folks. Folks."

7. Do you agree with Jem's assessment of Boo at the end of the chapter? Explain.

Summary

Atticus's mild response to Bob Ewell's threat is that he wishes Ewell didn't chew tobacco. Miss Stephanie tells Jem and Scout the story, and they are disturbed. They decide to ask Atticus to borrow a gun, but he won't. Jem suggests that Scout throw a fit and cry, but this doesn't move Atticus either. But he does notice a change in their behavior, and when he asks them why, Jem tells him, "Mr. Ewell." Atticus understands that Bob Ewell threatened him and spat in his face as a retaliation for his humiliation at the trial, but he believes that the catharsis has taken place and there's nothing more to fear. Aunt Alexandra doesn't agree and tells Atticus of her concern, but Atticus dismisses her fears, and Jem and Scout are calmed.

Atticus lets the children know that Tom's case is being reviewed, and he may go free or have a new trial. He says that there is a good chance. Jem questions whether rape should be a capital offense and points out that the jury could have given Tom twenty years. Atticus says that this jury had to acquit or invoke the full penalty of the law, but he adds that he objects to the death penalty being given in cases with only circumstantial evidence. He suggests a change in the law that would have the judge, rather than the jury, set the sentence in capital cases. Jem again argues against the injustice of the decision, and Atticus responds more emotionally than he has any time previously, telling Jem and Scout that a white man who takes advantage of a Black man's ignorance is "trash."

Jem suddenly asks why townspeople like Miss Maudie and the Finches don't serve on juries, and Atticus explains that, first of all, women can't serve on juries in Alabama. He explains that townspeople avoid jury duty to avoid offending their neighbors and having to make up their minds. Jem responds that Tom's jury decided quickly, and Atticus counters that they didn't—they took a few hours because one person—one of the Cunningham clan who had confronted Atticus at the jail—was holding out for acquittal. Jem is amazed that Atticus put that man on the jury, and Atticus replies that when everyone is certain to convict, a man who is unsettled is a bonus. In addition, he points to three Cunningham traits that swayed him: first, that they don't take anything from anyone. Second, once their respect is won, they support you wholeheartedly. Third, they rarely change their minds.

Scout decides that she should invite Walter over sometime when they go back to school, but Aunt Alexandra objects, encouraging Scout to be nice to Walter—but at a distance. When Scout asks her again, Aunt Alexandra replies, "Because—he—is—trash," and concludes by telling Scout "You're enough of a problem to your father as it is." Jem saves the sobbing Scout from further mishap by leading her to his room, where he comforts her and tries to explain Aunt Alexandra to her. She counters that it is the comment about Walter that bothers her—that the Cunninghams are not like the Ewells. Jem explains his theory of four kinds of people in Maycomb County: the townspeople, the rural folks, the people like the Ewells who live near the dump, and the Blacks. Each group despises the group below it. The conversation continues as Jem and Scout try to fathom the classes of people, until Scout says, "I think there's just one kind of folks. Folks." Jem responds that he used to think that as well, but wonders why, if there is only one kind of folks, they don't get along with each other? He concludes by saying that he thinks Boo Radley stays shut up "because he *wants* to stay inside."

Writer's Forum 10

Summary

A **summary** is a useful tool for focusing attention on the major points made in a piece of writing that is too lengthy to remember in its entirety. A summary is a selection with a purpose: The same piece of writing could be summarized in more than one way, depending on why you want to recall parts of it. You choose what is most important to you at this time for this reason.

Here are some steps you can take:

- Identify your purpose for summarizing.
- Using your purpose as a focus, review the material, noting the main ideas in your own words.
- Write a separate sentence for each main idea.
- Organize your notes in a logical order for your purpose. (Often this may be chronological order or the order of appearance in the material from which you are summarizing, but other orders are possible.)
- As you write your summary, use transitions to show the relation of one idea to another.
- Review your summary to be sure it fulfills your purpose.

1. Summarize the argument between Aunt Alexandra and Scout about Walter to "match it up" with Jem's and Scout's refutations. What are your conclusions?

Chapter 24   Missionary Circle Meeting

Vocabulary

yaws: 228, infectious and contagious tropical disease that causes ulcerating lesions
vocation: 230, occupation; career
commenced: 230, began
impertinence: 230, rudeness
duress: 230, pressure; force
devout: 230, religiously devoted
oppressed: 230, people burdened by abuses of power or authority
squalor: 231, degradation; filth
largo: 232, slow, stately musical tempo
sulky: 232, sullen; moody; temperamental
replenishing: 232, refilling
sibilant: 232, hissing
bovine: 232, cowlike
hypocrites: 234, those who pretend (1) to be what they are not or (2) to believe what they do not

Journal and Discussion Topics

1. Guns are shot twice in the novel. Compare and contrast the circumstances.
2. What irony is there in the missionary circle's fascination with the Mrunas?
3. What is the news about the preacher's wife? What does this part of the conversation reveal about the missionary circle?
4. What do you think has made Scout decide that she wants to be a lady?
5. Why is it ironic that Mrs. Merriweather is known as "the most devout lady in Maycomb" (p. 230)?
6. Why did Aunt Alexandra look at Maudie with gratitude?
7. Why is Mrs. Merriweather blurting out the word *hypocrite* ironic?
8. Calpurnia says, "First thing you learn when you're in a lawin' family. . . ." How does her choice of phrasing support what Atticus told his sister about Calpurnia's relationship to the family?
9. What does "background" mean in Miss Maudie's view?

Summary

Aunt Alexandra is hosting the missionary circle, and during the business section of the meeting Mrs. Merriweather gives a report on the Mrunas (Scout's understanding of the name) and their abysmal living conditions. Scout helps Calpurnia carry in coffee for the ladies' refreshment, and Aunt Alexandra invites her to stay. For a few moments the conversation revolves around Scout, and it comes out that she is wearing her britches under her dress. She is asked if she wants to be a lawyer when she grows up, but responds, "Nome, just a lady." At a question from Scout, Mrs. Merriweather launches into a eulogy to J. Grimes Everett, the missionary working with the Mrunas. The subject switches to some woman in Maycomb whom the church should help to lead a Christian life, and Scout assumes that Mrs. Merriweather is speaking about Mayella, but it turns out that she is speaking about Tom Robinson's wife (whose name she can't remember). Mrs. Merriweather goes on to complain about the local Black reaction to the trial verdict and tells how she chastised her cook.

Mrs. Farrow opines that Maycomb ladies aren't safe in their beds, and Mrs. Merriweather responds that there are "some good but misguided people in this town," who are only succeeding in stirring up the Black population. Recognizing an insult to Atticus, Miss Maudie steps in to defend him. Aunt Alexandra passes refreshments to get past the moment but looks her thanks to Miss Maudie.

Scout reflects on gender differences, asserting that she is more at home in her father's world. Her opinion that women can be hypocrites is emphasized by Mrs. Merriweather completing her thought by saying the word *hypocrites*.

Atticus suddenly comes in with a white face and asks Aunt Alexandra to accompany him to the kitchen because he needs to borrow Calpurnia for a few moments. Miss Maudie joins them, and he tells them that Tom Robinson is dead, shot seventeen times as he tried to escape over the prison fence. Atticus wants Cal to go with him to tell Helen. After a few moments for recovery, Miss Maudie, Aunt Alexandra, and Scout rejoin the ladies, and take over Calpurnia's service role. Scout concludes, "After all, if Aunty could be a lady at a time like this, so could I."

Strategy 22

Stock Characters and Character Foils

Directions: Read the explanation; then answer the questions.

Some characters in fiction are purposely created merely to fill a role in a story rather than to be fully developed and realistic. We even call such characters by generic names: the hard-bitten detective, the mad scientist, the damsel in distress—these are some of the **stock characters** we find in fiction. Stock characters are stereotypes and so are easy to recognize because of their flat depictions with no development. They create a kind of shorthand between writer and reader because just a few traits suggest the idea, and the reader can complete the picture him- or herself.

Sometimes a character may seem to be stock but break out of the role. Mr. Dolphus Raymond is an example. He looks and acts like a cross between the town drunk and the town eccentric. That's how Jem and Scout have him pegged, until in conversation with Dill and Scout we and they realize that his character is more complex and more realistic than we had previously thought.

Another technique writers use is to juxtapose two characters who stand for opposite points of view or ways of life. Called **character foils**, characters in sets of this kind highlight each other's features. Usually one of the characters is the protagonist. The protagonist may have more than one foil.

1. Find a name for the stock character that Mrs. Dubose at first seems to be. Then explain how she breaks out of the role.

2. Find names for the stock characters of Mrs. Merriweather, Mrs. Farrow, and J. Grimes Everett. Tell what led you to choose as you did.

3. Identify any character foils so far in the book. How do the foils offset each other?

Chapter 25

Vocabulary

There are no vocabulary words in this chapter.

Journal and Discussion Topics

1. Explain Dill's relationship with his father.
2. Reread the exchange between Dill and Jem about the turtle (p. 14) and the section about killing a mockingbird (p. 90). In the light of these ideas, what do you make of Jem's attitude toward the roly-poly? How would you respond to Scout's conclusion that Jem's "getting more like a girl every day"?
3. In the light of the roly-poly incident, how do you interpret Dill's observation that Helen Robinson " 'Just fell down in the dirt, like a giant with a big foot just came along and stepped on her. . . . like you'd step on an ant' "?
4. What kind of career do you think Dill would be suited for as an adult? Why?
5. Writer Walker Percy in his essay "The Loss of the Creature" (*The Message in the Bottle,* New York: Farrar, Straus & Giroux, 1976, p. 58) says, "As Kierkegaard said, once a person is seen as a specimen of a race or a species, at that very moment he ceases to be an individual. Then there are no more individuals, but only specimens." What light does this shed on Maycomb's reaction to Tom's death?
6. How does Mr. Underwood's editorial add to your ideas about the ultimate meaning (themes) of the book?
7. React to this statement: "Tom was a dead man the minute Mayella Ewell opened her mouth and screamed" (p. 241).
8. Do you think Jem's assessment of Bob Ewell is accurate? Explain your reasoning.

Summary

One night Scout is about to squash a roly-poly bug when Jem admonishes her to put it outside because it doesn't "bother" her. Scout gets comfortable on her cot and thinks of Dill while she waits to fall asleep. But the thought of Dill learning to swim sends her back to the day of the missionary circle meeting, the day Tom Robinson died. Dill had told her afterward that he and Jem were at Barker's Eddy so Jem could teach Dill to swim. They were walking home when they spotted Atticus and waved to him. After Jem pleaded, they were allowed to come if they stayed in the car, and on the way to the Robinsons', Atticus told them what had happened. When they arrived, Atticus asked Sam Robinson to fetch his mother. Helen arrived, greeted Atticus, looked at his face, and as Dill describes it to Scout later, Helen " 'fell down in the dirt, like a giant with a big foot just came along and stepped on her.' "

Calpurnia and Atticus helped Helen inside, and when Atticus finally came out, Calpurnia stayed with Helen. The narrator reports that the interest in Tom's death lasted about two days, and that it was considered "typical." Mr. Underwood wrote an editorial about Tom in which "he likened Tom's death to the senseless slaughter of songbirds." Scout concludes that "in the secret courts of men's hearts Atticus had no case. Tom was a dead man the minute Mayella Ewell opened her mouth and screamed." Bob Ewell's response to Tom's death was "one down and about two more to go," as Jem reported to Scout, adding that Mr. Ewell was more talk than action and that if she mentioned the comment to Atticus, he would never speak to her again.

Writer's Forum 11

A **eulogy** is a public tribute, written or spoken, often to honor a person who has recently died. It includes at least a brief biography of the person, and then highlights the most praiseworthy parts of his or her life, using examples and anecdotes to illustrate points. It may refer to his or her favorite or most cherished people, causes, interests, and possessions. Often, if the subject is an adult, there is elaboration of the person's role in and value to his or her community. Quotations of noteworthy sayings from the person being honored may also be included. With all these possibilities, it is clear that a eulogy may contain elements of description and narration, but it also can contain expressive writing, like poetry and literature.

An **anecdote** is a short, self-contained, interesting, humorous, or insightful story. Like any other narrative, an anecdote has a plot with a beginning, middle, and end. It also generally has characters, sometimes even a main character. But unlike most narratives, it often does not have a well-developed setting and very little, if any, character development. Also, unlike other types of narratives, it is likely to have a lesson or a punchline, or some other fairly explicit way of stating what the point is. And there usually isn't much room for interpretation of that point.

Anecdotes may include conversation. For punctuating dialogue, see Writer's Forum 9: A News Article (p. 109).

1. Write a eulogy for Tom Robinson from a persona of your choice. First, decide your relationship to Tom. Second, determine when and where and how the eulogy will be presented and to whom. (Reverend Sykes's church or Tom's burial are two possibilities.) Then write your piece, praising Tom. You may add details (such as his birthdate, birthplace, and family history) that are in keeping with the story.

Chapter 26 Hitler and Democracy

Vocabulary

recluse: 242, person shut off from society by choice

poise: 243, self-assured manner

spurious: 244, not considered to be legitimate

holy-roller: 244, member of a religious sect whose worship meetings are characterized by spontaneous expressions of emotional excitement

prosecutin': 244, dialect for *prosecuting*; bringing legal action for alleged criminal or law-breaking activities

persecuting: 244, causing suffering because of beliefs

dictatorship: 245, form of government in which absolute power is concentrated in one person

prejudiced: 245, holding preconceived judgments or opinions

enunciated: 245, pronounced carefully

maniac: 246, lunatic

undue: 247, excessive; more than proper

Journal and Discussion Topics

1. Scout learns that Atticus actually knew that she, Dill, and Jem had been at the Radleys' the night Jem lost his pants. What do you conclude about Atticus?

2. If people were so dissatisfied with Atticus, why do you think they continued to elect him to the legislature?

3. Scout lists a group of activities that "the state paid teachers to discourage" (p. 244). What conclusions can you draw about the State of Alabama's view of the role of education in the world of the story? How does it compare to the education you've experienced?

4. Why do you think Lee introduced the confusion between the words *prosecuting* and *persecuting*?

5. Miss Gates says, "Over here we don't believe in persecuting anybody. Persecution comes from people who are prejudiced" (p. 245). Why is this ironic?

6. What does Cecil's question, "They're white, ain't they?" (p. 245) imply?

7. Scout thinks, "Looked to me like they'd shut Hitler in a pen instead of letting him shut them up" (p. 246). What does this suggest about Scout's view of the responsibility for Hitler's actions?

8. Do you agree with Atticus's dictum, "It's not okay to hate anybody" (p. 245)? Explain.

9. Why does Jem get so angry when Scout explains Miss Gates's hypocrisy? What is he trying to forget?

Summary

School starts and with it the routine of walking by the Radleys', which leads Scout to reflect again about Boo, remembering their attempts to make him come out and the items found in the tree. She toys with looking for him and imagines a meeting sometime in the future but concludes that it is only a fantasy. Atticus warns her to leave it, pointing out that Nathan Radley shoots at trespassers, and commenting "You were lucky not to get shot," revealing to Scout that he knew all along what happened the night Jem lost his pants.

Scout tries to leave the events of the summer behind, but they are brought back by a discussion in school when Cecil introduces a news article about Adolf Hitler, prompting Miss Gates to explain that only prejudiced people persecute others, and that doesn't happen in America, which is a democracy where there are equal rights for all. Scout senses something wrong and asks Atticus if it's okay to hate Hitler. He says it's not okay to hate anyone. There is something else on her mind, but she doesn't say it to Atticus—she goes instead to Jem. To him, she explains that Miss Gates hates Hitler because it's not right to persecute anyone. But Scout recalls that when they left the courthouse after Tom Robinson's trial, she heard Miss Gates tell Miss Stephanie that the Blacks needed to learn a lesson to prevent them from thinking they could marry white people. Jem becomes furious and orders Scout to never again speak to him about the courthouse. Scout goes to Atticus who explains to her that Jem is trying to forget something until enough time had passed for him to be able to think about it.

Vocabulary

Look at each group of words. Tell why it is important in the story.

1. devout, sulky, sibilant, hypocrites _____

   _____

2. prosecutin', persecuting, dictatorship, prejudiced _____

   _____

Essay Topics

1. Atticus says to Aunt Alexandra that the trial was "just as much Maycomb County as missionary teas" (p. 212). What parallels do you see between the two milieus?

2. How did Atticus apply a theory of heredity and character in his jury selection? What, if any, other criteria did he use?

3. What was your reaction to Dill's story of how he tried to tell Miss Rachel where he was going the day of the trial? How does this fit with the picture of his life at home, as reported to Scout in Chapter 14?

4. What do you think of Scout's education?

5. Atticus opined that "things have a way of settling down." Do you think the matter of Tom Robinson's trial and Bob Ewell's threats are done? What loose ends in the story do you see that "need" to be tied up?

Chapter 27

Bob Ewell Trespasses at Judge Taylor's, Trails Helen

Vocabulary

WPA: 248, Works Progress Administration; program of the Second New Deal formed to create jobs and reduce unemployment

notoriety: 248, state of being well-known in a negative way

fruity: 248, overly sentimental

florid: 248, flowery and wordy

carcass: 249, worthless body, most often used of a corpse

assault: 249, threat or attempt to hurt someone that either puts a person in physical danger or causes him/her to fear harm

assessment: 250, evaluation; appraisal

radical: 250, extreme in views or opinions; advocating extreme measures

National Recovery Act/nine old men: 251, National Industrial Recovery Act (NIRA) passed in June, 1933 and ruled unconstitutional by the Supreme Court ("nine old men") in 1935

dog Victrolas: 251, record player with a dog as a trademark

purloined: 252, stolen

pageant: 252, a loosely unified drama

Ad Astra Per Aspera: 252, Latin phrase meaning "to the stars through difficulties" (state motto of Kansas)

contraption: 253, invented device, often with unusual qualities

tactfully: 253, politely

escort: 253, accompany; walk with (sometimes in order to protect)

Journal and Discussion Topics

1. Whom do you think trespassed at Judge Taylor's? What led you to this conclusion?
2. What in this chapter draws a connection between Boo Radley and Tom Robinson? How are they parallel?
3. Link Deas says to Bob Ewell, "If I hear one more peep outa my girl Helen" (p. 249). What do you think he's indicating by the use of the personal possessive *my*? How does this compare to Calpurnia's use of *my* in regard to Scout and Jem?
4. What does the success of Link's campaign to protect Helen suggest about Bob Ewell?
5. Analyze Aunt Alexandra's and Atticus's exchange about Bob Ewell. What assumptions about human nature and character are implicit in their conclusions?
6. How is what J. Grimes Everrett doing for the Mruna's social life with the support from people like Mrs. Merriweather similar to what's being done in the Maycomb schools with the rural white children?
7. What do you think of the whole tribe being "one big family"? Is it wrong/bad/immoral/cruel/misguided/inappropriate? How do people outside the immediate family in Maycomb act like family?
8. Are Misses Tutti and Frutti stock characters? Explain?
9. What do you think the last sentence of this chapter means? What evidence supports your conclusion(s)?

Summary

By October, the narrator reports, things had settled down except for three unsettling incidents. First, Mr. Bob Ewell got a WPA job, was fired within a few days, and publicly blamed Atticus. Second, Judge Taylor's screen door was cut by a trespasser who ran away before being identified. Third, Bob Ewell began stalking Helen Robinson, only giving up when Mr. Link Deas threatened him. Again, Aunt Alexandra is disturbed, but Atticus is calm.

One new October event was a Halloween pageant. Since the prior year some children had played a practical joke on two maiden ladies, Tutti and Frutti Barber (taking all their furniture and hiding it in their cellar), parents had decided that a planned Halloween celebration was in order. Organized by Mrs. Merriweather, the evening would provide activities for the children and a pageant about Maycomb County for the adults, featuring children dressed as the county's agricultural products. Scout is cast as a ham, and has a cloth and chicken wire costume.

Scout does a demonstration for Aunt Alexandra and Atticus who have decided to stay home, and Aunt Alexandra has a momentary twinge of apprehension. Then Scout and Jem, her escort for the evening, set out on what is to be, according to the narrator, their "longest journey together."

Writer's Forum 12   Possible Ending

The end of a book is a special part because it usually is meant to round off all the little details and plot bits, explain what needs an explanation, put a final exclamation point on the themes, leave the characters in a situation of equilibrium or show their disequilibrium in a striking way, noting what has happened to all the important characters, and send the reader off feeling that all loose ends have been tied up or that the situation is so complex and tangled that no neat ending is possible. The ending should make sense of the foreshadowings and plot development that has occurred so far in the book, and play out the main ideas that have been treated in the book so far.

1. Write an ending for *To Kill a Mockingbird*, picking up after Chapter 27 ends. Do not look ahead in the book while you do this.

Chapter 28

Halloween Pageant and Return Home

Vocabulary

incantations: 254, spells; a particular sequence of words believed to have magical powers
blissful: 254, joyful; happy
irascible: 255, hot-tempered
lament: 255, mournful sound
gait: 255, pace; stride; rate of progress
crap games: 255, gambling games played using two dice
ventured: 255, dared to come
component: 256, constituent part
billowed: 257, swelled outward; bulged
teeming: 257, full to overflowing with
lichen: 258, complex plant made up of algae and fungus
exploits: 258, notable or heroic acts
floundering: 262, thrashing about; moving clumsily or ineffectively
entangled: 262, tangled up; ensnared
pinioned: 262, restrained by having one's arms bound or held
hexagonal: 264, six-sided
distraction: 264, absent-minded state
boil-prone: 264, having a tendency to get boils (a type of skin inflammation)
untrammeled: 266, unimpeded; unrestrained
sought: 266, searched for

Journal and Discussion Topics

1. In what ways does Jem behave like a true gentleman in this chapter?
2. What do you think of the argument about bobbing for apples?
3. *Ad Astra Per Aspera* really means "to the stars through difficulties." What can you gather from Mrs. Merriweather's comments about the phrase?
4. How would you evaluate the entertainment value of Mrs. Merriweather's pageant? Be specific and explain your criteria.
5. Who is the "countryman" who brought Jem home?
6. How does Aunt Alexandra's behavior in this chapter differ from how she has behaved earlier?
7. Did you know before Heck's comment that the attack was made by Bob Ewell? If so, explain how you knew. If not, what did you think and why?

Summary

Scout and Jem set out, and hear a mockingbird as they pass the Radleys' house. Blinded by the lights of the auditorium, they look at the ground and are surprised by Cecil's jumping out at them in a sheet. Scout stows her costume and goes off with Cecil to enjoy activities until the pageant. They visit the House of Horrors, buy divinity, discuss bobbing for apples, and then it's time to prepare for the pageant. Scout's costume has been mashed, but Mrs. Merriweather quickly helps reshape it. The pageant begins with Mrs. Merriweather's account of the history of Maycomb County, including the embarrassing exploits of Colonel Maycomb, told at such great length that Scout falls asleep and misses her entrance. It is not until the finale that Scout awakens, decides she had better catch up, and bounds onstage as Mrs. Merriweather is parading the state flag. Mrs. Merriweather tells Scout afterward that her late entrance ruined the pageant, but Jem comforts her. Nevertheless, Scout is embarrassed; she decides to go home inside her costume, and they wait until pretty much everyone else is gone. Scout forgets her shoes, but Jem says they can get them the following day.

Suddenly Jem tells Scout to hush. He thinks he's heard something following them. Concluding that it's Cecil, they walk slowly so he'll know they're not scared. They call to him, but Cecil doesn't answer, and they figure it isn't him. Jem suggests that Scout change into her dress, which he has brought along, but she says it will be difficult in the dark.

They continue to hear the shuffling sound behind them. Suddenly when they are under the tree by the Radleys', the footsteps do not stop when the children do, but keep coming. Jem cries out to Scout to run, but she loses her balance, and feels the chicken wire costume crushed while metal rips through it, and she falls. Jem scuffles on the ground, then gets up and pulls Scout to her feet. Entangled in her costume, Scout moves slowly, and when they near the road, Jem is jerked back away from her, hits the ground, and then there is a crunching sound, and Jem screams. Scout runs to Jem and hits a male stomach, the owner of which grabs her and squeezes her till she begins to lose her breath. Then he is jerked backward and flung to the ground, making Scout think that Jem is up. The scuffle ends, and Scout hears only wheezing and then coughing.

Scout calls to Jem but receives no answer. The wheezing man moves around, and Scout realizes there are four people under the tree. She says her father's name, but receives no answer. The wheezing man is walking unsteadily toward the road. Scout tries to find Jem but finds a man lying on the ground who smells of whiskey. Scout attempts to find the road, and looking down toward the street light she sees a man carrying an overwhelming load—Jem, whose arm is dangling. Scout sees Atticus framed in the Finches' doorway and then running down the stairs to help the man bring Jem in. She follows and hears Atticus call, "Where's Scout?" and Aunt Alexandra affirms that Scout is there.

Dr. Reynolds and the sheriff are called, and Aunt Alexandra works Scout out of her costume, calling her "darling" and fetching her overalls to put on. Scout asks both Atticus and Aunt Alexandra if Jem is dead, and both tell her no, but they need to wait for the doctor. Dr. Reynolds arrives shortly. When he returns from Jem's room, Scout asks him the same question. He reports that Jem has suffered a bump on the head and a broken arm, but he's not dead. Scout, still concerned, asks him again, and he sends her in to see for herself. At the same time, Mr. Heck Tate comes in and accompanies her.

Scout looks at Jem and then notices the "countryman" who had brought Jem home, standing in the corner. She imagines that he was at the pageant and came running when he heard them scream. Atticus asks Heck if he found anything, adding that he can't conceive of anybody low enough to attack children. Heck invites Atticus to sit down, and Atticus fetches chairs so they can all sit. The sheriff begins to tell what he found: a dress (identified as Scout's), some muddy-colored cloth (identified as Scout's costume), and Bob Ewell lying dead with a knife stuck in his ribs.

Strategy 23   Adjusting Reading Rate

Directions: Read the explanation; then answer the questions.

How quickly or slowly we read may be an aspect of reading we don't think too much about. It may be automatic for us to adjust our speed to cope with different kinds of text and purpose. But let's just stop for a moment here and identify some of the indications that might lead us to purposely slow down our reading, and if necessary, reread material (for more on re-reading, see Strategy 26: Rereading a Book, p. 144).

Reading Situation	How to Adjust
Difficult vocabulary	Slow down to use context clues or consult outside sources for word meanings.
Long complex or compound sentences	Slow down to ensure that relationships between grammatical elements are well understood.
Unfamiliar subject matter	Slow down or reread to make sure that new ideas/concepts/insights are grasped.
Format	Slow down to read charts, maps, graphs, and other illustrations that require more inference than reading text.
Description of some unclear/confusing phenomenon	Slow down and reread when something by its very nature cannot be well or clearly described.
Varying importance of material in context	Slow down for more important material; increase reading rate for less important material.

Specific Purposes for Reading (some examples)	How to Adjust
Want/need to remember/memorize material	Slow down and reread to retain all details.
Need to correlate with other material	Slow down and mark the text with parallels and antitheses you've noted.
Preparing for a paper, class discussion, or test	Slow down and pay more attention to details, order of events, relationship among parts, etc.; reread as necessary.

In general, we might imagine the different varieties of text as being on a continuum. At one extreme would be texts that use words and sentences and sounds only to convey information, after which the particular words, sentences, and sounds have no special importance. After you have acquired the knowledge, it no longer is important how you acquired it. To convey the idea that the king is dead, it is probably not important whether the sentence that delivers that information is:

- "The king is dead" or
- "The king has passed away" or
- "The king succumbed to an illness" or
- "The king is no longer with us"

and so on. In any of these cases, the content of the message is conveyed, and the message itself no longer matters.

At the other end of the spectrum is poetry, in which the meaning cannot be separated from the particular words, word groups, and sounds the writer chose. Here sound and sense along with spelling and grammar and mechanics and usage are *one* thing. The experience of these particular choices makes the one thing that constitutes the poem for the reader. Information exists apart from the way it is conveyed; a poem does not.

In between these two outliers we find narrative fiction—what we call literature. Where on the continuum a particular work of literature, or a particular part of a particular work, lies depends on how it is written. We can only discover its place by the experience itself. But a good approach to literature is to start reading it as if it were written with the care and intentionality of poetry, as if "everything counts."

1. Without looking back, explain in as much detail as you can what happened to Scout and Jem on their way home from the pageant.

2. Reread the pertinent part of Chapter 28 and then write a detailed summary of what happened to Jem and Scout on the way home. Consciously make choices about your reading rate. Write about what happened on the way home and about how you adjusted your reading. Compare your two explanations. What conclusions can you draw?

Chapter 29

Scout Tells Her Story and Meets Boo

Vocabulary

bleakly: 267, grimly
turmoil: 267, agitation; distress
reprimand: 270, scold
indentations: 270, hollows
spasm: 270, involuntary muscle contraction

Journal and Discussion Topics

1. What's ironic about Heck Tate's statement, "He's good and dead"?
2. Why does Aunt Alexandra say it was her fault? Explain whether or not you agree with her and why.
3. What does the "shiny clean line" on Scout's costume indicate?
4. Atticus says Bob Ewell was crazy. Heck Tate disagrees and says Ewell was evil. What support do you find for each opinion in the story? What's your view?
5. When did you realize that the man who carried Jem home was Boo? If you knew before Scout greeted him, what clues led you to your conclusion?
6. Why did Scout have tears in her eyes when she said hello to Boo?
7. In retrospect, what are the functions of the mad dog scene besides revealing Atticus's ability with a gun?

Summary

Aunt Alexandra and Atticus are both shocked by Heck Tate's news that Bob Ewell has been killed. Atticus asks if Heck is sure, and Heck replies that Bob Ewell won't hurt the children again, but Atticus says that isn't what he meant. Alexandra apologizes for not following her premonition, and Heck says we can't always follow all feelings. Heck asks Scout to tell what happened.

Scout tells that as they started walking home, the lights at the school went out. Jem told her to hush because he heard something. At first they thought it was Cecil because he had scared them earlier dressed in a sheet and they yelled back at him, but got no answer. Heck interrupts to find out if Atticus heard them calling to Cecil, but he didn't since he had the radio on.

Scout mentions that she could hear the footsteps then, even in the ham costume, and the costume's construction explains to Heck the marks on Bob Ewell's sleeves and arms (from the chicken wire). Heck asks Atticus to bring him what's left of the costume, and his examination shows a rip mark where a knife cut through the costume. "Bob Ewell meant business," he remarks. Atticus responds that Bob Ewell was crazy, but Heck Tate counters that Bob Ewell was mean.

Scout continues that when they got under the tree, she was grabbed. Jem found her and they started toward the road; then Mr. Ewell yanked Jem down, there was a noise, and Jem hollered. The next thing Scout was aware of was Mr. Ewell squeezing the breath out of her, and then he was yanked away. Scout suggests that Jem got up and pulled Mr. Ewell away from her. Then she heard the wheezing and coughing. First she thought it was Jem and then Atticus. The sheriff asks who it turned out to be, and Scout points to the man standing in the corner. And now, Scout really looks at the man, who shyly smiles, and with tears in her eyes she says, "Hey, Boo."

Strategy 24

Logical Fallacies

A **logical fallacy** is a faulty argument in which something besides reason contributes to the conclusion drawn. Many fallacies have been named and categorized to make it easier to recognize and remember them. In this book, where the use of valid argument (as opposed both to prejudicial thinking and to violence) is an important topic, you can gain something from analyzing the logic of the characters' statements and conclusions.

Two basic forms of valid reasoning are deduction and induction.

Deductive reasoning moves from the general to a specific instance of the general cases being considered. If something is true in general, and an instance is really representative of that general class, then the truth will hold for the specific instance. Syllogisms are examples of deductive reasoning.

The standard syllogism form follows:

Every X is Y.	Something, Y, is true in general of a class called X.
C is X.	C is a member of the class called X.
Therefore, C is Y.	What is true in general of the class called X, is true of each of its members; therefore, Y is true of C.

Fallacies in deductive reasoning come about when the first statement of a syllogism is not true, or if C (whatever it is in the example) is assumed to be a member of X when it truly isn't.

Inductive reasoning moves from the particular to the general. It is harder to achieve certainty in this way because you have to determine when you've looked at enough particular examples to be able to draw a general rule that will hold good in all cases.

The following is not a complete list of logical fallacies, but it includes faulty arguments that are used in this book.

Insufficient Evidence
Hasty generalization—drawing a conclusion with too little evidence
Fallacy of exclusion—leaving out evidence that would change the outcome of an inductive argument
Oversimplification—making a complex issue simple by ignoring some of its aspects

Directions: Read the explanation; then complete the exercises.

Cause and Effect Mistakes
Gambler's due—assuming that after a certain number of events of a similar kind, things are "due" to change
Post hoc, ergo propter hoc—literally "after this, therefore, on account of it"; assuming that something that comes after is caused by what came before
Slippery slope—assuming that one thing inevitably leads to another
False analogy—assuming that because of some (superficial) resemblances, conclusions drawn from one case apply to another

Emotion Rather Than Reason
Appeal to hate—claiming that if people don't like an idea, it should be dismissed
Appeal to force—attempting to persuade the listener/reader by threat or actual force
Guilt by association—inferring that a person's character can be discovered by looking at the company he or she chooses
Special pleading—presenting a case as being outside the rules (Can contain a more specific appeal to emotion, such as an **appeal to pity**.)

Reread each section of the text that is quoted. In each case, decide which logical fallacy best describes the reasoning that is used to draw the conclusion.

1. " 'You never went to school and you do all right, so I'll just stay home too' " (p. 29).

2. " 'It's against the law, all right...and it's certainly bad, but when a man spends his relief checks on green whiskey his children have a way of crying from hunger pains. . . . Are you going to take out your disapproval on his children?' " (p. 31).

3. " 'You don't 'n' I'll tell Calpurnia on you!' Rather than risk a tangle with Calpurnia, I did as Jem told me" (p. 34).

4. "Jem told me I was being a girl, that girls always imagined things, that's why other people hated them so" (p. 41).

5. " 'It's bad children like you makes the seasons change' " (p. 65).

6. " 'Atticus, you must be wrong. . . . most folks seem to think they're right and you're wrong' " (pp. 104-105).

7. " 'Why's he sittin' with the colored folks?' 'Always does.' . . ."He doesn't look like trash' " (p. 161).

8. "I knew that Mr. Gilmer would sincerely tell the jury that anyone who was convicted of disorderly conduct could easily have had it in his heart to take advantage of Mayella Ewell" (p. 196).

9. "So many things had happened to us. . . . Atticus said that he didn't see how anything else could happen" (p. 243).

10. "Atticus said. . . that things had a way of settling down" (p. 243).

11. "He slowly squeezed the breath out of me. I could not move. Suddenly he was jerked backwards and flung on the ground, almost carrying me with him. I thought, Jem's up" (p. 262).

Chapter 30 Heck Tate Decides

Vocabulary

blandly: 271, showing no outward emotion; imperturbable in manner
self-defense: 272, the legal right to protect oneself against violence with reasonably necessary force
eluded: 273, escaped
connived: 273, failed to take action against
audible: 275, able to be heard
craw: 275, stomach, often of a lower animal
honed: 275, sharpened
bided his time: 275, waited

Journal and Discussion Topics

1. What explanations might account for Dr. Reynolds not having noticed Boo the first time he was in the room?
2. Do you think Atticus had second thoughts about having chosen to defend Tom Robinson as he did, sitting on the porch, knowing that Tom was dead, and believing that Jem had just killed Bob Ewell?
3. What was the "contest" between Heck and Atticus?
4. What was Mr. Tate going to say to Dr. Reynolds when he stopped and said, "deceased's under that tree" (p. 274)?
5. Where do you think Heck got the switchblade?
6. "Let the dead bury the dead" is from the New Testament Gospel of Matthew 8:19, 21-22. What does the phrase mean?
7. What caused Bob Ewell's death?
8. What do you think would have happened if Heck Tate had told the town "all about it"?
9. In your opinion, was Heck Tate justified in what he did?

Summary

Atticus formally introduces Jean Louise to Mr. Arthur Radley. Heck is about to speak to Boo when Dr. Reynolds comes back and sends them all away. Atticus suggests they sit on the front porch, and Scout assumes the role of Mr. Arthur's guide, sensitive to what circumstances he would find most comfortable.

Atticus begins speaking about Jem's age and the county court and self-defense, and it becomes evident to Heck that Atticus thinks Jem killed Bob Ewell. Heck immediately denies this, and Atticus argues with him, thinking that Heck is going to cover up Jem's action to protect him. Atticus keeps talking, thanking Heck, and saying that he can't live with a cover-up, and Heck announces that Bob Ewell fell on his knife, killing himself. Then Atticus starts in again, until Heck says he can prove that Bob Ewell fell on his knife. Atticus goes on, but Heck says again that Bob Ewell fell on a tree root and that he will demonstrate. He pulls a switchblade out of his pocket, sends Dr. Reynolds to examine Bob Ewell's body, and then demonstrates how Bob Ewell supposedly stabbed himself. He explains to Atticus that Scout was mistaken about part of what went on, but Atticus still counters him. Finally the sheriff explodes, *"God damn it, I'm not thinking of Jem."* This gets Atticus's attention, as well as Miss Maudie's and Miss Stephanie's, who hear the sound of Mr. Tate stomping on the floorboards of the porch. Heck says that Jem with his broken arm couldn't tackle and kill a grown man in the dark. Atticus suddenly asks where Heck got the switchblade, and the sheriff tells him he took it off a drunk man. It seems likely that he is equivocating and the drunk man was Bob Ewell, although when Atticus asks him again, he says he took it from a drunk man who was downtown.

Atticus is being unusually obtuse. Heck tells Atticus that it's his decision, not Atticus's, that Jem never stabbed Bob Ewell, and that it's time to let the dead bury the dead. He tells Atticus that it's not illegal for citizens to try to prevent crimes, but if the news got about, the man who killed Bob Ewell would become the center of attention in town, and shoving this man into the limelight would be a sin. Heck repeats that Bob Ewell fell on his knife and leaves. Atticus, finally understanding that Arthur Radley killed Bob Ewell, asks Scout if she can understand that Mr. Ewell fell on his knife. She says, yes, that the sheriff was right—identifying the man responsible by making the whole story public would be like shooting a mockingbird. Atticus hugs Scout, thanks Arthur for his children, and goes into the house.

Writer's Forum 13 Evaluation

Evaluation involves holding up something to a set of preestablished criteria and then judging it based on those criteria. It involves much more than "I like it" or "I don't like it," although that kind of personal, gut-level reaction can form a part of an evaluation. But after that, it's time to become analytical and describe why and how the object/idea/thing/work in question succeeded in or failed in meeting your approval as measured by the criteria.

It's time to look back at the definition of courage you wrote in Writer's Forum 8: Definition (p. 76), right after reading about Atticus facing the mad dog and Mrs. Dubose battling morphine addiction. Since then you have witnessed many other examples of behaviors that might qualify as courageous (this list is not complete).

Place in the Book	Examples of Courage
Chapter 13	Calpurnia confronts Lula; Reverend Sykes confronts his congregation with (a) their sins and (b) the need to support the Robinson family
Chapter 14	Dill runs away from home to the Finches
Chapter 15	Atticus sits outside the jail to protect Tom
Chapters 17–20	Atticus "really" defends Tom
Chapter 19	Link Deas bursts out in court to give his view of Tom's character
Chapter 22	Atticus reacts to Bob Ewell spitting in his face
Chapter 24	Miss Maudie defends Atticus; Tom Robinson risks his life for freedom; Aunt Alexandra, Miss Maudie, and Scout tend to the ladies despite their own distress
Chapter 27	Link Deas stands up to Bob Ewell to protect Helen
Chapter 28	Jem tries to protect Scout from attack; Boo saves Jem and Scout (as we learn later)
Chapter 30	Heck Tate takes the risk of doing what he thinks is right in handling Bob Ewell's death

Use these references (and any others you find relevant) and the following questions to evaluate your definition:

1. Is your definition broad enough to include all the examples of courage that you find in the book? If not, what do you need to change or add?

2. Which action(s) that you've seen represented in *To Kill a Mockingbird* show(s) the greatest courage in your opinion? Why? Which show little, or exemplify something different? Explain. How can you express these conclusions in your definition?

3. Is there any need for more specificity in your definition? If so, how can you improve it?

Chapter 31

Scout Takes Boo Home; Last View of the Finch Family

Vocabulary

raling: 277, rattling
sedative: 277, drug meant to calm or (in this case) to artificially induce sleep
apprehensive: 279, slightly anxious
silhouetted: 279, outlined

Journal and Discussion Topics

1. Reread the first paragraph of description on the opening page of Chapter 31. Recall the description of Mayella after she was beaten, presumably by Bob Ewell. Now imagine Boo going to try to save Jem and Scout from Bob Ewell. What thoughts come to mind?
2. What does Scout mean when she says, "I would lead him through our house, but I would never lead him home" (p. 278).
3. What do you think of Scout's definition of neighbors? Explain your thinking.
4. What did Scout understand from standing on the Radleys' porch?
5. Why do you think the book ends where it does?
6. Jem's injury creates a parallel between him and Tom Robinson. What do you think it means?
7. Compare and contrast Arthur with the children's fantasies about him.
8. In what ways does Atticus misjudge Bob Ewell? What do you think leads to his misapprehension?
9. Several important incidents in this novel take place at night. Write a stream of consciousness piece in which you muse on the possible connections and resonances between and among these incidents.
10. Do you think Jem will become a lawyer? Explain your reasoning.
11. Dill leaves in Chapter 25 and therefore is neither a participant in nor a witness of the winding up of the events that grew out of the trial or the final episode in the search for Boo Radley. What do you think of his absence?
12. Why do you think Boo didn't come out again after saving the children?
13. Explain the role of fear in the novel.

Summary

Boo arises from his seat, still coughing, and at his silent instigation, Scout leads him to Jem to say goodnight. Scout tells him that since Jem is asleep he can do what he clearly wants to do—caress him. Boo lightly touches Jem's hair. Again at his nonverbal sign, Scout leads him to the front porch so that he can leave, and he speaks to her directly for the first time, saying, "Will you take me home?" Scout avows that she will never lead him home and instructs him to offer her his arm, as if *he* were escorting *her*. They walk to the Radleys' porch. Boo turns the knob, releases her hand, goes in, and shuts the door. Scout never sees him again.

Scout reflects on neighbors, on the things Boo had given them, receiving, she thinks, nothing in return. Turning around to start home, Scout sees the neighborhood from Boo's point of view. She imagines the world as Boo has seen it—scenes that Boo would have seen of "his" children greeting their father, dragging a fishing pole, acting out a drama in their front yard, fighting in front of Mrs. Dubose's house, finding items in the oak tree, watching a house burn, watching their father shoot a mad dog, having their hearts broken by an unjust ver-

dict, and needing Boo to save their lives. She reflects that she doesn't need to stand in Boo's shoes—"standing on the Radley porch was enough."

Scout goes home, and seeks out Atticus in Jem's room. He sends her to bed, but she wants to stay with him. Atticus is reading *The Gray Ghost*, and Scout asks him to read it aloud. He does, and as he reads she falls asleep. But when he wakes her to help her to bed, she tells him how the boys in the book thought Stoner's Boy was messing up the club house, and how they tried and tried to identify him, but didn't know what he looked like. But when they found him, he hadn't done the things he was accused of, and he was nice. Atticus replies, "Most people are, Scout, when you finally see them."

Atticus turns off Scout's light and returns to Jem's room, where he will be when Jem awakens in the morning.

Strategy 25

Symbolism

Symbolism is a technique in which a person, place, thing, or idea represents not only itself, but also a deeper, more complex reality beyond itself. There are **universal symbols**, which are identifiable and used by people in many cultures and countries. There are **cultural symbols**, the meaning of which is shared by people with the same ethnic background, faith, or other cultural connection; and **national symbols**, the meaning of which are understood in a particular society, regardless of cultural group, station, or class a person comes from.

Many symbols involve allusion: you must know something else outside of the story to interpret the symbol. Many cultural symbols come from religious works and mythology, whereas many national symbols arise from a particular nation's history and practices.

Finally, there are **contextual symbols** whose meaning applies only in the context of a particular work or works. For example, a mockingbird is neither a universal symbol, nor is it—in our country at least—a cultural or national symbol. In *To Kill a Mockingbird*, however, because the mockingbird is referred to in the title and throughout the work, it takes on a symbolic meaning. Repetition is often a key to identifying items that have a symbolic meaning.

Identify the symbolic meaning of each item in this book.

1. The mockingbird

2. Tears/crying

3. Doors

4. Ghosts

Directions: Read the explanation; then complete the exercises.

Strategy 26

Rereading a Book

*Directions:
Read the
explanation;
then complete
the exercise.*

Think of a book you've known for a while and have read at least twice. How does your understanding of this book differ from the way you understand a book you've read only once?

- Do you remember details better?
- Do you remember the sequence of events better?
- Have you memorized parts of it?
- Can you imagine the characters in another setting?
- Do you return to the book when you feel a certain way or want to feel a certain way?
- Do you feel that all the parts of the book fit together to form a whole integrated experience?

Authors and critics alike suggest that reading fiction should be experiential. Novelist Joseph Conrad wrote, "My task, which I am trying to achieve, is, by the power of the written word, to make you hear, to make you feel—it is before all, to make you see. That, and no more, but it is everything" (Preface to *The Nigger of the "Narcissus,"* Oxford: Oxford University Press, 1984, p. xlii). Janet Burroway, a writing instructor, elaborates: "Written words are...at two removes from experience. . . . They are transmitted first to the mind, where they must be translated into images. . . . What it means is that...[the] fiction writer [must] focus attention, not on the words, which are inert, nor on the thoughts these words produce, but through these to felt experience, where the vitality of understanding lies" (*Writing Fiction: A Guide to Narrative Craft*, sixth edition, New York: Longman, 2002, p.54). In other words, we don't read literature for information; we read it in order to pass through (in our minds) the sequence of events the author proposes, allowing our minds and hearts to respond to these events.

But all of this doesn't happen without the extended and complex act that we call reading. And in our first reading of a text, we cannot give ourselves fully to experiencing the story because we have to

- Recognize black marks on the paper as letters and words
- Process the words in groups to construct meaning and figure out how paragraphs and ideas are connected
- Relate the perceived meaning to what we already know about stories in general, stories of the same genre as the one we're reading, earlier information from this particular story, and so forth
- Create in our minds the world of the story
- Apply prior knowledge of facts, experiences, other stories, ideas, feelings, sensory data, and the like, to help us understand what we have read
- Try to recollect a new sequence of events and many facts and details
- Fill gaps left by the text (no text tells absolutely everything that happened) with our own elaborations

Considering the enormous investment of energy required to read, author Vladimir Nabokov said, "one cannot *read* a book: one can only reread it. . . . When we read a book for the first time the very process of laboriously moving our eyes from left to right, line after line, page after page, this complicated physical work upon the book, the very process of learning in terms of space and

time what the book is about, this stands between us and artistic appreciation. . . .
In reading a book, we must have time to acquaint ourselves with it. We have no
physical organ (as we have the eye in regard to a painting) that takes in the
whole picture and then can enjoy its details. But at a second, or third, or fourth
reading we do, in a sense, behave towards a book as we do towards a painting"
(*Lectures on Literature*, New York: Harcourt Brace, 1982, p. 3).

Rereading is also important when we want to clarify, reexperience, or
check on our understanding of a link between different parts of a book.

Think about the events of Chapter 31. Did you remember, as you were
reading, when *The Gray Ghost* was mentioned earlier? Did you go back and
find the place so that you could reread and understand more about its
significance in the book? This is the kind of situation in which rereading is
important even before you've finished the story for the first time. The symbol
of the ghost is a crucial element and not consciously comprehensible to Scout,
but it should be to you. It was Dill offering to bet this book that convinced Jem
to touch the Radleys' house—he won the book by taking the dare. So the book
has been connected with Boo from the beginning. Your understanding depends
on having the earlier passage in mind when you read. (For more about *The
Gray Ghost*, see Strategy 28: Literary Allusion: Case Study, p. 148.)

1. Reread *To Kill a Mockingbird*. Keep track of things that you notice in
   your second reading that you bypassed without paying attention the
   first time. Write a brief compare and contrast essay, to show the similarities and differences in the two readings.

Strategy 27

Comparing and Contrasting a Book and a Movie

As you may recall from Writer's Forum 3: Compare and Contrast Essay, page 44, in such an essay you show the similarities and differences between two or more people, things, ideas, approaches, and so on, and draw some conclusions based on this examination. You choose the categories to compare and contrast based on your purpose, and these categories will change depending on your topic.

Sometimes, when considering literature, you will want to compare and contrast two different treatments of the same subject in different genres or media. You might want to do this if one work has been adapted or translated to create a new work, or if a work has inspired or influenced another work, or if they have the same subject and enough in common or such wide differences that you think it would be fruitful to see the similarities and differences in how they make meaning and achieve their effects.

In this particular case, you are going to contrast the book *To Kill a Mockingbird* with the movie made from the book. Usually it is easier to do this if you both read the book twice and watch the movie at least twice, once to experience it, and once to take notes for your paper. Here are some questions that would be useful to examine:

- A movie is usually no longer than two hours, so a movie adaptation of a book leaves out material included in the book. What is excerpted or compressed in this movie?
- A movie script may have additional material not included in the book, or it may make changes in the book. What additions and/or changes do you notice?
- How did your mental images of the characters, settings, and actions of the book resemble or differ from the way they were presented in the movie? Compare the characterizations and the plots carefully.
- Apart from the book, did the movie work as an experience in itself? Did it hold your interest? Was it worthwhile?
- Did the theme(s) you identified in the book come out in the movie? If not, what message(s) did the movie give?
- Did you like the book or the movie better? Why?

Source words that can help you express concepts of similarity and difference include

- as well as
- similarly
- differ
- whereas
- however
- likewise
- alike
- while
- but
- on the contrary
- at the same time
- resemble
- conversely
- though
- on the other hand

1. Write an essay comparing and contrasting the book and the movie of *To Kill a Mockingbird* (Robert Mulligan, 1998).

Writer's Forum 14   Book Review

In a **book review**, you identify the work you are considering by its title, author, and genre; briefly summarize the plot; and then state your evaluation of the work.

When you write the summary, it is a good idea to include the names of the main characters, the basic plot conflict, the setting, and the background of the situation (see Writer's Forum 10: Summary, p. 118).

Your statements of judgment should include your general evaluation of the work as a whole (or so far, if you have read only a portion of the work) and show how your reaction to elements of the work led you to that response (see Writer's Forum 13: Evaluation, p. 140). For example, you might respond positively to the following:

- The plot is suspenseful and interesting.
- The themes resonate with what you believe.
- You like or admire one or more of the characters.
- The vivid description catches your interest.
- The book is amusing and enjoyable.
- You learn something valuable.
- You are so absorbed that you can't wait to read more.
- You find insights or understandings that enrich your life.

Your evaluation does not need to only include favorable responses, however. You may judge the work unfavorably, if you think, for example, that the

- Dialogue is unbelievable
- Characterization is weak
- Characters' motivations are not believable
- Plot is convoluted or unbelievable
- Attitudes expressed seem inappropriate to you
- Genre doesn't appeal to you

It is also possible to present a situation in which you began with one point of view, but as your reading developed, your evaluation changed.

1. Write a review of *To Kill a Mockingbird*. Use these criteria, as well as pertinent criteria of your own.

Strategy 28

Directions:
Read the
explanation; then
answer the
questions.

Note: Page references to To Kill a Mockingbird are marked TKAM. References to The Gray Ghost are marked TGG.

The *Gray Ghost* shows up in the very first chapter of *To Kill a Mockingbird* when Dill bets Jem *The Gray Ghost* against two Tom Swifts that Jem won't go inside the Radleys' gate (*TKAM*, p. 13). Ghosts, not necessarily gray, come and go in the book as well, as indicated in Strategy 25: Symbolism (p. 143). Every time the name *Boo* appears, the ghostly theme is invoked. Recall that Atticus says of Boo that he was not chained to the bed, but "there were other ways of making people into ghosts" (*TKAM*, p. 11). Cecil, dressed in a sheet, scares Jem and Scout on the way to the pageant (*TKAM*, p. 255; retold on *TKAM*, p. 268). And although the word *ghost* is not used in the description of Boo (*TKAM*, p. 270), his white face, hollow cheeks, colorless eyes, and "dead" hair certainly put one in mind of a ghost. And then again at the end (*TKAM*, p. 280), Atticus reads *The Gray Ghost*.

Here is some more information about *The Gray Ghost*, which is very hard to obtain, being out of print with very few copies left in public libraries.

The Gray Ghost is a book in the series of "The Books of Seckatary Hawkins" from the Cincinnati publisher, Robert F. Schulkers. Other books in the series include *The Red Runners; Stormie, the Dog Stealer; Stoner's Boy; Knights of Square Table; Ching Toy; The Chinese Coin; The Yellow Y;* and *The Cazanova Treasure.* They were published in the 1920s and 1930s.

The inside cover reads, "Your boy—and girl, too, for that matter—will certainly thank you for this book. It is the most absorbing story of boyish adventures that has come to our notice. It is chuck full of adventure, mystery, and humor from cover to cover. Also, which is an important thing with boys' books, it will teach the reader the importance of thinking for himself, and playing fair and square at all times."

The book is endorsed by *The Cleveland Times, Fairmont West Virginian, America, Pittsburgh Sun, American Hebrew, Portland Oregonian, Cincinnati Enquirer,* and Father Finn. It was copyrighted in 1926.

The books are about a boys' club and the adventures they have. As Scout indicates in her sleepy remarks, Stoner is an unknown and an outsider, and the club members spend a lot of their time trying to figure out who he is and what his qualities are. They confuse him with others and suspect him of things he hasn't done. In other words, as indicated by the connection of the book with Jem's touching Boo's house, there are close links between the experience of the club with Stoner's Boy in the book and the experiences of Dill, Scout, and Jem in trying to discover Boo Radley.

In both books, there is a desire to see the mysterious person. In *The Gray Ghost*, one of the boys asks, "You never saw Stoner's face, did you?"..."No, I never did...because he always has it covered up to the eyes with a gray handkerchief," is the answer (*TGG*, p. 49).

Like Boo's father, whom Calpurnia calls "the meanest man ever God blew breath into" (*TKAM*, p. 12), Stoner has a villainous father who is blamed for Stoner's going bad. The sheriff of the town says, "I am right about Stoner's Boy. I knowed his pappy—not a single good thing to say about his pappy— worst villain I ever turned the lock on. It's a pity, too, on account of the boy. Such a pappy for a little boy. What do folks expect from such as that?" (*TGG*, p. 220).

Like Boo, Stoner's Boy missed the chance to go to the state reform school, which might have done him good. The sheriff says with regret, "I always hoped that we might catch him some day and let Judge Granbery send him up to the school where bad boys must go. If he had the right kind of training, I bet you, Doc, Stoner's Boy would turn out to be a fine fella" (*TGG*, p. 222).

What Scout says about Stoner's Boy is telling: he is thought to be responsible for a great deal of mischief, and chased, but never caught, because it wasn't known what he looked like. But when he was finally known, it was discovered that he hadn't done anything that he had been suspected of..."he was real nice" (*TKAM*, pp. 280-281).

But there is more. With the sighting of Stoner's Boy, the club comes to realize what he has meant to them: they discover, as Scout, Jem, and Dill experienced with Boo Radley, that this mysterious figure was the focus of their lives: "What Stoner was to us, we realized now. He was the life and soul of our very existence. He had gone out of our lives forever, and we would miss him and the excitement that he had brought always with him" (*TGG*, p. 287).

And like Boo, when Stoner was gone, he was gone forever. Seckatary Hawkins ends the book by saying, "The rain still beat against the windows—the wind still shrieked around the clubhouse—and there seemed to be something in all the wild sound that said to me that we would never more see Stoner's boy. Which we never did" (*TGG*, p. 288).

1. How does this information enhance your understanding of the story?

2. How might you use this experience to inform your approach to reading other works?

Strategy 29

Theme

*Directions:
Read the
explanation;
then complete the
exercise. Answer-
ing requires
reflection on your
own experience
and knowledge.*

The **theme** of a story might be thought of as the story's point or its message. A theme is usually a generalization about life or human behavior or values; it is true, but not a truism. In general, a theme is the author's insight into the way things are that he or she wants to share with readers. Theme is an important part of a story's meaning and is developed throughout the story. It is important to note that a story can have multiple themes and meanings.

A persuasive or didactic piece of writing (such as a fable) might have an explicit moral—a clear statement of theme. Such a statement can both clearly convey the author's idea of what the story means and limit interpretation of the piece on the part of the reader. However, a piece of writing that was written with experience or aesthetic response in mind is more open to interpretation. Certainly the author may have had a theme or themes in mind, but the readers bring their own understandings. In this case, different readers may legiti-mately find different meanings based on patterns and messages in the text combined with their own interpretations and insights. But we seek for a balance between what is in the text and what the reader brings to the text. The message, however the reader interprets it, is always shaped by the author's intention and purpose.

Besides patterns and symbols in the story (which often point to the theme), certain parts of a story often refer to the theme: the title, the beginning and the very end. An important character's first and final words or thoughts are also likely to carry powerful indications of theme.

In a story such as *To Kill a Mockingbird*, which deals with complex issues, you will likely find multiple themes. But also try looking for a single, overarching theme.

1. Review your revised hypothesis from Strategy 21: Revising Hypotheses (p. 106). The more evidence from the story your hypothesis accounts for, the more likely it is to be a thematic statement.

2. State the theme or themes you find as you review the novel in your mind. Explain how you concluded that these statements are thematic.

Vocabulary
Look at each group of words. Tell why it is important in the story.

1. floundering, entangled, pinioned _____
   _____

2. fruity, florid _____
   _____

Essay Topics

1. In what ways have Jem and Scout become like Atticus?

2. How are Tom Robinson and Boo Radley alike?

3. At the very beginning of the story (p. 3) Jem and Scout disagree about what led to Jem's injury. Scout said the Ewells started it, while Jem said it was trying to get Boo to come out. Write a justification for each point of view.

4. Crucial decisions affected the outcome of the plot. Choose one of the decisions and write about what might have happened had the person taken a different course.
   a. Atticus chooses to really defend Tom.
   b. Heck decides to shield Boo from prosecution.
   c. Scout decides to try to be neighborly to Mr. Cunningham in front of the jail.
   d. Mayella lies to the jury.
   e. Jem accepts Dill's dare to try to make Boo come out.
   f. Tom Robinson tries to escape from prison.

5. Consider the narration of the book and elaborate on how you imagine it would have been different in one of the following cases:
   a. Narrated by Scout without the benefit of her adult perspective
   b. Narrated by Jem
   c. Narrated by Atticus
   d. Narrated by Boo Radley
   e. Narrated by Calpurnia
   f. Narrated by Aunt Alexandra

6. Miss Maudie says in Chapter 5, "The things that happen to people, we never really know" (p. 46). Write an essay in which you both
   a. Tell what, from your experience, we can and can't know about other people and how this affects our relationships with them.
   b. Tell the value of reading both fiction and nonfiction in light of this separation between ourselves and other people.

7. Write a characterization of Aunt Alexandra. Has your view of Aunt Alexandra grown/changed/developed? If so, explain how and why.

8. How does Atticus's statement about standing in another's shoes resonate in the last two chapters of the book?

9. In retrospect, what do you think the morphodite symbolizes?

10. How are Jem and Scout "Boo's children"?

History of Social Thought Pages

Introduction

The term **history of social thought** refers to part of what makes up our social and historical context—the ongoing give and take across time and across cultures about important social issues in our world. The best judicial system, the appropriate means and ends of education, the nature of human beings, the role of human beings toward each other, and the definitions of *culture* and *community* are some of the important topics about which peoples' ideas have evolved over time.

Every artist lives in a social and historical context. Writers incorporate the issues, ideas, and popular culture of their day in a variety of ways in their works. It can be helpful to the understanding of a work of literature to know more about the historical context in which the author's thought was formed.

The following pages will give you an introduction to some of the social ideas that shaped the period in which Lee grew up and were reflected in her book about the trial of a Black man accused of raping a white woman in a Southern town in the 1930s. Please be aware that the comments necessarily simplify the events and ideas Lee experienced, and if you want to *really* understand the thoughts and history of the time, you should study far more extensively.

Social Inequality and Racial Inequality

Social classes are groups of people who are differentiated by their power in society, the courtesies accorded them, the kinds of employment they can hold, their economic conditions, their working and living conditions, their life-styles, and their education. There may be other factors, as well. In the South in the 1930s, the social scale and the racial scales were interrelated. The lowest group socially was people of mixed race ("They don't belong anywhere. Colored folks won't have 'em because they're half white; white folks won't have 'em 'cause they're colored, so they're just in-betweens, don't belong anywhere," p. 161). Then came Blacks, who had social strata within their race ("Calpurnia says that's nigger-talk," p. 37). Blacks who worked, often for white landowners as field hands or for whites who lived in town as servants, were ranked above the unemployed. Blacks sometimes owned small houses or shacks, but usually had neither running water nor electricity. In any case, white people could refer to Blacks as "Negro" or "Colored" or "Nigger"; call them by their first names, and address them with belittling terms such as *boy*, while expecting Blacks to address them with a title of respect. White society ranged from "trash" ("He doesn't look like trash," p. 161; "Because-he-is-trash," p. 225) through various levels of working-class whites from poor farmers to those with town jobs to professionals (notice that Atticus often calls the sheriff "Heck," but the sheriff never calls Atticus anything other than "Mr. Finch") and a kind of aristocracy composed of families who were established in the area and usually were (at least at one time) wealthy. It is in the face of this elaborate system that Scout comes up with her own theory that there are "just folks" ("I think there's just one kind of folks. Folks," p. 227).

1. Use information from the novel to differentiate the social classes Lee presents in the categories of differentiation indicated (courtesies accorded them, work opportunities, economic conditions, working and living conditions, life-styles, and education).

A Little History

Although the Emancipation Proclamation freed the slaves in 1863, and the Thirteenth Amendment abolished slavery in 1865, it wasn't until 1868 and the ratification of the Fourteenth Amendment that citizenship was granted to all persons born in the United States, and not until 1870 when the Fifteenth Amendment was passed that freedmen, as freed male slaves were called, were guaranteed the right to vote. In 1896, the Supreme Court decision in *Plessy v. Ferguson* created a legal sanction for the separate-but-equal approach. (You may have noticed that there were no Blacks living in the Finches' neighborhood and no Black children in their school.) The separate-but-equal approach to public schooling was banned in 1954 in the Supreme Court's decision in *Brown v. Board of Education*. The following year, Rosa Parks refused to give up her seat on a Montgomery, Alabama, bus to a white woman, and the year of protests that followed resulted in desegregation in that city's bus system. It was at the time of these changes that Harper Lee began writing her novel.

Of course, racism affected the ability of Black people to receive a fair trial. The Scottsboro Case, argued before the Supreme Court in 1931, in which nine young Black men from Alabama were falsely accused of raping two white women on a train, brought to public attention the fact that Blacks were systematically excluded from jury duty, despite being legally allowed (obliged) to serve, and there being qualified Blacks available.

2. Read about the Scottsboro Trial—a good introductory article "The South Speaks" by John Henry Hammond, Jr. can be found at: http://newdeal.feri.org/nation/na33465.htm

   Write a short essay detailing similarities between the Scottsboro Boys Trial and the trial of Tom Robinson.

Miscegenation

Miscegenation, meaning to mix races, was coined in 1864 to refer to marriage or sexual relations between people of differing races, often between whites and Blacks. Many states carried laws on their books to prevent "mixed" marriages. The Virginia Code, for example, read: "All marriages between a white person and a colored person shall be absolutely void without any decree of divorce or other legal process." In 1967, the United States Supreme Court heard the case *Loving v. Virginia*, in which antimiscegenation laws were found to violate the Equal Protection and Due Process Clauses of the Fourteenth Amendment. The case evolved from the marriage of a Black woman and a white man in 1958 that was found to be in violation of Virginia law. California had rescinded a miscegenation statute in 1952, followed by Arizona, Colorado, Idaho, Indiana, Maryland, Montana, Nebraska, Nevada, North Dakota, Oregon, South Dakota, Utah, and Wyoming. But at the time of the Supreme Court decision, there were still fifteen states besides Virginia with antimiscegenation legislation on the books, according to *Time Magazine* ("I'm Just Who I Am," May 5, 1997, Vol. 149, No. 18, by Jack E. Whitec). Mr. Justice Stewart, in a concurring opinion, said briefly, "it is simply not possible for a state law to be valid under our Constitution which makes the criminality of an act depend upon the race of the actor."

3. Antimiscegenation laws were in force during the 1930s. How does knowing that such laws existed help you understand the attitudes of the townspeople and the jury toward the Robinson case?

History of Social Thought

Antimiscegenation laws bring up the question of "who is Black?" Scout raised this question when she asked Jem, "Well how do you know we ain't Negroes?" (p. 162). The legal answer may surprise you—at least in one case. The same *Time Magazine* article cited above reports that by law in Louisiana until 1983 you were counted as legally Black (with a note on your birth certificate to that effect) by the "one thirty-second rule." That is, if you had one single great-great-great-grandparent who was Black, then you were legally Black. If you then married a certified white person, your child, being less than one-thirty-second Black, would be officially "white." Before 1970, the Louisiana law reportedly said that if you had a "trace" of Black ancestry, that made you Black.

4. In your opinion, should people be asked to identify their racial make-up? Their ethnic loyalties? If so, in what situations and why? If not, why not?

Gender Equality

With the ratification of the Fourteenth Amendment to the Constitution in 1868, citizens and voters of the United States were expressly defined as male. An amendment to give women the right to vote was introduced in 1878, but it was not passed until 1919, forty-one years later, and ratified in 1920. As you have seen in the discussion of jury eligibility, women were not serving on juries in Alabama in the early 1930s (p. 221).

5. Do you think Atticus or Aunt Alexandra would have thought about raising Scout differently if they knew that when she grew up she would serve on a jury? Explain your answer.

Theme Page

Personal Quality

1. What behaviors are indicative of good manners in Maycomb?

2. Jem, imitating Atticus's instructions to him (p. 100), tells Scout to "be a gentleman" (p. 101); this might seem incongruent. But perhaps a gentleman and a lady have similar attributes. Consider this possibility while you read and react to this quotation:

   "Thoughtfulness for others, generosity, modesty, and self-respect are the qualities which make a real gentleman or lady, as distinguished from the veneered article which commonly goes by that name." — Thomas Henry Huxley

   If you believe that the attributes of gentleman and lady differ, explain how they differ.

3. Is being a gentleman or lady a matter of class? Aunt Alexandra thinks so (she doesn't think Walter Cunningham can be a gentleman, pp. 224–225); Scout doesn't (she thinks Little Chuck Little is a gentleman, p. 26, and she compares Tom Robinson's manners to Atticus's, p. 195). Read these comments and then give your opinion.

   "Education begins the gentleman, but reading, good company, and reflection must finish him." —John Locke"

   "A gentleman?...Individual conscience will rule his social acts. By love of quality as against quantity he will choose his way through life. He will learn to know the difference between the curious and the beautiful. Truth will be a divinity to him. As his gentlehood cannot be conferred, so it may not be inherited. This gentleman of democracy will be found in any honest occupation at any level of fortune, loving beauty, doing his best and being kind." —Frank Lloyd Wright

   "A man may be outwardly successful all his life long, and die hollow and worthless as a puff-ball; and he may be externally defeated all his life long, and die in the royalty of a kingdom established within him. A man's true estate of power and riches, is to be in himself; not in his dwelling, or position, or external relations, but in his own essential character." —Henry Ward Beecher

4. In the following quotations, is Gandhi talking about being a gentleman or lady, or something else? What kind of person is he describing? What is character, as he uses the term?

   "All your scholarship, all your study of Shakespeare and Wordsworth would be in vain, if at the same time you do not build your character, and attain mastery over your thoughts and actions. When you have attained self-mastery and learnt to control your passions, you will not utter notes of despair. You cannot give your hearts and profess poverty of action. To give one's heart is to give all. You must, to start with, have hearts to give. And this you can do if you will cultivate them." —Mahatma Gandhi

   "There are eternal principles which admit of no compromise; and one must be prepared to lay down one's life in the practice of them." —Mahatma Gandhi

Theme Page   Maturity and Adulthood

1. What do you think is the difference between being a boy and a man? A girl and a woman? Does Jem deserve to be called "Mr. Jem"?

2. Adulthood is partially defined in our society by law. At age sixteen or so, one is able to earn a driver's license. Then, at age eighteen one can vote, and at twenty-one one gains other privileges. How would you define an "adult"?

3. Would you consider adulthood different from maturity? How would you explain the relationship? Use people from *To Kill a Mockingbird* as examples.

4. Read the following quotation as you answer the question: What is the relationship between maturity and character? Then write your answer.

"Not education, but character, is man's greatest need and man's greatest safeguard." —Herbert Spencer

Theme Page

1. Read the following quotations. Define educational equality, economic equality, political equality, and equality before the law. Explain the relationships between and among them.

   "Political freedom or political equality is the very basis on which you build up other equalities. At the same time political equality may cease to have meaning if there is gross economic inequality." —Jawaharlal Nehru

   "Until justice is blind to color, until education is unaware of race, until opportunity is unconcerned with the color of men's skins, emancipation will be a proclamation but not a fact." —Lyndon Baines Johnson

2. Read the following quotation. Do you believe that we have achieved equality "before the law" in our country? Explain.

   "We believe, as asserted in the Declaration of Independence, that all men are created equal; but that does not mean that all men are or can be equal in possessions, in ability, or in merit; it simply means that all shall stand equal before the law." —William Jennings Bryan

3. What does this quotation mean?

   "Justice delayed is justice denied." —William Ewart Gladstone

4. What does the following quotation mean? What does it have to do with justice?

   "always treat others as you would like them to treat you." —Jesus (New Testament, Matthew 7:12)

Theme Page   Education/Reading

1. What is education? What is its purpose? Does education in a democracy have particular requirements? How does education relate to adulthood and maturity? Consider these quotations:

   "I have never let my schooling interfere with my education." —Mark Twain

   "Education comes to us from nature, men, or things. The inward development of our faculties and organs is the education of nature; the use which we are taught to make of this development is the education of men; and what we gain from our own experience of the objects around us is the education of things." —Jean Jacques Rousseau

2. Read the following quotations. Who are the educators in our society? What kind of people should they be?

   "Educators should be chosen not merely for their special qualifications, but more for their personality and their character, because we teach more by what we are than by what we teach." —Will Durant

   "Those who educate children well are more to be honored than even their parents, for these only give them life, those the art of living well." —Aristotle

3. What are the goals of education in *To Kill a Mockingbird* as delivered by (a) the schools, (b) Atticus, (c) Aunt Alexandra.

4. Consider these quotations. What role does reading play in education?

   "Every reader, if he has a strong mind, reads himself into the book, and amalgamates his thoughts with those of the author." —Goethe

   "Eating words has never given me indigestion." —Sir Winston Churchill

5. What did you learn from this book? Has the experience of reading and thinking about *To Kill a Mockingbird* contributed to your education? To your becoming a mature individual? To your becoming an adult? Explain how.

Theme Page

Neighbor/Community

1. Scout gives her definition of a good neighbor at the end of the book. Read these quotations. What is a good neighbor in your estimation?

   "Many times I realize how much my own outer and inner life is built upon the labors of my fellow-men, both living and dead, and how earnestly I must exert myself in order to give in return as much as I have received." —Albert Einstein

   "The race of mankind would perish did they cease to aid each other. We cannot exist without mutual help. All therefore that need aid have a right to ask it from their fellowmen; and no one who has the power of granting can refuse it without guilt." —Sir Walter Scott

2. How does Boo's approach to community differ from the approach taken by the rest of his family?

3. Why does Boo care about Scout and Jem when they spent so much time teasing him?

Theme Page Courage

1. Courage is an important quality in *To Kill a Mockingbird*, and you have been asked to consider it several times. Based on the understanding you've achieved, react to these quotations.

   "Courage is rightly esteemed the first of human qualities because it is the quality which guarantees all others." —Sir Winston Churchill

   "Courage consists not in hazarding without fear, but being resolutely minded in a just cause." —Plutarch

2. Is the following an elitist view? Explain.

   "Far better it is to dare mighty things, to win glorious triumphs, even though checkered by failure, than to take rank with those poor spirits who neither enjoy much nor suffer much, because they live in the gray twilight that knows neither victory nor defeat." —Theodore Roosevelt

3. Harper Lee's book was published in 1960, three years after Rev. Martin Luther King, Jr., began to lead a resistance movement working through the Southern Christian Leadership Conference, the year that the sit-in movement started to force desegregation of public places, four years before the passage of the Civil Rights Act, and five years prior to the passage of the Voting Rights Act. Consider writing and publishing *To Kill a Mockingbird* as an act of courage. What thoughts come to mind?

Theme Page

Status and Reputation

1. How important are status and reputation in the world? How can a good reputation be a benefit to an individual or to society as a whole? How important are status and reputation in your life? Do you think your reputation reflects your true character? If there is a difference, how do you account for it?

2. Are hierarchies necessary in society? In work? In family life? How are these three situations similar and how are they different? Explain your thinking.

3. Explain the hierarchies at work in Maycomb. What were the most influential factors in forming the hierarchies?

4. Who has status in the community of Maycomb? Why?

5. Atticus risks his reputation to follow his conscience. What advice would you give to someone who faced a choice between reputation and conscience?

6. Edgar Watson Howe, an American editor and author, said, "What people say behind your back is your standing in the community in which you live." Which characters in the book are talked about behind their backs? What kinds of things are said about them? How does this affect their standing in the community?

7. Henry Ward Beecher said, "A man's character is the reality of himself. His reputation is the opinion others have formed of him. Character is in him;—reputation is from other people—that is the substance, this is the shadow." Did your judgments of characters as you read rely on their character or on their reputation or the separation between the two? Explain.

8. Words have the power to ruin a reputation and to send a man to his death. Discuss the power of words in this book, with the following quotation in mind:

    "It is with a word as with an arrow—once let it loose and it does not return." —And-el-Kader, Algerian leader

9. In the end, which do you think had more influence on the community: Atticus or Bob Ewell? Explain your thinking.

Answer Pages

PART ONE

Strategy 1: Beginning a Book, pages 23–24

1. Students' reactions will depend partly on the associations they have with mockingbirds.

2. Without knowing that the mockingbird is used in this book as a symbol of generosity and innocence, students are unlikely to make accurate guesses about the title. Students may think that it sounds like a purpose clause, that killing a mockingbird is somehow the goal of the book. They may think that the story has to do with hunting or a quest.

3. Answers will vary depending on the edition. The Warner paperback shows the knot-hole with a gold watch and a ball of twine, a bird in flight against an evening sky, and a thinner-than-crescent moon rising above the treetops. Students' conclusions will vary.

4. The book was copyrighted in 1960; the correct answer will depend on the current year.

5. Answers will vary. Some students may have seen the movie.

6. Harper Lee won the Pulitzer prize. Students may think that this reflects a work of high quality or importance.

7. Answers will vary. Students may suppose that the book will show how the mature and logical thought of a lawyer gets its start in youth.

8. Answers will vary. Possible responses: Jem seems like a not atypical jock. Simon seems to have been hardworking but greedy and hypocritical, following his religion when it suited him and suiting himself when it didn't. Atticus is generous to his brother, and seems to be a fair and sensitive man.

9. This suggests that the narrator has an unusual relationship with her father.

10. Answers will vary. Possible response: The narrator is telling what is, in the world of the story, an autobiographical tale. She is revealed to be intelligent and ironical and to have a sense of humor. We have the opportunity to check the narrator's judgment in at least one case—she refers to the name Haverford as being synonymous with "jackass," and their behavior reveals this to be an accurate judgment. Although her assessment of Simon, as well, is given with a blend of cynicism and sarcasm, she speaks with affection of Atticus, but her description of both her father and brother seems more objective than emotional. For these reasons, she seems to be trustworthy.

11. The story takes place in Maycomb, Maycomb County, Alabama. Though students cannot be expected to know this unless they do research, it is not a real setting, but a fictional town based on the real town of Monroeville, Alabama. A map can be found on the Internet at: http://www.educeth.ch/english/readinglist/leeh/map.html
The setting is special in that it is an old town, steeped in tradition, impoverished by the Depression.

12. The detailed description of the setting and the fairly objective tone suggest historical, realistic fiction.

13. The first paragraph suggests that the incident in which Jem broke his arm might be crucial to the story. The title may make students suspect a hunting accident. The epigraph suggests that it might be about lawyers. Students will likely have difficulty pulling these pieces together without more information.

14. Answers will vary. Students may pick one of the starting points suggested by the narrator or Jem as the likely beginning after the general background of Maycomb is set.

15. Answers will vary. Possible responses include how Jem broke his arm, more about the family, who the Ewells are, who Boo Radley is, and who Dill is.

Strategy 2: Marking a Text, page 25

1. If possible, students should have an opportunity to put into practice the suggestions, if not in a book, then perhaps on photocopied material that is original or within the fair use clause of the copyright law.

Chapter 1: Dill Arrives, page 27

1. Scout is five, and Jem is nine.
2. Calpurnia spanked the children with her hand.
3. The first sentence, taken alone, gives the impression that he was not a competent lawyer. This idea is dispelled by the realization that the deaths of his clients were due to their own stubbornness, not any failure on Atticus's part.
4. He is a native, tied to Maycomb by birth and history, related to nearly everyone, and sharing a mutual understanding with them.
5. To protect Boo from the "degradation" (in his mind) of being housed with Negroes in the jail, the sheriff has him confined in the courthouse basement, a damp, moldy space that makes Boo sick and would have led to his death had his father not taken him home, apparently under a sort of informal house arrest.
6. They are set apart, not by Boo's offenses, but by their refusal to participate in the social and religious life of the town.
7. Students should be able to figure out the basic layout of the neighborhood through clues in the book. For a map superimposing this on the map of Monroeville, see http://www.educeth.ch/english/readinglist/leeh/map.html
8. Scout: ability to read, observant; Jem: love of football, daring; Dill: imaginative, sensitive.
9. Possible answers: take away their prerogatives, confine them to a less than full life, hamper their personal growth so that they never fully develop. Atticus may have been thinking of threats (including religiously-based threats), punishments, intimidation, and the like.
10. Answers will vary. Later evidence, including the two soap dolls and Scout's awareness of laughter after the tire incident, suggests that there really was movement—Boo was watching them.
11. Answers will vary. Possible responses: His imagination is piqued. He identifies with Boo who is, like him, different and unwanted by his parents.

Strategy 3: References and Allusions—Consulting Outside Sources, page 30

1. Students should see the connection between Roosevelt's reference to "nameless, unreasoning, unjustified terror" in the nation and the children's reactions to Boo Radley. They may also see parallels between "leadership of frankness and vigor" in the nation and the behavior of Atticus and Heck Tate.
2. Students' lists will vary depending on which topics they pursue.

Strategy 4: Plot—The Design of a Story, page 31

1. Possible response: Students may identify the exposition as including the first eight chapters of Part One and the complication as beginning with Chapter 9, which shows the beginning of how the trial affected the children's lives. The complication continues into Part Two, with the crisis coming at Chapter 28 with Ewell's attack on Jem and Scout. The falling action finishes Chapter 28 and continues until the end of the porch discussion in Chapter 30, which introduces the resolution.

Strategy 5: Forming Hypotheses, page 32

1. Possible hypothesis: Boo has something to do with Jem's broken arm. Evidence: Jem says the story of his arm begins with trying to get Boo to come out. Astute students may catch the connection between the book title that gets Jem to touch the house—*The Gray Ghost*—and Atticus's comment that people can be made into ghosts, and formulate a hypothesis relating these two pieces of evidence.

Strategy 6: Rhetorical Figures, page 33

1. Parallelism: "was probably the beginning of my father's profound distaste for the practice of criminal law. During his first five years in Maycomb, Atticus practiced economy more than anything" (p. 5)—parallel use of *practice* has the effect of a pun.
   Hyperbole: "Scout yonder's been readin' ever since she was born" (p. 7)
   Simile: "The Radley Place . . . drew him as the moon draws water" (p. 8)
   Personification: "From the day Mr. Radley took Arthur home, people said the house died" (p. 12); "The old house was the same, droopy and sick" (p. 15)
   Euphemism: "Mr. Radley went under" (p. 12)
   Idiom: "bought cotton" (p. 9)

Chapter 2: Scout's First Day of School, page 34

1. Possible response: School is different from home and requires a different outlook and set of behaviors; Scout finds that the rules of school are arbitrary, if not senseless, contrary to the familiar expectations of home, contrary to education, and unfair.
2. He seems to have had a crush on her based on her appearance.
3. She misjudges their level of knowledge and skill, particularly Scout's; their interests; the meaning of Walter's failure to bring a lunch and refusal of her quarter; the intention of Scout's intercession for Walter.
4. Miss Caroline claims that Scout has been improperly taught reading and that she (Miss Caroline) will have to undo the damage caused by Atticus's teaching. Miss Caroline tells Scout to stop writing because in first grade printing is the accepted mode of communication, and she's supposed to learn handwriting in school, not at home.
5. The Dewey Decimal System is the system of categories used in many libraries to organize books. Jem is referring to the educational theories of John Dewey.
6. Possible response: Miss Caroline would like a docile, illiterate, impressionable child who speaks only when spoken to.
7. Scout bases her opinion on how Miss Caroline conducts herself.
8. Scout uses her knowledge of the Cunningham family situation and family history.
9. Country folks and farmers have no money. As a result, professional people, like doctors, lawyers, and dentists are poor because their clients can't pay them in cash. But the clients find ways to pay in kind.
10. Possible response: None of her expectations were met, and she is frustrated.
11. Answers will vary. Students may think that Scout will make even greater mistakes or that she will refuse to return for the afternoon.

Strategy 7: Characterization, page 36

1. Crucial questions posed by Chapter 1 are: Who is Boo Radley? How do we come to know a person? Also important is: What are the effects of two different characterizations of Scout—the young girl told about in the story and the voice of the narrator? In this book, characterization is not only a tool of the author, but also a subject of the book. This theme will be developed through the trial in which there are two different presentations of Tom Robinson's character.
2. Students should note that the characterization of the Radleys depends very little on words, in that we have no access to their thoughts. Their setting (their yard and their house, which is said to have died) and their lack of interactions with the town are

informative. While there is some physical description of Mr. Radley, the information about Boo's physical appearance is obviously made up. The name "Boo" and the few of his actions and interactions that seem factual build up a different picture than the rumor/gossip/fantasy. Students may question whether either represents the true person.

3. Answers will vary. Possible responses: His authority does not rest in a title. He respects his children as he respects other adults, and his choice shows this. It is symbolic of the "courteous detachment" with which he treats his children (p. 6).

4. Answers should include the following: Jem is open to persuasion (taking the dare); respectful to elders (Mr. Radley); leader in the group of himself, Dill, and Scout (we can infer that he gets all the starring roles in their productions).

5. Students should note Miss Caroline's attractive appearance; how ill-equipped she is to teach and particularly to teach the class she has; how she fails to consider her audience (this may be contrasted with Atticus's speaking to the jury later); her inability to adapt her knowledge to a situation; her refusal to let her convictions be influenced by experience.

6. Possible response: Dill is sensitive, gentle, kind, imaginative, able to put himself in another's place; Jem is analytical, self-assured, matter-of-fact, unimaginative, defensive.

7. Students may note the following: only direct quote so far is, "Mm, mm, mm" (p. 11), although there have been several indirect quotations. No physical description, a brief summary characterization (p. 6) and a brief biography, no interior thoughts, the anecdote about his first clients, the comments about his relationship to the town, no change or development so far, a name that suggests the democracy of Athens and Solon the lawgiver.

8. In the anecdote about Atticus's first clients, we are told that "Haverford is synonymous with jackass" (students may fail to make the connection with Miss Rachel); she grows collards; she has a rat terrier; and she is generous enough to take on her unusual nephew as a permanent summer guest.

Writer's Forum 1: Description, page 37

1. Students should particularly note Dill's name, that he is displaced from what would be his ordinary setting (his home), as well as his words, his appearance, and what can be inferred about his motives, choices, and thoughts.

Strategy 8: Plot—Conflict, page 38

1. Students may have trouble identifying the protagonist with certainty. They may argue for Jem, the first character mentioned and the breaking of whose arm is the beginning and end of the story and who wants to be a lawyer (perhaps this is an example to match the epigraph—the future lawyer, Jem, as a child). They may argue for Atticus, who is the moral center of the book and the central figure in the prime conflict in the book—the trial as well as in the greater conflict of trying to bring up his children well under the circumstances he finds himself in. They may argue for Scout, who shows perhaps the greatest character development and is central because she is the character from behind whose shoulder the author has chosen to look out, as well as the narrator. Some students may look at the Finch family as a whole as the protagonist.

2. Students may argue for the trial, which begins affecting the children in Chapter 9 and is responsible for the attack on them. They may also propose that the conflict is trying to bring up children in a world that is not just, honest, or fair.

3. Students should identify the conflict or conflicts in each chapter.

Writer's Forum 2: Journal, page 39

1. Answers will vary. Entry should show consistent characterization and be recognizable as belonging to the character of Scout in point of view, tone, language, maturity, and so on.

Chapter 3: Walter Cunningham and Burris Ewell, page 41

1. Students may suggest that he is following Atticus's model or that he has natural generosity (based on this incident or Jem's hospitable response to Dill or both).
2. Possible response: It is an indication that Walter feels comfortable enough to have lost his self-consciousness—that all the stigmas and cultural limitations attached to the family were dispelled by Jem's (and maybe Scout's) openness to him as an individual.
3. Scout's ideas of company are linked to social class—only certain people qualify as company; Calpurnia's are based purely on location—someone who comes to your house is your company, period.
4. She believes that she is valued by Calpurnia and that losing her would hurt Calpurnia. This is both true and shows the self-centeredness of Scout's five-year-old mind.
5. Answers will vary. Students may equate the term *gentleman* with adult males of high social standing, or with a particular kind of manners. Scout's view of gentleman is more egalitarian (like Calpurnia's view of company): a male of any age who behaves with courtesy, kindness, gentleness, respect, thoughtfulness, and understanding is a gentleman.
6. Answers will vary. Students should be clear that Scout learns little or nothing in her academic subjects but that she gains an understanding of human interactions. Miss Caroline learns that there is wisdom in local knowledge in two cases, but she learns little or nothing about how to teach the first grade to which she is assigned, or how to educate Scout. She is still of the opinion that the children must fit into the system, rather than adapting the system to fit the children. Students may form the opinion that Scout is receiving a far superior education at home than at school.
7. Both Dill and Atticus see the value of trying to understand another point of view.
8. Answers will vary. Students may say that "the end justifies the means" as a general principle, or that "the innocent shouldn't suffer for the sins of the guilty." Explanations should be cogent and to the point.
9. Answers will vary. This is a tough issue because even though we do not wish to stereotype people, we do wish to understand behavior patterns so that we can act accordingly. Students may point to the treatment of Walter and say that even if general information about a family or other group is found to be valid and informs your understanding, each individual should be treated as an individual when you are interacting one on one.

Strategy 9: Irony, page 42

1. Answers will vary. There are many examples of irony in the story. For example, it is ironic that although the general population thinks Mr. Dolphus Raymond is drinking alcohol because he is depraved, he is actually drinking soda, but in a manner that he intends to seem as if he's drinking alcohol so that people will have a ready-to-hand explanation of why he acts the way he does (Chapter 20). It is ironic in Chapter 24, when Scout is contemplating the differences she has noted between the behavior of men and of women, that the word she is searching for is supplied by Mrs. Merriweather (*hypocrites*), who may be the biggest hypocrite in the book.

Strategy 10: Point of View, page 43

1. Page 7 in the sentence "Scout yonder's been readin' ever since **she** was born."
2. Answers will vary. Possible response for the child Scout: "her hand was wide as a bed slat and twice as hard" (p. 6); "Mrs. Dubose was plain hell" (p. 6); "I thought she was going to spit on it" (p. 21). Possible response for the adult Scout: "an occasion that was probably the beginning of my father's profound distaste for the practice of criminal law" (p. 5).
3. No, the point of view is limited.

Writer's Forum 3: Compare and Contrast Essay, page 44

1. Possible responses include size, pace of life, age, appearance, and climate.
2. Students should use the techniques of characterization to demonstrate the similarities and differences between Burris and Walter. Overall, students may realize through this exercise, if it hasn't already occurred to them, that although Burris and Walter have similar backgrounds in some ways, they are very different people—Walter is diffident, mature, and responsible; Burris is crude, rude, and recalcitrant.

Chapter 4: Gum in the Oak Tree, page 45

1. We go from the child Scout's perspective to a retrospective view of the adult Scout on her entire schooling experience.
2. Answers will vary. Students may have thought another child was storing things for him- or herself or leaving things for others.
3. Their attitudes toward personal property are less strict for items that are not money— they borrow/share/steal milk, flowers, and grapes and do not give something back unless a person can prove ownership—but they feel an obligation to return money. Students' descriptions of their own ethics will vary. Some may feel that the distinction between money and other items is false—something that belongs to another person should be respected, whatever it is.
4. Students may have difficulty finding language to discuss this issue with sensitivity. Calpurnia seems to be referring to an uneducated and superstitious point of view. Students may have differing views of what this means.
5. The children are tired of the games they have played previously (based on the Rover Boys), and Jem is tired of making up plots. These two facts, coupled with the incident with the tire, probably are the factors that work in Jem's mind to evolve the new game.
6. She had heard someone inside the house laughing when the tire she was in rolled into the yard. Jem and Dill think she's scared.
7. They were imitating an adult story they had heard exploring various facets of the same family's existence week after week.
8. Possible response: Yes, because he asks them if their game has to do with the Radleys.

Strategy 11: Setting and Mood, page 48

1. Students should show awareness of the various uses of setting. They should note how people act in unfamiliar or forbidden settings (white children in the colored balcony and at Calpurnia's church; Tom Robinson on the Ewells' property as reported at the trial; Jem in Mrs. Dubose's yard; Boo at the Finches', etc.)

Strategy 12: Foreshadowing and Flashback, page 49

1. Possible response: Scout recalls her lack of recollection of learning to read (pp. 17-18).
2. Possible response: "There was more to it than he knew, but I decided not to tell him" (p. 38); "Jem was a born hero" (p. 39). Students may not be able to recognize this as foreshadowing until later in the story.
3. Answers will vary. Some examples include: "A nightmare was upon us" (p. 144); "But I must have been reasonably awake or I would not have received the impression that was creeping into me. . . . A deserted, empty, waiting street. . ." (p. 210).

Chapter 5: Miss Maudie; The Fishing Pole Note, pages 50–51

1. Students should see that Jem's thinking fits the concept of following the letter, whereas Scout is following the spirit.

2. Scout is referring to Miss Maudie's different styles of dress to suit her work in her garden or her presence on her porch in the evening.

3. The ten plagues: 1 water turned to blood; 2 frogs; 3 gnats; 4 flies; 5 pestilence; 6 boils; 7 hail; 8 locusts; 9 darkness; 10 death of the firstborn. The plagues were disasters of tragic proportions. During World War I, the Second Battle of Marne was fought July 15–August 4, 1918; French and Americans under General Foch defeated the Germans. This battle was the turning point in the war that ended with Allied victory. Lee is using a simile comparing Miss Maudie to the Allies and the nut grass to the Germans.

4. Possible response: Because some people are taught to be private about health matters and may even consider them embarrassing, and because of the social gap between adults and children, Scout considers it a great concession and display of generosity on Miss Maudie's part.

5. Students may mention that it limits the preferential treatment that one might give oneself over others, encourages sharing and general thoughtfulness, and may discourage competition.

6. Possible response: Although whiskey seems more dangerous than words in a book because a drunk person may act dangerously or irresponsibly, a person could use the words of the Bible to cause even greater damage to other people—to scapegoat, ostracize, intimidate, or shame people, for example.

7. Answers will vary. This question follows up on Question 4 in Chapter 4 and is, like that question, a challenging one to discuss. Issues to raise: Are generalizations about people ever valid? If so, how can they be stated truly (i.e., without overgeneralizing) and without being insulting? Is it different for Calpurnia to refer to information that is uneducated and superstitious as being from a particular class and race of people (her own race) than it is for Miss Maudie (a white woman) to do the same?

8. Students may word their analyses differently. A possible listing of Scout's categories include tone, good works, trustworthiness, honor, honesty, commitment, and general reasonableness.

9. Scout gains a more balanced and reasonable view from someone who can help her sort out hearsay, rumor, and gossip from fact. She also learns that it is, in Maudie's opinion, the unhealthy, repressed attitude in the household that led to Boo's (Mr. Arthur's) notorious behavior. Astute students may suggest a parallel between Calpurnia's talk to Scout about Walter and Maudie's talk to Scout about Boo in suggesting people are to be treated with respect (he's Mr. Arthur, not Boo) no matter what their background and social status.

10. Possible responses: Dill is curious about Boo, not just to know things about him, but to meet him. Some of his curiosity may come from reading *The Gray Ghost*, in which Stoner's Boy is the elusive subject of rumors and gossip and imagination, and is finally revealed in the end. Dill also feels a bond of sympathy with Boo ("I figure if he'd come out and sit a spell with us he might feel better," p. 47).

11. It seems likely that Scout was about to reveal what she heard (laughter) after the tire fell into the Radleys' yard.

12. Possible responses: They don't know who might answer. It would be scary to meet him face to face. It would be less exciting and romantic.

13. Answers will vary. Possible answer (after the fact): Lee didn't want to have Atticus give a lecture in first person so that he would not sound harsh and bossy and to keep his speech at the trial the centerpiece of the book.

14. By denying only one aspect of what Atticus said, Jem inadvertently admitted the other aspect.

15. He is able to get his feelings "off his chest" without endangering his relationship with his father or earning a punishment for himself.

Strategy 13: Dialogue, p. 53

1. Answers will vary.
2. Answers will vary. Possible responses:

Idiom or Dialect	Source	Meaning
I declare if I will.	Scout (p. 38)	I won't.
rang changes every day	Narrator (p. 39)	performed variations
'fore you fry alive	Calpurnia (p. 38)	before you get sunstroke
slicked up	Jem (p. 35)	shined
fall from grace	Narrator (p. 25)	misbehaving

3. Possible responses: Calpurnia's grammar as pointed out by Scout (p. 24); change from Boo to Mr. Arthur in Scout's reference when speaking to Miss Maudie (p. 43).
4. Possible responses: Dill is embarrassed about his father in some way, or perhaps his father has abandoned the family, or his mother is not married.

Writer's Forum 4: Dialogue, page 54

1. Atticus hardly has any direct discourse in the early part of the book. Students may gather later that this is to allow for increased drama when the long courtroom scene is reached. In general, his speech is more formal (less colloquial) than Scout's and Jem's. Students may refer to the narrator's remark that, "When she was furious, Calpurnia's grammar became erratic. When in tranquility, her grammar was as good as anybody's in Maycomb" (p. 24), although they have not seen an example. There is further discussion of Calpurnia's use of language on pages 125–126.
2. Answers will vary. Each character in the dialogue should have consistent characterization through his or her speech.

Test 1: Chapters 1–5, page 55

Vocabulary

1. Descriptions of Boo Radley
2. Characteristics of Simon Finch
3. Description of Dill Harris
4. The confrontation between Burris Ewell and Miss Caroline
5. Words having to do with Miss Maudie Atkinson

Essay Topics

1. Answers will vary. Students should show refinement of their thinking based on new information.
2. Answers will vary. Students should justify their choices.
3. Answers will vary. Students should support their preference with details.
4. Possible response: earning a living and raising children with integrity.
5. Answers will vary. Students should note the signs of Dill and Jem growing closer and the cordial argument between Jem and Scout expressed at the beginning of the book. Answers should relate to information in the text.
6. Students should note the suggestion by Atticus that Boo has been intimidated by his father and his brother and the references to the peculiarities of the Radleys' religious practices.
7. Lack of integrity is shown by Mr. Ewell who traps out of season and gets drunk rather than feeding his children; by Jem who can be very generous and friendly to Scout or aloof and distant when he prefers to hatch plots with Dill; and Simon Finch who is selective in his application of Methodism. Examples of people with integrity are Atticus, Calpurnia, and Miss Maudie.
8. Answers will vary. Students should support answers with details from the book.

Chapter 6: Jem Loses His Pants . . . and Recovers Them, page 56

1. Scout says that when Jem invoked her gender against her, she had "no choice" but to join them.
2. Since the description of the front of the house (p. 8) is less than appealing, it seems that this reference is ironic.
3. Answers will vary. Students should explain their responses.
4. Jem's agility at picking up Dill's explanation and reinforcing it is compared to an outfielder who catches a ball without looking.
5. Possible response: It is important to Jem how he appears in Atticus's eyes—he doesn't want to lose status with his father.
6. Scout thinks that "A lickin' hurts but it doesn't last" and that being whipped is a better choice than returning to the Radleys' for his pants. Jem is willing to brave even the Radleys' in order to avoid damaging his relationship with his father.
7. When students reach page 104, they will see that it is a phrase that Atticus uses and they may infer that the children have picked it up from him.
8. Answers will vary. Students should support their ideas with details from the text.
9. Answers will vary. Accept reasonable hypotheses that fit the text so far.

Writer's Forum 5: Persuasion, page 59

1.
    a. Courteous discourse that meets community standards
    b. Purposeful violation of community standards; point made several different ways
    c. Appeal to shared principle
    d. Appeal to fear on different levels or threats
    e. Address the other person's point of view
    f. Appeal to reason
    g. Threats
    h. Appeal to authority
    i. Appeal to reason
    j. Appeal to authority
    k. Courteous discourse that meets community standards; appeal to emotions
2. Answers will vary. Students should use an assortment of valid techniques to persuade.

Chapter 7: Soap Figures; Thank You: Filling the Knot-hole, page 60

1. She applies Atticus's suggestion to try to look at a situation from the other person's perspective, and she tries to wait patiently to see what Jem will do.
2. The pants were waiting for him as if someone knew that he would return for them, and he doesn't believe that anyone else can know what he is going to do without knowing him.
3. Possible response: That the pants are mended and returned points to someone who is benevolent; the location of the pants suggests someone in the Radleys' household; the poor stitching points to someone who is not accustomed to sewing. The closest description of a person that fits this is Miss Maudie's description of young Mr. Arthur Radley. The motivation is not at all clear, but it is certainly friendly.
4. They invented, not "toilet paper," but paper, and not "perpetual embalming," but embalming.
5. Possible response: The items seem clearly intended for Jem and Scout once the dolls are found. As with the return of Jem's pants, the location seems to indicate someone in the Radleys' household, and the motivation seems benevolent. Since Mr. Nathan Radley fills up the knot-hole, he is definitely eliminated; the items seem too generous, and the carving too skillful for a child. It seems possible that it is Boo.
6. He is probably considering telling about the items in the knot-hole.
7. Answers will vary. Possible response: He is cutting Arthur off from the outside world, isolating him from society, keeping him a "ghost."

8. Answers may vary. Possible response: Jem realizes that Boo has been contacting them and has been cut off, and he is terribly sorry. He also may realize how wrong he, Dill, Scout, and the townspeople have been about who Boo is. He may feel that now, again, he has no way to contact Boo.

Writer's Forum 6: Thank-you Note, page 62

1. Answers will vary. Notes should have the appropriate thank-you note elements and show consistent characterization (which may include remarks "authored" by both Jem and Scout) and be recognizable as Jem's and Scout's work in their style, tone, language, maturity, and so forth.

Chapter 8: Snow and Fire, page 63

1. They had hoped for more melodrama and excitement.
2. Students should recognize that Eula May has an important function in conveying information throughout the community.
3. Because Scout is happy with the snow, she does not see it as a punishment, but as a pleasure—so if Mr. Avery is right, that the snow results from children's badness, then the logical conclusion is, paradoxically, that badness is good.
4. Jem is being careful not to kill the worms.
5. We know from Chapter 7 (p. 60) that Mr. Avery is constantly whittling stovewood, and so this prop helps to clearly establish the snowman's identity.
6. Jem is trying to do a portrait and is satisfied with the resemblance, and so with the snowman. Atticus is considering Mr. Avery's feelings and doesn't want him to feel insulted.
7. Jem concludes that the fire could cross the street and reach the Finches' home.
8. Scout said the same thing in Chapter 6 (p. 57).
9. The shape of Jem's snowman is one of its chief identifying characteristics, and Mr. Avery's size is what gets him stuck in Miss Maudie's window.
10. His comments to Scout about Atticus (p. 70) when she is worrying about their house show his trust in Atticus to know and communicate if and when it's time to worry. And his "babbling" everything about the knot-hole and pants to his father shows that he trusts him to understand the situation with Boo.
11. Students should understand that Jem realizes that if Mr. Nathan finds out what Boo did, Jem fears he will act in some retributive or harsh way, as he did when he discovered the knot-hole. Jem wants to make sure Boo is spared that. Atticus understands perfectly, but Scout doesn't think Atticus does because she expects him to be angry about Jem's pants and the knot-hole. Atticus clearly isn't angry, and she doesn't understand why, because she hasn't yet figured out that it was Boo who fixed the pants and left the items in the knot-hole.
12. Answers will vary. Students should realize that Miss Maudie is not suffering or mourning her loss.
13. He suggests that she could get a colored man or that he and Scout could help her. The worth of a Black person, it seems, is equated with the worth of children—this may possibly show the low value placed on a Black person.
14. Students should understand that Scout has misunderstood what Miss Maudie said to Atticus on page 68. Maudie used the word *hermaphrodite* to indicate that the snow person had a combination of male and female characteristics, being a combination of Mr. Avery's body with Miss Maudie's hat and hedge-clippers. Miss Maudie finds Scout's mispronunciation, "morphodite," very funny.

Writer's Forum 7: Parody, page 65

1. Answers will vary. Parodies should highlight the style, diction, or other elements of the original in a way that is recognizable and treat it humorously in some way.

Chapter 9: Atticus Accepts the Robinson Case; Scout Fights Francis, pages 66–67

1. She means an unpleasant or difficult time.
2. Since Scout was "almost six" in the summer before first grade, and she is now in second grade, she is probably just about seven. Students may suggest that Atticus thinks that fighting is childish, an irrational approach to problem solving, or both.
3. Scout is about to say *niggers* but thinks better of it and uses what in her community is considered a more polite and respectful term.
4. Answers will vary. Accept reasonable responses.
5. Students should understand that Atticus is suggesting that the issue at stake is one about which people who are generally good-willed and neighborly to each other cannot agree, so that the usual, everyday understanding Scout has acquired of who is with them and who is against them won't hold. (Scout will also find that some of those whom she thought to be "against," like Mr. Raymond and Boo, are actually with them. You may wish to bring this up later.)
6. "Then Christmas came and disaster struck."
7. She meant that he didn't behave like other doctors she knew, or like her stereotype of doctors, which seems to suggest that Scout saw other doctors as dishonest, sneaky, condescending, and humorless.
8. Students may note the difference in intention—the story about Boo is intended to both thrill and horrify the audience; the story about Rose Aylmer is not intended to be believed.
9. She swears and says "please" in the same sentence; she is offensive and polite at the same time.
10. Students should understand that Uncle Jack means a woman who is well-mannered, genteel, and courteous. To Scout—being motherless, living in a situation in which "being a girl" is anathema, and whose most admired adult woman is Miss Maudie (who spends a good deal of her time in men's clothing)—defying custom, being a lady may seem like giving up life and being a doll or a puppet.
11. Answers will vary. Students may have the opinion that "white lies" or "social lies" are appropriate and a way to smooth human relationships or that they are still lies and therefore a breakdown of human relations.
12. Answers will vary. Students may conclude that Atticus misses his wife very much; that he respects Scout's choice of overalls although it doesn't seem appropriate to Alexandra; that he is more concerned about other aspects of Scout's development than about her taste in clothing; that he is very concerned about his children's upbringing.
13. Students may point out that although Alexandra never had a girl, she had been one herself. They may also suspect that any daughter of Alexandra's would have fallen sway to Alexandra's example and seemed ideal to her, just as Francis did. Possibly Atticus just meant that it's easy to criticize someone when you have no experience.
14. She is referring back to Uncle Jack's comment (see p. 78) when he is able to pull her splinter without her noticing because he has distracted her with a funny story.
15. Students should come to understand, though they may not at this point, that Atticus is, as Miss Maudie makes clear (p. 215), putting himself in the crucible on behalf of the many others, doing for them what they cannot do for themselves, making an enormous sacrifice, not for the sake of suffering, but because it is the right thing to do. In this he can be seen to be following Christ's model. See also the conversation between Maudie and Alexandra (p. 236).
16. He used the conversation to tell her several things indirectly: what's wrong with using bad language; why her hot-headedness is a problem; that she does well to follow Jem's example; and that he knows that she tries; and that when she has doubts or questions arising from the court case, he hopes she will trust him.
17. Cecil Jacobs and Francis use the term *nigger* to refer without differentiation to all Black people. Calpurnia uses it to refer to small-minded, superstitious, gossipy, uneducated Black people.

Strategy 14: Names and Characterizing Terms, pages 69

1. The symbolic interpretation of all the names listed is supported:
   Atticus—his behavior in court and his closing argument
   Calpurnia—her behavior when the mad dog arrives
   Scout—her quelling of the lynch mob; role as narrator
   Jean Louise—her protective care of Boo at the end
   Ewell—his attacks on Atticus, Scout, and Jem
   Finch—the attack on Jem, particularly links the Finches to the mockingbird of the title
   Alexandra—her arrival to aid the family in time of need; her imperious behavior
   Arthur—his defense and rescue of Jem and Scout

2. The following pages have comments relating to being a girl or feminine identity. Students should note the change in attitude from Part One to Part Two. They should discuss the elements of being a girl or lady that seem unchangeable and those that seem subject to interpretation (Miss Maudie's approach differs from Aunt Alexandra's). Students' personal responses will vary. Many students may find the narrator's comment concerning women serving on juries problematic.
   "Ladies bathed before noon, after their three-o'clock naps, and by nightfall were like soft teacakes with frostings of sweat and sweet talcum." (p. 5)
   " 'I swear, Scout, sometimes you act so much like a girl it's mortifyin'.' " (p. 38)
   "but Jem told me I was being a girl, that girls always imagined things, that's why other people hated them so, and if I started behaving like one I could just go off and find some to play with." (p. 41)
   "She was . . . a chameleon lady who worked in her flower beds in an old straw hat and men's coveralls, but after her five o'clock bath she would appear on the porch and reign over the street in magisterial beauty." (p. 42)
   " 'Thing is, footwashers think women are a sin by definition.' " (p. 45)
   " 'Scout, I'm tellin' you for the last time, shut your trap or go home—I declare to the Lord you're gettin' more like a girl every day!' " (pp. 51–52)
   " 'You want to grow up to be a lady, don't you?' I said not particularly. " (p. 79)
   "I could not possibly hope to be a lady if I wore breeches; when I said I could do nothing in a dress, she said I wasn't supposed to be doing things that required pants. Aunt Alexandra's vision of my deportment involved playing with small stoves, tea sets, and wearing the Add-A-Pearl necklace she gave me when I was born; furthermore, I should be a ray of sunshine in my father's lonely life. I suggested that one could be a ray of sunshine in pants just as well, but Aunty said that one had to behave like a sunbeam, that I was born good but had grown progressively worse every year." (p. 81)
   " 'Grandma says all men should learn to cook, that men oughta be careful with their wives and wait on 'em when they don't feel good.' " (p. 82)
   ". . .what are you doing in those overalls? You should be in a dress and camisole, young lady! You'll grow up waiting on tables if somebody doesn't change your ways.'. . ."
   'Don't pay any attention to her, just hold your head high and be a gentleman.' " (p. 101)
   " 'It's time you started bein' a girl and acting right!' " (p. 115)
   ". . .watching her I began to think there was some skill involved in being a girl." (p. 116)
   ". . .he warned his flock against the evils of . . . strange women. Bootleggers caused enough trouble in the Quarters, but women were worse. Again, as I had often met it in my own church, I was confronted with the Impurity of Women doctrine that seemed to preoccupy all clergymen." (p. 122)
   " 'We decided that it would be best for you to have some feminine influence. It won't be many years, Jean Louise, before you become interested in clothes and boys—' I could have made several answers to this: Cal's a girl, it would be many years before I would be interested in boys, I would never be interested in clothes . . . but I kept quiet." (p. 127)
   "I know now what he was trying to do, but Atticus was only a man. It takes a woman to do that kind of work." (p. 134)

" 'For one thing, Miss Maudie can't serve on a jury because she's a woman—' 'You mean women in Alabama can't—?' I was indignant. 'I do. I guess it's to protect our frail ladies from sordid cases like Tom's. Besides,' Atticus grinned, 'I doubt if we'd ever get a complete case tried—the ladies'd be interrupting to ask questions.' . . . Perhaps our forefathers were wise." (p. 221)

" 'You know she's not used to girls,' said Jem, 'leastways, not girls like you. She's trying to make you a lady. Can't you take up sewin' or somethin'?' 'Hell no.' " (p. 225)

"The ladies were cool in fragile pastel prints: most of them were heavily powdered but unrouged; the only lipstick in the room was Tangee Natural. Cutex Natural sparkled on their fingernails, but some of the younger ladies wore Rose. They smelled heavenly. . . . 'You're might dressed up, Miss Jean Louise . . . . Where are your britches today?' 'Under my dress.'. . . 'Whatcha going to be when you grow up, Jean Louise? A lawyer?' 'Nome, I hadn't thought about it. . . .' 'Don't you want to grow up to be a lawyer?' Miss Maudie's hand touched mine and I answered mildly enough, 'Nome, just a lady.' Miss Stephanie eyed me suspiciously, decided that I meant no impertinence, and contented herself with, 'Well, you won't get very far until you start wearing dresses more often.' " (pp. 229–230)

"Aunt Alexandra stepped back. She gave Miss Maudie a look of pure gratitude, and I wondered at the world of women. Miss Maudie and Aunt Alexandra had never been especially close, and here was Aunty silently thanking her for something. For what, I knew not . . . . But I was more at home in my father's world. People like Mr. Heck Tate did not trap you with innocent questions to make fun of you; even Jem was not highly critical unless you said something stupid. Ladies seemed to live in faint horror of men, seemed unwilling to approve wholeheartedly of them. But I like them. There was something about them, no matter how much they cussed and drank and gambled and chewed; no matter how undelectable they were, there was something about them that I instinctively liked... they weren't—'Hypocrites. . . .' " (pp. 233–234)

"After all, if Aunty could be a lady at a time like this, so could I." (p. 237)

3. Students should note terms like "Nigger-lover" (p. 83), "trash" (pp. 161, 220), and "hypocrites" (p. 234).

Chapter 10: Mad Dog, page 70

1. He can make airtight wills, he's the best checker-player in town, and he can play the Jew's Harp. He is a skilled and careful worker, intelligent and a good strategist, and musical. Jem and Scout don't value these characteristics.

2. Answers will vary. Students should recognize that Atticus's idea of sin involves injuring what is defenseless, generous, innocent, and beautiful.

3. Scout thought that dogs did not get rabies in February, only in August.

4. He could mean either that in an emergency those social conventions fall by the wayside, or that it's too late because she's already done it, or that the Radleys aren't going to answer the door anyway, so they won't have to deal directly with Calpurnia's disregard for society's rules.

5. His behavior doesn't fit any of her expectations and, therefore, seems more menacing. If you know what danger looks like, you can avoid it. If it can appear in a completely different form than what you expect, then you can't prepare or avoid it.

6. Atticus's glasses, usually so necessary to him, in the emergency become, not only useless, but an impediment to him. He drops them because it is the quickest way to get rid of them. Symbolically, the smashing of the glasses might represent the smashing of Jem's and Scout's vision of Atticus and the beginning of seeing him in a new light, so to speak.

7. Answers will vary. Miss Maudie equates talent with a "gift from God," and one has no reason to revel in having a gift. Besides, Atticus's talent is one that can destroy, and he has used it, after 30 years of disuse, only to save the community. In this, and in

carrying out his moral convictions in the courtroom, Atticus puts his talents at the service of the community. Students should consider whether talents benefit the individual or the community (or both), and the possible roles of God, genetics, environment, and hard work in developing talent.

8. They judged/misjudged him by his age, job, nearsightedness, chosen forms of entertainment. Answers will vary. Possible response: immaturity.

9. Possible responses: his principles; his community-mindedness; his selfless behavior; his maturity.

10. Answers will vary. Possible response: Maycomb depends on Atticus to do its dirty work.

11. Possible response: He didn't want them to see him in the role of one enabling them to kill.

Strategy 15: Characterization Continuum, page 72

1. Students' answers should be expanded beyond these brief notes.

daredevil/courageous—Jem's feats in the beginning of the book (e.g., touching the Radleys' house and the trip into their yard during which he loses his pants) are nothing more than daring. Going to find Atticus as he guards Tom's cell and protecting Scout and himself as best he can from Robert Ewell are courageous. Jem grows through the book.

insensitive/compassionate—Dill's interchange with Jem about the turtle shows his compassion from very early in the book. It is underlined when he cries in the courthouse and in the conversation with Mr. Raymond. Scout is compassionate from the start, but at first doesn't have the manners to interact gracefully with the community, as is pointed up in the situation with Walter Cunningham. By the time Boo Radley stands in her house, she is sensitive to his every need and able to graciously create the most hospitable atmosphere for him.

shy/intrepid—Boo's retiring nature is a constant subject of discussion in the greater part of the book, as the children try to induce him to show himself. There is so little sign of him in their world at first that they are not even sure he is still alive. When he does begin to interact with them—watching them, leaving items in the knot-hole—he himself remains separate and apart from them. When Jem returns for his pants, he finds them, but Boo is not in evidence. When Jem and Scout are uncomfortable from the cold night air as they stand out and watch Miss Maudie's house burn, he ventures out, not to speak with them; but to soundlessly wrap Scout in a blanket to protect her from the cold. Only when they are in mortal danger from Bob Ewell does Boo's fearlessness manifest itself, as he rushes to their assistance and (what is, perhaps, even harder for him) enters into company in order to bring Jem home. He then submits himself to their presence for a while and speaks to them, before returning to the seclusion of his home forever.

obtuse/discerning—Scout's obtuseness as a child—her misunderstanding of certain things around her (like "morphodite" and her inability to interpret the conversation between Jem and Atticus following Atticus sending Jem for the wrapping paper to return the blanket) is characteristic of her age. As she grows compassionate, she also grows discerning, as her comment about mockingbirds (p. 276) shows. Atticus is most discerning except when it comes to Bob Ewell and the fight at the end of the book. He is completely obtuse about the danger Ewell poses, and it takes Heck Tate a lot of work to finally get Atticus, usually so perceptive, to understand what happened during the fight. Even Scout seems to grasp the situation more quickly than Atticus does.

2. Answers will vary depending on the character chosen.

Chapter 11: Mrs. Dubose, pages 73–74

1. You may wish to ask this question before Atticus's explanation (p. 100). Answers will vary. Students should give cogent reasons for Mrs. Dubose's vicious insults.

2. They can't stand the vicious, hateful way she speaks about them and their father.

3. Possible response: Scout holds this opinion because he faces Mrs. Dubose and deals with her courteously. It should appear ironic as students read because they know that there is far worse to face in the world than a malicious neighbor. Later, students may see it as ironic because Atticus himself will have to face far worse—the deadly malice of Bob Ewell, in particular.

4. Possible response: She says things that aren't true; she makes personal attacks; she speaks about topics that are none of her business. Students will vary in how far they think the demands of courtesy extend. Some may say that when we know her circumstances, her behavior seems more deserving of compassion and understanding. Some may say that we should always be polite, no matter what. Others may think that Atticus goes too far, and that we have no obligation to people who are rude and insulting. Students may point out that our own courteous behavior may serve as a model for others.

5. It is ironic because "gentleman," not "lady," is the model given Scout for her behavior, and the model she follows. Students may reflect back on this advice when they reach Scout's comments about the two worlds of gentlemen and ladies when she is at Aunt Alexandra's meeting (pp. 233-234), and Scout's decision to be "a lady" (pp. 230 and 237).

6. They are too upset to enjoy it; they know that what Jem did was wrong, and are awaiting the consequences. This takes away their enjoyment of what otherwise would have been a treat.

7. Answers will vary and may follow along the lines of the response to Question 4. Students should state their opinions clearly and support them.

8. He means that our most important decisions—those about what kind of person we choose to be and whether we choose to do right or wrong—are deeply personal and should be decided by our own moral sense, not by others' choices, because, in the end, we have to answer to ourselves.

9. Answers will vary. Students may recall Scout's attitude toward Jem after the incident and that Scout even made a move to accompany Jem when Atticus sent him to talk to Mrs. Dubose on the day of the incident, and find a consistency in her sticking with him.

10. Some students may respond along the lines of "sticks and stones can break your bones, but names can never hurt you." Others may think that the emotional and psychological pain of name-calling can be heartbreaking.

11. Jem is using "well" simply as an interjection—it doesn't have much meaning, just fills up space. Atticus is using it as an adjective meaning "cured or healed."

12. Possible response: A woman who does what she thinks is right, no matter how great the odds against her; a woman of courage and conviction.

13. Students should recognize the difference between courage that comes from power and courage when one is nearly powerless; between courage that faces almost certain success and courage that faces the real possibility of defeat; between courage that makes one look good to others and courage that makes one look (as Scout said of Mrs. Dubose) horrible to others.

14. Scout and Jem both respond with violence to insults and learn parallel lessons.

Writer's Forum 8: Definition, page 76

1. Answers will vary. Students' first definitions will likely reflect the examples of Atticus and Mrs. Dubose. The second may reflect the examples of Atticus in the trial and in sitting outside the jail; Boo Radley in defending the children; Jem in trying to protect Scout; Heck Tate in making a decision to protect Boo. Students' reflections should identify the changes their thinking underwent.

Test 2: Chapters 6-11, page 77

Vocabulary
1. Uncle Jack's response to Scout
2. Jem's mud-and-snow caricature of Mr. Avery
3. Mrs. Dubose's diatribes against the Finch family

Essay Topics
1. Students should discuss whether right actions must be done, regardless of whether the desired outcome is assured or even possible, or whether an action that cannot accomplish the desired end is not necessary. They may also discuss whether virtue is its own reward.
2. The juxtaposition of freezing and burning in this chapter might make a symbolic interpretation attractive.
3. The Radley place is generally considered the most dangerous place in the neighborhood, but under these circumstances, it is considered the safest.
4. Answers will vary depending on examples students choose. The alternatives offered should be socially acceptable in the milieu of the novel.
5. While Alexandra reportedly says that she won't be able to walk in the street if Atticus *does* defend Tom Robinson, Atticus himself says that he couldn't hold up his head in town if he *doesn't* (p. 75); in other words, their responses are diametrically opposed. (This will make Alexandra's support for Atticus later in the novel more noteworthy.)
6. Answers will vary. Possible response: Atticus's lack of concern to impress his children (or anyone else) helps establish his simplicity, honesty, and, most of all, integrity.
7. Students should realize that this chapter directly addresses courage, fighting, community, the meaning of being a neighbor, the nature of education, respect, prejudice, manners, and so on—many or all the themes that have been introduced so far, (for a definition of theme, see p. 150).
8. Most students will likely identify with Atticus as the protagonist, given the upcoming trial, although some may continue to identify and give reasonable explanations for other choices, such as Scout or Scout and Jem.
9. Answers will vary. Students should support their responses and connect them to the text they've read so far.

PART TWO

Chapter 12: Calpurnia's Church, page 78
1. It casts light both on Jem's entry into adolescence and the early stages of being recognized as a "young man" rather than as a "boy" and on the irony of Calpurnia, who is a grown woman, being called by her first name with no title of respect because she is Black, while she has to use a title with a young white male.
2. Scout is affected both by the change in Jem's attitude ("It's time you started bein' a girl and acting right!", p. 115) and by beginning to see that there is some skill involved in being a girl (p. 116).
3. Scout has the strong and short-lived emotions of a child, even though she has some of the vocabulary to speak of her relationship with Dill in terms of adult romance.
4. Possible response: It refers to cleaning up accumulated problems. The sentence alludes to the larger world outside Maycomb County, which is rare in this book.
5. Shadrach was a Hebrew captive of the Babylonian king Nebuchadnezzar, who along with two others was put into a fiery furnace but miraculously escaped death. His story is told in Daniel 3 in the Hebrew Scriptures/Old Testament. The class was testing Eunice Ann's faith by reenacting the trial of Shadrach.
6. Answers will vary. Students may think it natural that being at their home and having responsibility for them all day, five days a week, Calpurnia would naturally look on Jem and Scout as "hers" to some extent. She is their disciplinarian (p. 6) and their model (pp. 31-32). Here, she is emphasizing that their appearance and presentation reflect on her.
7. This chapter shows Jem's lack of prejudice in his behavior at Calpurnia's church, that is, it shows his color-blindness in the figurative as well as in the literal sense.
8. She chooses the appropriate and comfortable dialogue for each (this is called "social registers"). Answers will vary. Students should give details that clearly differentiate the two situations and the language use within the two contexts.

9. Reverend Sykes sets the moral tone, encouraging virtue and reproving individual failings. He also makes sure that community members support each other in need.
10. Answers will vary. Students may suggest that she bears herself as if she were wearing armor.

Strategy 16: Prior Knowledge, page 80
1. They judge her language to be a falling off from the standards she exhibits in the milieu in which they know her.
2. The similarities between the service Scout is used to, including the design of the service and the tone of the sermon, and the service at First Purchase helps make it accessible.
3. She dismisses it as being wrong and inappropriate.
4. Students should include at least the following facts: Atticus has been asked to defend a Black man, Tom Robinson, who is accused of raping one of Bob Ewell's daughters.

Chapter 13: Aunt Alexandra Comes to Stay, page 81
1. Answers will vary. Students may indicate that she is bossy and critical and acts as if she owns the place.
2. Possible response: It seems likely that Aunt Alexandra would interpret such a comment as rude and, given her attitude toward Calpurnia (i.e., that the family does not need her), which will become clearer in subsequent chapters, she would have been very angry.
3. Answers will vary. Some students may agree with the necessity of the "social" or "white" lie, while others may suggest that any misrepresentation of truth is wrong. The discussion may include questions of whether equivocation or partial truths are acceptable, and the relative importance of motive and action in determining whether an action is good or bad, right or wrong, appropriate or inappropriate, may come up.
4. Students should realize that Atticus is speaking figuratively about the effects of the trial, not about a weather prediction.
5. Aunt Alexandra believes that character is a result of family background rather than individual development and education, the result of genetic passing on of years of gentle breeding and good behavior and community standing rather than something acquired by any one person. She believes that some of the effects of family history are inescapable trends toward particular physical characteristics and behaviors, ranging from a particular way of walking or a stooped shoulder to lying, drinking, gossiping, and having a good sense of humor.
6. Students should recognize that the narrator is conveying Aunt Alexandra's point of view, not the narrator's own views. The preceding sentence ending "I knew I was in for it" (p.132) intimates that a lecture from Aunt Alexandra is coming. The following sentence has "she"—Aunt Alexandra—as the subject.
7. Aunt Alexandra closely links identity with standing and role in the community. She understands Jem and Scout as Finches, and the Finches are people who have played an important role in the development of Maycomb and the State of Alabama. Jem and Scout have a duty to continue to live out this legacy, which they can only do by first understanding it and then acquiring the manners and behavior that will allow them to fulfill their continuation of it.
8. Possible response: He changes from being a spokesperson for Aunt Alexandra to just being himself again.
9. *Note:* This is a difficult question to answer, particularly at this point in the book. Perhaps—in the light of the changes we see in Scout in Chapter 24, in which the examples of Aunt Alexandra and Miss Maudie become Scout's guidance for acting "like a lady," despite her stated preference for the male world—she is referring to the modeling needed for a young woman to become a lady, even on Atticus's terms. That is, even though Scout ultimately rejects Aunt Alexandra's views on background and

character in favor of Atticus's, she still needs a feminine model of something like Atticus's principles.

Strategy 17: Distinguishing Fact and Opinion, page 84

1. Opinion—Atticus's assessment of Mrs. Dubose's courage
2. False fact—Jem's mistaken belief about turtles' nervous systems
3. Irony—Jem's ironic extension of Aunt Alexandra's opinions on family
4. Figurative language
5. Opinion—Miss Maudie's generalization rests on her personal valuation of what it means to be in one's "right mind."
6. Figurative language—Miss Maudie is not speaking literally
7. Fact—Judge this statement in terms of Jack's agreement with it later--there is evidence to uphold it, so we can take it as fact, not opinion
8. Opinion—aesthetic judgments can be more personal or more philosophical (and based on accepted principles and criteria) depending on the situation

Chapter 14: Dill Runs Away, page 85

1. Because Atticus is defending Tom Robinson, he and his children are getting attention.
2. Answers will vary because although he does answer Scout, as he suggests adults should always answer children, he uses words that he knows she cannot possibly understand. Scout, however, does not pursue the topic, and perhaps this is his guide for judging how far to go with the topic.
3. Possible response: Yes, Atticus does not seem to have a problem with Scout and Jem seeing other people's realities (as long as they're invited).
4. Atticus and Alexandra had a serious disagreement.
5. He refers to himself as one of the "grown folks" (as opposed to Scout), and she cannot bear his "maddening superiority."
6. Students may conclude that Maycomb/the Finches' home was Dill's "real" home because he did not feel at home at his parents' house.
7. Jem broke the code of not telling Atticus; he broke it earlier after the fire when he told about the Radleys and Boo.
8. Possible response: Dill runs away because his folks aren't interested in him, whereas Scout considered running away to avoid excessive interest in shaping her life. Dill is seeking love; Scout is seeking respect.
9. Possible response: Dill's sensitivity, born of his own difficult situation, allows him to "put himself in Boo's shoes" and apply his compassionate understanding to Boo's situation.

Chapter 15: Friends in the Yard; Mob at the Jail, pages 87–88

1. Possible response: The first sentence created suspense by foreshadowing what was to come. The second created a false expectation.
2. Possible response: Link is thinking of Atticus's professional life, his reputation, and the danger to which Atticus and his family might be subjected to if he pursues this case. But for Atticus, taking this case is a matter of conscience. When he says that he couldn't go to church and worship God if he didn't defend Tom (p. 104), he is saying that his soul is at stake in this case. And when he says that if he didn't defend Tom, he couldn't hold up his head in town (p. 75) or face his children (p. 88), he is saying his self-respect and his fatherhood are at stake. And in his view, those are the most important things; and his soul, his self-respect, and his children's respect are the three things he is guaranteed not to lose if he defends Tom, win or lose the case.
3. If you put together this statement with what Atticus said to Uncle Jack (p. 88), it seems that for Tom, telling the truth has no value as far as justice in this world. He will die in any case. He will not be believed because it is his word against a white person's word.

4. He is Jewish.
5. It suggests that the person whose word will be opposed to Tom's is a woman, and—since we know that he is accused of rape—it seems that a white woman has accused Tom of raping her, although he did not. That Atticus says "polite fiction" suggests that perhaps she, rather than Tom, was the aggressor in an encounter, and what is being preserved is a (false) image of a pure, innocent female.
6. Answers will vary. Some students may suggest that he sees his relationship with God as private and between the two of them.
7. They know Atticus's habitual behaviors and choices.
8. They want to kill Tom, but follow Atticus's admonition in order not to disturb Tom's sleep.
9. Possible response: It created suspense and foreboding.
10. Scout thinks that the men gathered around Atticus are friends, but they are strangers. Because of this misapprehension, she abruptly enters the scene, and ultimately resolves it. Scout takes the gathered men to be "cold-natured" because their sleeves are buttoned, not rolled up. Perhaps they have unrolled their sleeves in preparation for a scuffle, or so that they might not accidentally touch their skin to the skin of a Black person. Scout's innocence contrasts with their calculating prejudice. Scout assumes afterward that Atticus is paying Jem out for not leaving, but she is wrong. This shows that she doesn't yet have an understanding of what happened at the jail.
11. Possible responses: Maybe being treated as a human individual, not a member of a mob, pushed him to make an individual human response. Perhaps being welcomed by a child of a different strata of society made him embarrassed by his own prejudices. Possibly Scout's conversation recalled to Mr. Cunningham all that Atticus had done for him without monetary compensation—this could make him feel more kindly toward Atticus and also, perhaps, give him something in common with Tom, another of Atticus's clients.

Strategy 18: Historical Fiction/Autobiography, page 90

1. Choose:

Inventions	
Dewey Decimal System, p. 18	A system of classifying published materials into categories (using three-digit numbers) and subcategories using numbers after a decimal point. It was invented by librarian Melvil Dewey in 1876, and is still used today to organize materials in libraries.
	Jem has confused this Dewey and his system with John Dewey, a leading philosopher in the progressive education movement.
Documents	
Rosetta Stone, p. 63	A stone discovered in 1799 and inscribed in hieroglyphics, demotic characters, and Greek; famous for having given the first clue to the meaning of Egyptian hieroglyphics.
	Mr. Avery either is having fun at the children's expense or doesn't know what he's talking about. In either case, he makes Jem and Scout feel guilty.

Missouri Compromise, p. 76	In 1817, when Missouri asked to be admitted to the Union as a slave state, it would have upset the balance of eleven slave states and eleven free states. Henry Clay proposed a compromise—the number of slave states and free states must remain equal, and the 36 degrees 30 minutes parallel would be the dividing line for new states with no slave states north of this line and no free states south of it. Maine, a free state, entered with Missouri, a slave state, and the balance was maintained. The law was repealed in 1854 by the Kansas-Nebraska Act. The reference to this 116-year-old piece of legislation shows how much Cousin Ike (and others like him) were holding on to the glory of the Confederacy and its hopes.
Indian-head pennies, p. 34	Pennies minted in the beginning of the 1900s with a Native American wearing a headdress. Because they were minted for a short time, they are relatively rare, and therefore very special.
Events	
Second Battle of the Marne, p. 42	A battle in late July and early August, 1918, in which, after German successes by Reims, the French and Americans joined to counterattack, and under the leadership of Foch, defeated the Germans. Miss Maudie has the fierceness of Foch when she attacks nut grass.
Spanish American War, p. 257	An 1898 conflict between Spain and the United States. Due to a variety of circumstances, including the strategic importance of Cuba, the United States supported Cuban patriots' demands for independence from Spain. When the U.S. Battleship *Maine* was sunk in Havana harbor on February 15, the United States demanded that Spain withdraw from Cuba. In retaliation, on April 24, Spain declared war on the United States. The war was fought in Cuba and the Philippines (where the Spanish fleet was defeated on May 1) until July, when U.S. troops captured Santiago de Cuba and subsequently destroyed the Spanish fleet there. The Treaty of Paris, signed December 10, freed Cuba, ceded Puerto Rico and Guam to the United States, and gave the Philippines to the United States in exchange for $20 million. It is a symbol of pride in violence, which in this book is continually counterbalanced with words as instruments of change.

Creek Indian Wars, p. 258	Tecumseh, the Shawnee chief, convinced the Creeks, whose land was being encroached on by settlers, to unite with other tribes against the settlers in 1813. The Creeks' leader, Red Eagle, led an attack on a stockade, and ignoring Red Eagle's attempts to stop them, the warriors massacred 500 whites. The United States responded on November 3 by destroying the Creek village of Talladega in Alabama, also killing about 500. The war ended with General Andrew Jackson defeating Red Eagle and the Creeks at the Battle of Horseshoe Bend in March, 1814. About 900 of the 1000 Native Americans who fought in the battle were killed. In this important episode in local history, Colonel Maycomb looks downright foolish. That Mrs. Merriweather chose the "fearless" leader Colonel Maycomb to sing about casts doubts on her judgment.
People	
Dixie Howell, p. 103	An All-American quarterback on the Alabama Crimson Tide, Howell was the star of the 1935 Rose Bowl and made the All-Time Rose Bowl Squad. Scout was giving Jem the best compliment possible, which was extremely generous after what he'd done to her, and showed great compassion for the trouble into which he had gotten himself.
William Jennings Bryan, p. 160	Bryan (1860–1925) was a lawyer and famous and persuasive orator who was pro-Prohibition and worked to pass legislation banning the teaching of evolution. By 1925, legislation had been proposed in fifteen states and passed in three, including Tennessee. Bryan was on the prosecution team in the Scopes Trial, insisting that the Bible was literally true, and that evolution was fiction. He died five days after the trial ended. Stephanie's comment suggests that people were going to court as if someone really important and impressive was giving a speech—and the effect is to treat the trial as a performance which seems completely inappropriate when we consider that Tom Robinson's life is at stake.
Things	
Prohibition ticket, p. 159	The Prohibition Party, begun in 1869, is the oldest minor United States political party still in existence. Although a Prohibition Party candidate

was never elected to high office (at best, the presidential candidate got 2.2 percent of the popular vote in 1888 and 1892), their main purpose was realized from 1920 to 1933, when the manufacture, transportation, and sale of alcoholic beverages was illegal in the United States.

Knowing that the Prohibition Party contained mostly Protestant evangelicals, and that people who vote a straight ticket (for all the candidates of one party) may be thinking in black-and-white terms means that Dill could actually conclude something about Mr. Tensaw Jones's character from Jem's brief comment.

	Places
Appomattox, p. 65	Town where General Robert E. Lee surrendered to General Ulysses S. Grant on April 9, 1865, ending the Civil War.
	The defeat of the South is still being used as a time-marker by Mr. Avery.
Bellingraths, p. 73	The Bessie Morse Bellingrath house and gardens, known for their azaleas and chrysanthemums, are one of the largest tourist attractions in Alabama.
	The comparison signals what a wonderful garden Miss Maudie is planning to have.
	Organizations
Ku Klux, p. 147	The Klan as known in the twentieth century was begun by Colonel William J. Simmons in 1915 near Atlanta, Georgia. It's membership reached 4,000,000 in the 1920s and declined during the Great Depression.
	The Ku Klux Klan (which has come back, despite Atticus's prediction) shows how prejudice grows from private conversations into established and organized action.
CSA, p. 99	Abbreviation for Confederate States of America
	Here is another sign of the continued importance of the Civil War and all it stood for to the Southerners of the 1930s.
	Food
Scuppernongs, p. 35	A variety of grape that can be used to make wine.
	Scout and Jem distinguish natural and replenishable goods from money.

2. (a) This is the foundation of the character of Boo Radley. (b) This (along with the Scottsboro Trial) is the foundation of the trial in *To Kill a Mockingbird*, with the white girl, Mayella, falsely accusing the Black man, Tom, of rape. If students read more widely from Moates' book, they will find the seeds of the stories about the Klan marching against Samuel Levy and Scout being attacked while dressed in her costume from which she was unable to free herself easily.

Test 3: Chapters 12-15, page 92

Vocabulary
1. Aunt Alexandra's world view
2. Description of the Maycomb jail
3. Reverend Sykes's sermon

Essay Topics
1. Students should recognize that attention, commitment, concern, mentoring, taking responsibility, being there, and other forms of human interaction and involvement, above and beyond biological family, are extensions of the fundamental "belonging" that is often the result of blood ties.
2. Students should recognize the differences in attitude, intention, behavior, morality, and so forth, but they should also recognize the common humanity that all the men share. This is what Scout's effect on the mob at the jail shows.
3. Scout's consistent application of the principles taught by Alexandra, in the case of Samuel Levy, for example, allows her to avoid being blinded by prejudice and bias. It does not allow her to understand the prejudice and bias of others.
4. Students should recognize that the church sets the standard and holds responsibility for enforcing community mores.
5. It shows the poverty of the Black community, both in material goods and in education. It reveals a strong sense of community and initiative that encourages them to "do the best they can with the sense (and resources) they have."
6. The focus has shifted from Scout and Jem's community and lives to the trial, including Tom's community and Aunt Alexandra's arrival (an indirect result of the trial).

Chapter 16: The Courtroom, page 93
1. She belatedly realizes the similarity between Atticus facing the mad dog and Atticus facing the mob outside the jail—that is, she realizes the danger they had been in.
2. Possible responses: He did it for Atticus's sake; he placed basic rights (e.g., the right to a trial) over his personal opinions and prejudices.
3. Answers will vary. Students should realize that the word *them* is distancing; Alexandra doesn't even call Calpurnia by name. The statement makes no differentiation among Blacks. Although Calpurnia is a longtime employee, daily entrusted with the Finch children's welfare, she is lumped in with all other Blacks. Some students may feel that Alexandra speaks as if Blacks are a lower form of being.
4. Answers will vary. Students should support their opinions with information from the text. Some students may say that no friend would turn on a friend ever. Others may say that his behavior at the end of the encounter shows what was truly in his heart and the way he acted up until then is attributable to being in a group, not revealing of his true nature and attitudes.
5. That he sits with the Black community is told us by the narrator (Jem affirms that he always does). Considering that the rest of the information comes through Jem, and we know something about his accuracy from his "reasonable description" of Boo Radley (p. 13), it is not clear what is true and what is not true.
6. The time of Lent leads up to Good Friday when Jesus died as a criminal, hung on a cross. Carnival is the time of celebration before it. This "celebration" may also end in someone's death.

7. Answers will vary. Students should note the following: Dill assumes that Raymond should fit into the category "trash" because he sits with Blacks; Jem, in correcting him, offers that he owns property and is from an old family to prove that Raymond is *not* trash. Students may find significance in the fact that you can't "tell" by looking what racial mix someone is and that, as Uncle Jack says, we don't know exactly who our ancestors include, if you go far enough back.

8. Students may note that (a) the Idlers' Club, like Jem and Scout, seem to be making the mistake of underestimating Atticus ("He reads all right, that's all he does," p. 163); (b) the Idlers and Scout following them, make a distinction between being appointed to defend and actually defending. We find out that Atticus *has* to serve as Tom's attorney, having been ordered to, but he didn't make that clear to Scout, as if it didn't matter. The original reason for Atticus's defending Tom may have been a court appointment, but once his conscience was engaged, the fact that he "had to" no longer mattered.

9. Students should see that convention is being broken here—Jem and Scout are welcomed into the Black community, breaking the otherwise well-defined color barrier; just as Jem was shown to be literally color-blind before he and Scout attended Calpurnia's church where they were shown to be figuratively color-blind, so here they are again, welcomed by and mixed in with the Black community on account of Atticus's choosing to follow his conscience.

Chapter 17: Heck Tate and Robert E. Lee Ewell Testify, pages 95–96

1. Students should include the following: He calls Mr. Gilmer "cap'n"; he makes an "obscene" comment in response to the question of whether he is Mayella's father; he does not use language or manners befitting the courtroom in his testimony (hence Judge Taylor's sharp glance, p. 172); he omits "Mr." in front of the sheriff's surname ("I run for Tate . . . ," p. 175); he uses the name *Jesus* in a curse in his testimony; he uses the crude and loaded term *ruttin'* rather than a more formal and acceptable term for sexual intercourse or even *raping*; he descends the witness stand without waiting for cross-examination; and he is defiant and rude to Atticus. Ewell's behavior reveals his lack of familiarity with the courtroom, his lack of common courtesy and good manners, his irreverence and hypocrisy (calling himself a "Christ-fearing" man rings hollow after his curses), his lack of respect for sexuality and for his wife (from his comment about Mayella's ancestry). By juxtaposing descriptions of the sheriff's appearance and behavior (note the details surrounding Heck's leaving the witness stand) with Ewell's appearance and behavior, Lee underlines Ewell's inappropriateness.

2. Answers will vary. Students will only be able to speculate until page 186 when it is revealed to the reader that Tom's arm is useless, a fact that Heck would already know. Heck realizes that it is physically impossible for Tom to have inflicted the injuries that Heck himself described Mayella as having. But the reader doesn't know this yet.

3. Heck was going to say "with one hand." Students will only be able to speculate about why Atticus stopped him until page 186, when they realize that Tom has only one good hand. Atticus is stopping Heck to prevent the introduction into the jury members' minds of the possibility that Tom, even with only one usable hand, could have inflicted Mayella's injuries.

4. She says it was dull because nobody "thundered," and the opposing counsels weren't arguing with each other.

5. Possible response: No, her prediction is not believable because it is based on a faulty premise: that the lack of courtroom drama and an environment in which people operate outwardly under the laws of civility, rationality, and courtesy signals that people's (the jury's) inward behavior will mirror this. She seems to have forgotten or not understood the deep nature of the prejudice toward Blacks in Maycomb. Beyond this, she seems to have lost sight of the fact that a man's life is on the line (which is

dramatic whatever the outward appearances of the process may be) and to be ignoring the brutal details of the vicious beating she just heard described.

6. The geraniums set Mayella apart from her heritage and surroundings. They show some interest in and ability to care for and nurture something, some taste for beauty, and some sensitivity to living things.

7. Answers will vary. Students may gain an understanding of where the word *trash* as used in the book to describe a certain group of poor white people comes from. They may reflect on how much more civilized, orderly, and so on, the nearby Black community appears. They may consider that it makes Ewell's comments about the "nigger-nest" ironic.

8. Answers will vary. Students may find this single instance of direct address odd, or it may have just flowed in with the rest of the narration for them. Accept reasonable responses.

9. Ewell is suggesting the possibility that Mayella's mother may have had sexual intercourse with a man other than himself, and therefore he may not, in fact, be Mayella's father. Students who have read *The Odyssey* may contrast Telemachus' serious questioning about who his father is ("My mother says I am his son; I know not surely. Who has known his own engendering?" translation by Robert Fitzgerald, p. 8) to Ewell's prurient speculation.

10. Answers will vary. Some students may think that Reverend Sykes is showing prudent concern and community spirit by acting *in loco parentis* and taking responsibility for children who, being present because he made it possible, are more or less in his care, even though they are not "his."

11. (a) When Ewell looks on the disorder and chaos he has caused, the word "handiwork" which suggests the product of an art or craft creates a contrast, thus irony. (b) From the narrator's description, it seems more likely that *he* is devaluing *their* property. (c) In denying that he is ambidextrous, Ewell characterizes himself with precisely the traits that make a person ambidextrous.

12. (a) Attempting something that is not difficult but in this case is rendered impossible because one has not used prudence and foresight. (b) Assuming an ending that is not guaranteed.

13. The judge realizes that Ewell is the most likely person to have inflicted the injuries that Mayella sustained.

14. Bob Ewell says he saw Tom Robinson having sexual intercourse with his daughter, and he and the sheriff say that she was beaten. There was no physical examination to corroborate that intercourse took place, and there are intimations that Bob Ewell may have beaten Mayella.

Strategy 19: Sensory Language, page 98

1.

Hush (p. 166)	angry muffled groan (p. 173)
Sh-h (p. 168)	banged (p. 173)
scraped (p. 169)	murmuring (p. 173)
whispered (p. 169)	taps (p. 173)
thundered (p. 169)	pink-pink-pink (p. 173)
husky voice (p. 169)	rapping (p. 173)
booming voice (p. 169)	silence (p. 174)
crowed (p. 170)	squallin' (p. 175)
laughter (p. 172)	laugh (p. 175)
screamin' like a stuck hog (p. 172)	whispers (p. 177)
raisin' this holy racket (p. 173)	chuckles (p. 177)

2. **Touch:** smooth-faced (p. 166), corrugated (p. 170), flat (p. 170), greasy (p. 170), and so on
   Sight: strutted (p. 170), shiny (p. 170), crepey neck (p. 170), snaggle-toothed (p.170), scrawny orange chickens (p. 170), dirty-faced (p. 171), and so on
   Smell: stale whiskey (p. 169), barnyard smells (p. 169), bacon frying (p. 171), fragrant gardenia in full bloom (p. 177), and so on

Chapter 18: Mayella Ewell Testifies, page 99

1. It contrasts the phrases "young girl" and "somehow fragile-looking" with "thick-bodied girl accustomed to strenuous labor."
2. Possible response: Courtesy extended to someone who is considered by society unfit to receive the particular honor in question has historically been used as mockery—think of Jesus with the "crown" of thorns and the purple cloak. Such an act can be seen as calling attention to the difference between what the person is (or thinks him- or herself to be or is perceived to be) and what the honor is meant to recognize.
3. It is easy to imagine that she has little or no experience with either concept.
4. Mayella is suggesting that Atticus wants to sway her from the path of truth and make her lie, while Atticus is suggesting that Mayella has not yet done anything *but* lie.
5. Possible response: It shows his compassion for her and his attempt to get inside her defenses.
6. It suggests that her tears before were part of an act.
7. The more questions Atticus asks, the more Mayella lies. Students may come to realize after some consideration that either Mayella lied to her father and said that Tom was the instigator in the situation, or Bob Ewell may have known that Mayella was instigator and compelled her to say that Tom raped her to cover up the truth. In either case, Atticus knows that if she told the truth, she would face more of the same or maybe worse from her father when she went home. By his questions, Atticus shows that he knows the truth, and Mayella is naturally terrified. Her choice is this: to lie and put an innocent man to death or to tell the truth and face her own guilt, and likely more brutal treatment from her father.
8. Likely he, too, believes that Bob Ewell rather than Tom Robinson was responsible for beating Mayella.

Strategy 20: Imaging, page 101

1. Images and quality of the students' drawings will vary. They should portray elements of the story with detail and understanding.

Chapter 19: Tom Robinson Testifies, page 102

1. It emphasizes the uselessness of his left arm and hand.
2. She is accusing and, it seems, lying about, the only person who was ever kind to her.
3. Answers will vary. Some students may think that manliness doesn't reside only in physical wholeness. They may argue that as he was, without qualification, Tom was a fine specimen of a man. Others may point out that the narrator says "specimen of a man," rather than "specimen of a Black man" and draw conclusions from that.
4. Apparently Bob Ewell committed incest with his daughter Mayella. Students may comment on the fact that Atticus does not pursue this so as to further call Mayella's motives into question.
5. He treats him in a variety of demeaning ways: he calls Tom "Robinson" without any title of respect and "boy"; he makes insinuations about Tom's motives for helping Mayella, jumps on his wording, and as Dill says "sneered at him an' looked around at the jury every time he answered."
6. The first pronunciation emphasizes the audacity of someone lower on the social scale pitying someone higher when it would properly be the other way around; the second pronunciation emphasizes that of all the feelings Tom might have had toward Mayella, he felt pity, emphasizing the inappropriateness of his choice of words and emotions.

7. Scout views Mr. Gilmer's behavior in terms of courtroom roles and expectations; Dill judges by the demands of civility and courtesy and humanity, with no reference to the fact that they are in the courtroom.

Chapter 20: Dill and Mr. Dolphus Raymond Meet; Atticus's Closing Speech, page 104

1. Students should note and comment on the following points:
   a. **individual and community**
      " 'Some folks don't—like the way I live. . . . I do say I don't care if they don't like it, right enough—but I don't say the hell with 'em . . . . I try to give 'em a reason, you see. It helps folks if they can latch onto a reason.' " (p. 200)
      " 'Cry about the hell white people give colored folks, without even stopping to think that they're people, too.' " (p. 201)
   b. **appearance and reality**
      "Mr. Dolphus Raymond was an evil man" (p. 200)
      "evidently taking delight in corrupting a child" (p. 200)
      " 'It'd ruin my reputation if you [told]' " (p. 200)
      " 'That ain't honest, Mr. Raymond, making yourself out badder'n you are already—' " (p. 200)
      "I had never encountered a being who deliberately perpetrated fraud against himself." (p. 201)
2. The statement "after all he's just a Negro" is racist, assuming that there is something lesser about the being of a person who is Black than a person who is white, and therefore it is not such a great evil to mistreat him. The statement, "Cry about the hell white people give colored folks, without ever stopping to think that they're people, too" comes from an understanding of the right of all individuals to be treated with respect for their inherent human dignity.
3. The cliched phrase can be taken to refer not only to the contrasts diametrically opposed pairs of dark/light; absence of light/light; evil/good; but also to the way that the two races are opposed in this particular case. This is emphasized where Atticus says, "And so a quiet, respectable, humble Negro . . . has had to put his word against two white people's" (p. 204).
4. She is guilty of trying to get rid of her own guilt for tempting a Black man by initiating a romantic physical relationship with him. Students may question/disagree about whether Mayella actually pretended to her father that Tom was the instigator of the relationship and/or that she was raped OR whether Bob Ewell pursued the case because of his own prejudice and compelled Mayella to comply.
5. Possible response: In the end, the case is not about Black versus white (people), but about character as it has been revealed by testimony; character is not determined by race or heredity, but by choice.
6. It means the president's wife, Eleanor Roosevelt.
7. Most students will agree that all people are not equal at birth or in life in terms of talent, ability, strength, virtue, or intelligence but should be equal in their right to a fair trial.
8. Answers will vary. Students will have varying notions regarding the relative importance of social development, the development of the intellect, and the ways and means of developing self-esteem and about whether this development takes place primarily in the school, in the home, or in both places.
9. Answers will vary. Accept reasonable responses. Some students may think that Atticus's remarks were too intellectual for the people he was addressing.

Strategy 21: Revising Hypotheses, page 106

1. Boo Radley (Chapter 1, pp. 8–15, etc.)
   Mr. Dolphus Raymond (Chapter 16, pp. 160-162; Chapter 20, pp. 199–201)
   Tom Robinson (Chapter 19, pp. 196–199)
   Miss Maudie (Chapter 5, p. 44; Chapter 16, p. 159)
   Scout (Chapter 13, pages 127–128)
   Finch family, particularly Atticus (Chapter 11, pp. 99–112)
   Atticus (Chapter 10, pp. 89–92)
2. Among students' records, these two statements should be included:
   Mr. Dolphus Raymond (Chapter 20, p. 201), "Cry about the simple hell people give other people—without even thinking. Cry about the hell white people give colored folks, without even stopping to think that they're people, too."
   Atticus's summation (Chapter 20, pp. 204–205)
3. Answers will vary. Accept reasonable responses.

Chapter 21: The Jury Decides, page 107

1. Students' assessments may vary according to whether they think the concerns are valid.
   a. This statement reveals the idea that fitness is not decided by common standards of civility and courtesy, but by consequences. Alexandra aims to control negative reactions by containing the truth and, at the same time, lumps Calpurnia in with all other Black people.
   b. This is an acknowledgment of good manners as the sole basis for deciding whether remarks are fitting.
   c. and d. These statements show concern for the appropriateness of material based on psychological development (and on parental permission as well).
   e. This statement may be primarily due to concern about Scout's age, gender, or both.
2. Jem argues based on logical conclusions drawn from the evidence presented and the sexual assault laws of the State of Alabama and from a belief in the power of the truth. Reverend Sykes argues from real world experience and an understanding of the role of prejudice in people's thinking and discernment.
3. Answers will vary. Students may conclude that the spectators were showing a certain reverence or awe.
4. It is the incident with the mad dog. Answers will vary. Possible responses: It is a simple foreshadowing of the verdict. Unlike the mad dog situation, in this situation Atticus is powerless to stop the evil that is approaching. It is a portent of the death of an innocent victim of circumstances: like Tim Johnson, Tom Robinson will die. Evil like that in the Ewells is like a mad dog and can only be stopped by death. There are some battles that no words can win—they can only be fought with violence.
5. The statements are all definitions of courage that acts on principle no matter what the likelihood of success or possible consequences to oneself.
6. "Atticus opened his mouth to answer, but shut it and left us." (p. 207)
   "I ain't ever seen any jury decide in favor of a colored man over a white man.... " (p. 208)
   Scout's sense of foreboding (p. 210)
   "but watching all the time knowing that the gun was empty" (p. 211)
   "A jury never looks at a defendant it has convicted, and when this jury came in, not one of them looked at Tom Robinson." (p. 211)
7. As a sign of respect/reverence/gratitude/honor for Atticus's courage/dedication/honesty.

Writer's Forum 9: A News Article, page 109

1. Students may choose to write for a local Maycomb paper, for the whole State of Alabama, or for the world. The first paragraph should succinctly sum up the main information about the trial: who was on trial, what was the charge, what was the jury's finding. Details should be presented in a reasonable order, and made-up facts should be consistent with the characters and the situation. Made-up interviews should have characters speaking from an appropriate point of view, and capitalization and punctuation for quotations should be accurate.

Test 4: Chapters 16-21, pages 110–113

Vocabulary
1. The atmosphere on the day of the trial
2. Description of Robert E. Lee Ewell
3. Atticus's summation

Essay Topics
1. Students should raise issues of loss of individual identity in the community, the protection of the individual by the community, the outcast, and the responsibility of individuals to the community and of the community to individuals.
2. Scout cries because she realizes that her father was in danger; Dill cries because Mr. Gilmer treats Tom with condescension; both are crying on account of someone else. Mayella cries over her own discomfort because she is lying in public.
3. Tom would likely have been charged with rape in the first degree because Mayella argues for forcible compulsion, and he would have received a sentence of hard labor for between ten years and life. Students' attitudes toward the reduction of the maximum penalty to eliminate capital punishment will vary—accept reasonable responses. Mayella might have been charged with sexual abuse (depending on the definition of sexual contact and information that we do not have about what actually occurred between Mayella and Tom), and received a sentence of a year and a day to 10 years of hard labor, or with criminal coercion and received a sentence of up to a year in jail at hard labor, or with unlawful imprisonment in the second degree, resulting in not more than 3 months in jail at hard labor, or possibly a combination. Students may point out that she likely would also have been in contempt of court for lying under oath.
4. Joseph is falsely accused of rape by the wife of his employer Potiphar, when he refuses her attempts to seduce him. He is imprisoned, but later freed because he can interpret dreams. He becomes the highest ranking official in Egypt. The main similarities are the accusation to cover up an attempt at seduction by a woman of one race against a man of another and the imprisonment of the victim. The main difference is that Joseph will live and his fortunes will rise again. Students do not yet know Tom's fate, but only that he has been found guilty of a crime that can carry the death penalty as its sentence.
5. Answers will vary. Students should support their opinions with details from the text. Some students may think that since the accusation of incest rests on Tom's report of what Mayella told him, it would not have been an effective trail to follow. Others may think that it would have been the surest way to separate the jurors' sympathies from the Ewells.
6. Possible response: Dill ran away because he felt unwanted. But the focus never gets to what his parents have/haven't done—instead it's on Dill's "crime" of running away. In Dill's case and in Tom's, the person/people who are truly responsible for the problem are let off, while the victim takes the blame.

Chapter 22: Reactions to the Verdict; Bob Ewell Threatens Atticus, page 114

1. They were influenced by personal prejudice and possibly their sense of what the community would expect and the feeling of obligation to meet that expectation (and possibly fear of the consequences of not meeting it).

2. Possible response: He misjudges the inhabitants of Maycomb, having seen them from a white child's eyes; he has been unaware of the prejudice they harbor.
3. Jem cries from righteous indignation; Atticus, from enormous gratitude. All the characters who cry (even Mayella—remember the geraniums) show unusual sensitivity.
4. He feels that he shares in responsibility for the state of Maycomb's attitudes.
5. There is still the possibility of an appeal.
6. Dill is distrustful of people and their motives in some cases, which a cynic is, but he is not contemptuous, nor has he (yet) given up on human nature. Jem is much closer to being cynical in this chapter.
7. Miss Maudie means that people in Maycomb are rarely called on to show heroic virtue, and that a few individuals answer the call on behalf of the community when such virtue is required.
8. Possible response: He's probably saying that he's going to leave Maycomb, based on his disillusionment with the residents of Maycomb.
9. Answers will vary. Some students may think that, just as he strutted like a bantam cock at the trial, this is more strutting and not meaningful. Others may suggest that a man who would beat his daughter so savagely (and rape her) is easily capable of hurting another human being.

Chapter 23: Picking the Jury in Retrospect; Folks, page 116

1. Possible response: He sticks to his principles, whether at home or in public, even if the situation might, in others' views, warrant a change. He gave up using a gun many years before, he took no gun on the night that the lynch mob came to the jail, and he won't get a gun now.
2. Answers will vary as to whether Atticus or Aunt Alexandra has accurately assessed the danger of Bob Ewell acting on his threat. Accept reasonable responses. Jem and Scout appear to be calmed by Atticus's reasoned responses.
3. Answers will vary. Accept reasonable responses.
4. Answers will vary. Students should respond thoughtfully to the argument.
5. Wording may vary somewhat: Atticus—a person who takes advantage of another's ignorance; Aunt Alexandra—a person who is not of "gentle breeding"; Scout—people like the Ewells (characterizations will vary); Mrs. DuBose—people like the Cunninghams (since she refers to Atticus's non-Black clients and these are the clients we know); Dill— hard to tell, seems to presume that anyone who was welcomed into a "higher" class would prefer to mix with them, and only a very lower class white would want to be in community with Black people. Answers will vary about whether any of these categories are useful and, if so, what they should be called.

   At issue are these points: Is *trash* an indication of socioeconomic status, of culture, of chosen behavior (e.g., subverting community by defying the law or refusing to work, as Bob Ewell does), or a combination of these? Is there ever any reason to use a disrespectful term to describe a human being? What if the human being one is describing acts in a way that is truly disrespectful or injurious to others?
6. Answers will vary. Accept reasonable responses. Most students will agree that people are fundamentally similar.
7. Answers will vary. Accept reasonable responses. Students may think that, similar to Dill at the end of Chapter 14, Jem offers his interpretation of Boo Radley based not so much on his knowledge of Boo as on his own experience.

Writer's Forum 10: A Summary, page 118

1. Students should enumerate Alexandra's points and match them up with Jem's and Scout's points. Conclusions will vary. Accept well-reasoned responses.

Chapter 24: Missionary Circle Meeting, page 119

1. Atticus shoots the mad dog once to protect the community and as a last resort; the guards shoot Tom Robinson seventeen times to prevent his escape from prison where he is not even allowed to see his family. Students should consider if the violence is necessary, helpful to the community, and/or ordinate.
2. If Mrs. Merriweather is any indication, the missionary society is condescending to the Black people in their own community, indifferent to their feelings, and uninterested in improving their situation.
3. The preacher's wife is pregnant. They are gossiping; their higher purpose and holy thoughts seem to be limited to the business part of their meeting, when they consider people in other regions of the world, not to the social part in which matters nearer home are discussed.
4. Answers will vary. Accept reasonable responses. (See answer to Question 9, Chapter 13, p. 179)
5. The label reveals that devotion among those who gave the label is measured by externals, not by an interior disposition of charity. Mrs. Merriweather is shallow, rude, and unfeeling: She doesn't know Helen's name and acts as if Helen is at fault for what happened, so that when she's speaking of Helen, Scout thinks she's speaking about Mayella; she shows no understanding for the Black community's reaction to Tom's conviction and is ready to fire her cook over it; she has the nerve to criticize Atticus in his own home.
6. Mrs. Merriweather's comment about "good but misguided people" is aimed at Atticus, and Miss Maudie defends him. "His food doesn't stick going down" means that he has a peaceful conscience.
7. It completes Scout's thought, and Mrs. Merriweather is a prime example of a hypocrite.
8. Calpurnia doesn't say "when you work for a lawin' family," but "when you're *in* a lawin' family"—she speaks as a member of the family.
9. It seems to be equated with people who have humility, gratitude, compassion, and understanding.

Strategy 22: Stock Characters and Character Foils, page 121

1. Answers will vary. Possible responses: She is a nasty neighbor, a bitter old woman. Mrs. Dubose has one virtue—courage—that raises her above the limitations of her incivility and her prejudices.
2. Possible responses: Mrs. Merriweather, self-righteous prig; Mrs. Farrow, sycophant; J. Grimes Everett, do-gooder. Focus on each character's main trait and attitude.
3. Atticus and Bob Ewell contrast in their attitudes toward work, education, parenting, community, and so on; Mayella and Tom Robinson are brought into contrast by their opposing testimony, by their demeanor in court, and by the irony of Mayella accusing the one person who was ever kind to her. Miss Stephanie and Miss Maudie are put into the reader's mind as foils by Scout's comparison of them (p. 44). Students may suggest other valid foils as well, for example, Bob Ewell and Boo Radley or Bob Ewell and Tom Robinson.

Chapter 25: The Death of Tom Robinson, page 122

1. Dill appears to have been abandoned by his biological father, accounting for his embarrassment when the subject comes up (p. 8). It seems that he makes up stories to make himself feel better, as well as to impress his friends, but sometimes he forgets exactly what he's said (p. 47). Eventually his mother remarries, but his stepfather doesn't like Dill (p. 140), not in an outright unpleasant way, but in his lack of acceptance of and interest in Dill (pp. 142–143).
2. Possible response: Jem has understood Atticus's principle and is trying out its application in everyday life. Responses to whether this attitude is girl-like will vary. Students may respond that compassion is not exclusively a feminine trait and respect

for others is different than squeamishness, though it might lead to a similar response in some cases.

3. Students should see the parallel between the two incidents, realize the wider implications of the Ewells', the juries', and the guards' responses to Tom Robinson, and contrast the attitude Jem has developed with that of the adults whose actions ultimately affected Helen in that way.

4. Answers will vary. Possible response: Students may imagine Dill as a storyteller or artist of some other kind because he has a wonderful imagination and others find his inventions attractive.

5. Possible response: By extending what Percy says, we might conclude that we do not mourn a specimen: just as Scout would have quickly forgotten the roly-poly she had killed (had Jem not intervened) since it was, to her, only a specimen of a kind of insect. Maycomb, likewise, can quickly forget Tom's death, since to most of the population he was a specimen of a Black man ("typical," p. 240), not an individual, a father, a husband, a person named Tom.

6. The editorial reinforces the mockingbird theme and relates Tom Robinson to the mockingbird.

7. Answers may vary. Students are likely to agree that in a community so riddled with prejudice, the accusation, rather than the evidence presented in court, sealed Tom's fate.

8. Answers will vary. Some students may agree, whereas others may think that Jem, like Atticus, is underestimating Bob Ewell's hostility/insanity/capacity for evil.

Writer's Forum 11: Eulogy/An Anecdote, page 123

1. Accept reasonable responses that follow the guidelines.

Chapter 26: Hitler and Democracy, page 124

1. Possible response: Atticus doesn't find it necessary to reveal everything he knows or directly punish his children for every transgression. In this case, he let the natural consequences have their effect and left it at that.

2. They may have continued to elect him because they didn't want to serve in the legislature themselves, and they knew that Atticus would follow his conscience, even if he did take disreputable stances on cases closer to home.

3. Students should note that the kinds of behavior include artistic appreciation, diet, religious practice, and pronunciation (the one item most reasonably under the purview of the school). Students will find their own experience more or less similar or different. Some may find that the current interpretation of "separation of church and state" shows a similarly intrusive policy by the state in the practice of religion. Students may find that these items go beyond what they see as the subject matter of education. Some students may be reminded of the reeducation plans that were enforced in China or Vietnam in the twentieth century.

4. Possible response: Lee wants to draw attention to the fact that in the case of Tom Robinson, as in similar cases, prosecuting turns out to be synonymous with persecuting.

5. Scout's observation clearly shows that Miss Gates is herself prejudiced.

6. Cecil's statement may reveal the preconception that only people of color are persecuted or that race is what gives people a cause for persecuting others.

7. Scout is holding the community responsible for the actions of its leaders.

8. Answers will vary. Some students' opinions may run along the lines of the quotation from Robert Frost: "You've got to love what's loveable and hate what's hateable—it takes brains to see the difference," suggesting that there are some things to which the ordinate response can only be hatred. Other students may agree with Atticus.

9. Possible response: The verdict was a rude awakening for Jem because he had "always thought Maycomb folks were the best folks in the world, least that's what they seemed like" (p. 215) and his realization that these folks could condemn an innocent man has so shocked him that he is planning to leave Maycomb as soon a he's grown (p. 216). His

explanation of why he thinks Boo Radley stays inside ("because he wants to stay inside," p. 227) reveals his own desire to avoid seeing the people whom he no longer trusts. In bringing Miss Gates' hypocrisy to Jem's attention, Scout is reopening this painful subject for him.

Test 5: Chapters 22-26, page 126

Vocabulary
1. The missionary circle meeting
2. The class discussion of Hitler and democracy

Essay Topics
1. Students should note the atmosphere of prejudice in both places.
2. He used three things he knew about the Cunningham family: that they don't take anything from anybody; that once you earn their respect, they support you; and that they rarely change their minds. Besides that, he used his understanding of psychology.
3. Answers will vary. Students will probably believe this story and mostly be empathetic. They may conclude that his treatment in Maycomb isn't much different from his treatment in Meridian.
4. Answers will vary. Students may suggest that Scout learns considerably more from Atticus and experiences like going to court than she does at school. They may criticize her school for trying to undo what Scout has already learned and failing to develop Scout's talents, and the system for hiring unprepared/inadequate teachers.
5. Answers will vary. Students may suggest that some resolution is needed in the matter of Boo Radley and in whether Bob Ewell actually will carry out or attempt to carry out his threats.

Chapter 27: Bob Ewell Trespasses at Judge Taylor's, Trails Helen, page 127

1. Answers will vary. That the first and third incident clearly involve Bob Ewell may be suggestive that the second does as well—Aunt Alexandra and Atticus clearly draw that conclusion (p. 250). Students may recollect Jem's report of Bob Ewell's comment at the end of Chapter 25 ("one down and about two more to go," p. 241) and conclude that Ewell is referring to Atticus and Judge Taylor, possibly the two people besides Tom Robinson that he figured had injured him.
2. The narrator says that they are both forgotten but states that there was an exception for Tom—Mr. Link Deas didn't forget him. Students may conclude that Jem and Scout provide the parallel for Boo—they are they ones who haven't forgotten Boo.
3. This is another relationship that, like Calpurnia or Reverend Sykes with Jem and Scout, shows bonds that cross beyond bloodlines and race and link members of community.
4. It suggests that Bob Ewell is a coward and bows to force. Students may note the differences between Link's approach (or Judge Taylor's) on the one hand and Atticus's approach on the other. They may also recall that those whom Bob Ewell has hurt so far have been weak or unable to protect themselves from him (Mayella, Tom, and Helen) and wonder what the outcome will be.
5. Although she doesn't understand his motives, Aunt Alexandra seems sure of Bob Ewell's continuing ill-intention. Atticus, while clearer about what has moved Bob Ewell to act, continues firm in asserting that his feelings will pass. Aunt Alexandra is reasoning about Bob Ewell's character inductively from the instances she knows of his behavior; Atticus seems to be taking a "Gambler's Due" attitude (see Strategy 24: Logical Fallacies, p. 135).
6. His goal seems to be, not to educate, but to enculturate—to make the Mrunas like a certain class of white Americans.
7. Answers will vary. Students may express that thoughts like "it takes a community to raise a child" capture the importance of having an attitude like the Mrunas, which is

more evident in Maycomb in the Black community's care of Jem and Scott than in the white community's activity.

8. Many students may agree that they are stereotypes of prejudiced, elderly, forgetful, unmarried women.

9. Students should recognize the sense of foreboding and foreshadowing, noting Aunt Alexandra's sense of apprehension in support, as well as Bob Ewell's threat.

Writer's Forum 12: Possible Ending, page 129

1. Answers will vary. Students' endings should provide a conclusion for Bob Ewell's threats, the long attempt to see Boo Radley, and the pageant.

Chapter 28: Halloween Pageant and Return Home, page 130

1. Some instances that students may mention include escorting Scout to the pageant, carrying Scout's costume, trying to help Scout when she trips, guiding Scout in dealing with the bright lights, making Scout feel better about her late entrance, and calling to Scout to run.

2. Students may have difficulty fathoming Aunt Alexandra's response. It is possible that Aunt Alexandra may think that Cecil's mother is being prissy and new-fangled over an old and time-honored tradition.

3. Her incorrect translation shows her ignorance—most people who are going to translate something in public would be sure to get it right.

4. Possible points: The punctuation by the bass drum seems pretentious; the story of Colonel Maycomb is hardly heroic; Scout falls asleep. On the other hand, Judge Taylor seems to have been mightily entertained by Scout's late entrance.

5. Boo Radley, a town dweller, brought Jem home.

6. She fetches Scout her overalls and calls her *darling*—students may conclude that the trauma has brought out a side of her that was unseen before.

7. Answers will vary. Accept reasonable responses.

Strategy 23: Adjusting Reading Rate, page 133

1. The level of detail in students' summaries will vary.

2. Students may find that they understood the passage much better—inasmuch as that is possible—the second time.

Chapter 29: Scout Tells Her Story and Meets Boo, page 134

1. "Good and dead" is an idiom meaning dead without question. It is ironic because he is hardly a person whom one would call "good" under any circumstances, and until the phrase is completed, it might seem for an instant that the sheriff is saying Bob Ewell is good (i.e., morally upright).

2. She feels that she overlooked her premonition and concerns about Bob Ewell too easily. Students' opinions will vary, but they may agree with Heck Tate's observation that we can't always follow our feelings.

3. It's a knife cut and indicates that Bob Ewell tried to cut or stab Scout.

4. Answers will vary. Accept reasonable responses supporting insanity or psychological ill health (students who hold this view may site the mad dog incident and draw parallels) and evil.

5. Answers will vary. Accept reasonable responses.

6. Possible responses: Her long-awaited dream of seeing him was being fulfilled; she was so grateful because he had saved her; she was overcome with emotion by the whole traumatic situation; she was embarrassed by the things she had thought, said, and done based on her misconceptions about Boo; some combination or all of the foregoing.

7. Possible responses: It parallels Bob Ewell stalking Helen and stalking Scout and Jem; they both show that sometimes only violence can stop the violent.

Strategy 24: Logical Fallacies, pages 136–137

1. False analogy
2. Special pleading with an appeal to pity
3. Appeal to force
4. Oversimplification
5. Post hoc, ergo propter hoc
6. Appeal to hate
7. Guilt by association
8. Slippery slope
9. Gambler's due
10. Fallacy of exclusion
11. Hasty generalization

Chapter 30: Heck Tate Decides, page 138

1. Possible responses: He didn't notice Boo because of his overriding concern with Jem; Boo's ghostlike quality; Boo's shyness.
2. Answers will vary. Accept reasonable responses. Possible response: No, although he might regret not having taken Bob Ewell's threats seriously, I don't think he would ever regret having followed his conscience.
3. The contest was about what story of the death of Bob Ewell was going to be told to the world. Students should note that the contest actually begins when Atticus asks Heck, "Are you sure [that Bob Ewell's dead]?" (p. 267), and in response to the answer which assures him that his children won't be hurt again says, "I didn't mean that"—Atticus is already thinking that Jem had wielded the knife and is thinking of the charge that Jem would have to face in court.
4. He was likely going to use the term "son of a bitch."
5. It seems likely that he got it from Bob Ewell. Very likely Ewell had been carrying the switchblade, and Boo had brought the kitchen knife out of his house.
6. Heck is saying that Bob Ewell's death provides closure and a kind of justice for Tom Robinson's death, and he wants to end the story there.
7. Arthur Radley killed him.
8. Answers will vary. Accept reasonable responses. Possible responses: Some people would have made Arthur a hero; some would have moved to have him prosecuted; one way or another, his whole life would have been disrupted.
9. Answers will vary. Students should support their opinions with reasons.

Writer's Forum 13: An Evaluation, page 140

1-3. Students should improve their definitions by following the suggestions.

Chapter 31: Scout Takes Boo Home; Last View of the Finch Family, page 141

1. Students may realize (if they haven't previously) how much courage Boo had to step into a fight with Bob Ewell.
2. Possible response: Scout is indicating that it would be rude/unladylike. By taking his arm, she allows him to assume the role of gentleman.
3. Answers will vary. Accept reasonable responses. Some students may say that not everything neighbors share is material; perhaps Jem and Scout gave Boo something by recognizing his existence and by receiving the gifts he gave them.
4. Answers will vary. Accept reasonable responses. Possible responses: She understood how Boo participated in the life of the community from behind the closed door of his house; she understood that Boo loved Jem and her.
5. The wish to see Boo Radley was granted, and his true character was revealed. At the same time, the events surrounding the trial of Tom Robinson were wrapped up, and the injury of Jem's with which the book began has been explained.

6. Possible response: Jem's injured arm symbolizes how deeply and lastingly the circumstances of Tom's trial and conviction hurt and changed him in a way that he would always carry with him.

7. Students should conclude that the wild suppositions had nothing to do with the reality. Jem, who cried when the knot-hole was blocked up and prevented Atticus from returning the blanket, may have had a clearer notion of who Boo is than Scout and/or Dill.

8. Possible responses: Atticus, perhaps in trying not to judge harshly or give way to unreasonable fear, underestimates Bob Ewell's determination to injure those who, by his reckoning, hurt him. Because he thinks of Bob Ewell as disturbed, rather than evil, Atticus fails to recognize the harm Ewell can do.

9. Answers will vary. Students may mention Jem losing his pants and recovering them, the fire at Miss Maudie's, the men gathering in the front yard and the mob at the jail, Bob Ewell at Judge Taylor's, and the aftermath of the pageant.

10. Answers will vary. Accept reasonable responses.

11. Students may feel that Dill was "gotten out of the way," or that the focus rightly returned to the Finch family proper. Accept reasonable responses.

12. Possible responses: Having hurt the community a long time before, he had now made reparation. Saving Jem and Scout had taxed him almost beyond his strength.

13. Students should recognize the connection of fear and prejudice and Atticus's attempts to quell fear and instill understanding.

Strategy 25: Symbolism, page 143

1. Possible response: The mockingbird symbolizes the innocent victim who serves the community but is made to suffer by that same community. Tom Robinson is linked to the mockingbird by Mr. Underwood; Boo Radley is, by Scout. The mockingbird is quiet before the mad dog is shot, and Jem and Scout hear a mocker on the way to the pageant.

2. Possible response: Tears and crying symbolize moral sensitivity. Jem, Scout, Dill, Atticus, and Mayella cry. Scout thinks Aunt Alexandra might cry, but she doesn't.

3. Possible responses: Doors symbolize important moments that we pass through in life; doors also symbolize shutting others out. Important moments with doors include Jem touching the Radleys' door, Atticus guarding the jailhouse door, Tom Robinson running out Bob Ewell's door, Boo Radley closing his door for the last time, and Scout seeing the view from the Radleys' door.

4. Possible response: Ghosts are the people who we ignore, who are not fully members of community. Boo's name links him to ghosts, and Atticus says of him that he was not chained to the bed, but "there were other ways of making people into ghosts" (p. 11). Cecil, dressed in a sheet scares Jem and Scout on the way to the pageant (p. 255; retold on p. 268). And although the word *ghost* is not used in the description of Boo on page 270, his white face, hollow cheeks, colorless eyes, and "dead" hair certainly put one in mind of a ghost. And then again at the end (p. 280), Atticus reads *The Gray Ghost*, a book that Jem won from Dill by daring to touch the Radleys' front door. For more on this connection, see page 148.

Strategy 26: Rereading a Book, page 145

1. Students' second reading should in general be smoother and easier than the first since they have already dealt with the conceptually and emotionally difficult material. What is lacking in suspense the second time through may be compensated by their ability to take in more of the detail and appreciate more of the artistry used in constructing the text.

Strategy 27: Comparing and Contrasting a Book and a Movie, page 146

1. Students should address the questions given for guidance. Facts and opinions should be clearly stated, and opinions should be supported by evidence. To extend this exercise, have students develop criteria for comparing and contrasting a book and an audio recording, and then compare the book with one of the audio renditions listed in the Bibliography on page 21.

Writer's Forum 14: Book Review, page 147

1. Students should include the title, author, genre, and summary but should also include their evaluation and the criteria they used to reach their judgment.

Strategy 28: Literary Allusion: Case Study, page 149

1. Students may find the references to *The Gray Ghost* more meaningful after using this worksheet.
2. Students may be encouraged to follow up allusions and references in other works.

Strategy 29: Theme, page 150

1. Students should review their prior work.
2. Answers will vary. Students will likely focus on topics such as justice, innocence, community, love, belonging, responsibility, and integrity.

Test 6: Chapters 27-31, page 151

Vocabulary
1. Bob Ewell's assault on Jem and Scout
2. The book Judge Taylor was reading when someone trespassed at his house

Essay Topics
1. Students should mention that they have both internalized Atticus's teaching about standing in someone else's shoes, and the figurative meaning of not harming mockingbirds.
2. Both are misunderstood by prejudiced people, are accused of crimes they did not commit, are used as scapegoats, and suffer for the community.
3. Focusing on the Ewells puts the emphasis on the actual agent of the injury and the subplot that concerns the trial. Focusing on Boo shifts the focus to the other main subplot—that of making Boo come out. By claiming status for both, the two threads are tied together from the outset of the book.
4. Answers will vary. Accept reasonable responses.
5. Students should accurately detail the character traits of the new narrator and the possibilities and limits of that character's knowledge and insight and suggest how these traits would shape the telling of the story.
6. Students should express an understanding of how, even in the best circumstances, our knowledge of each other has limits, and how reading accounts of people, places, and times beyond our experience, whether fictional or real, can enlarge our understanding beyond the boundaries of our own experience and help us to be more compassionate and understanding.
7. Although less dramatically than Jem and Scout, Aunt Alexandra is changed by the trial and Ewell's attack on the children. Students should recognize the character development.
8. Students should mention the great acuity with which Scout is able to understand what Boo would want and that she literally gets the view from the Radleys' that Boo has had all these years.
9. Possible response: The morphodite is both male and female, both Black and white. Its creation is symbolic of the erasure of racial and gender bias in Jem.
10. Possible response: They are Boo's in that Boo takes responsibility for their happiness, their comfort, their safety, and their lives.

Answer Pages

History of Social Thought Pages, pages 152–154

1.

Power in Society	Mixed Race	Blacks	White "Trash"	Rural Whites	Town Whites
Courtesies accorded	—	—	—	Titles of respect on certain occasions	Titles of respect depending on class (Atticus, yes; Heck no)
Work opportunities	?	Field hands or servants in town	Government jobs	Farming	Professions, service jobs
Economic conditions	?	Poor	Poor	Poor	A little less poor and up
Working and living conditions	?	Shacks/ shanties	Shacks	?	Houses with phones, indoor plumbing, running water, electricity
Life-styles	?	Church-oriented community	Dirty; pick garbage; skip school; not enough to eat	Fiddling, syrupy biscuits, pot liquor, holy rollers	Football, gardening, church, knowledge of history, missionary work, etc.
Education	?	?	—	Sporadic	Nine-month school

2. Students should mention a false accusation of rape by a white woman against a Black man, a jury with no Blacks, and a guilty verdict, among others similarities.
3. Students may gain in understanding of why the jury acted as it did.
4. Answers will vary. Some students may say that calling attention to race and granting positions and the like based on race maintains racism. Others may say that ignoring racial make-up would allow widespread discrimination to go unchecked.
5. Possible response: Atticus would likely do as he does. Aunt Alexandra might have had to reconsider the limits she placed on Scout's behavior.

Theme Page: Personal Quality, page 155
1. Students should mention some of the following: greeting and visiting neighbors and family, Sunday visits, belonging to the missionary circle, and going to church.
2. Answers will vary. Some students may believe that "good manners" or "character" or some other nongender-specific set of behaviors is at the root of being a gentleman or lady, and therefore there is little to distinguish them. Other students may focus on gender-linked definitions and therefore find differences between the two concepts.
3. Answers will vary. Accept reasonable responses.
4. Possible responses: He is talking about the best way to live; he is describing a person of integrity; your commitment to virtue is your character.

Theme Page: Maturity and Adulthood, page 156
1. Students may discuss both age and maturity as contributing to the transition to adulthood. They may differ concerning whether titles of respect should be given strictly by age, or whether they should be accorded when deserved by behavior.
2. Answers will vary. Accept reasonable responses.

3 People can be adults without having attained maturity. Stephanie Crawford might serve as an example. Mayella Ewell is an example of someone who hasn't yet decided to take responsibility for her own actions.

4. Possible response: Character is one of the most telling signs of maturity.

Theme Page: Justice, page 157

1. Students may differ on whether educational equality means equal access to education or access to education appropriate to each child's needs. Economic equality includes fair working conditions and hiring practices and equal pay for equal work. Political equality means the right to vote and fair voting practices to encourage representation. Equality before the law means the right to a fair trial. Students will likely agree that the various kinds of equality are interrelated.

2. The debate about the uneven application of the death penalty may lead students to say that equality before the law is not yet established.

3. Possible response: Spending time under suspicion, in jail, awaiting trial, filing an appeal, and the like, are unjust for an innocent person, but they are part of the system to deal with those who engage in, or who are suspected of engaging in, criminal activity.

4. It indicates that justice does not just apply to transactions that take place in court.

Theme Page: Education/Reading, page 158

1. Answers will vary. Students may suggest that education takes place anywhere a person is—if they're willing to learn: School is only one educational setting. Students may say that education includes some or all of the following: learning of skills (e.g., reading or athletic skills or social skills), facts (e.g., the multiplication table), methods (e.g., how to research), tools (e.g., calculator, computer), strategies (e.g., rereading), modes (e.g., aural, visual, kinesthetic), values (e.g., equality, justice), development of whatever talents/gifts are in the student. Education in a democracy creates, not only skilled workers but also good citizens, voters, and jury members. Answers will vary about the relationship between education and both adulthood and maturity. Students may raise the issue of people the extent of whose formal education is limited by circumstance or disability, but who nevertheless reach adulthood and/or maturity.

2. Students may mention those paid to teach, as well as parents, ministers and other religious authorities, peers, community members, family, neighbors, and so on. Answers will vary about the type of people who should be educators. Some students may claim that there is something to be learned from anyone. At the same time, students may believe that those hired to educate should have qualifications in their subject area and possibly other qualifications, if they agree with Durant. Students may object to Aristotle's assumption that parents have no part in the education of their children to live well.

3. Possible responses: Schools—to enculturate, to use a particular methodology; Atticus—to convert prejudice, fear, and superstition to knowledge and tolerance with the result being humane, sensitive, perceptive, thoughtful adults; Aunt Alexandra—to create ladies and gentleman, people who carry on the tradition of gentle breeding.

4. Possible response: It allows one to share another's point of view intimately for a brief time, to consider different perspectives dispassionately, to broaden one's experience with little danger or expense. Students may think that there are some books that could give one "indigestion"—such as books that spread prejudice or hatred, particularly books that try to persuade young people to actions that are not in the best interests of themselves or others or other books written or published with evil intent.

5. Answers will vary. Accept reasonable responses.

Theme Page: Neighbor/Community, page 159

1. Students should take this opportunity to reflect/expand on their answers to Question 3 on the Chapter 31 Page. Einstein's emphasis on those who have gone before, and Scott's reference to the "right" to ask for aid might be sources of new insights.
2. Students should expand on the contrast between Nathan Radley's withdrawal and aloofness from community and Boo's participation with Jem, Dill, and Scout, even when living reclusively.
3. Answers will vary. Accept reasonable responses. Possible response: They acknowledged—in their own way—his existence, his continued importance as a member of the community. They showed interest in him and in tried to contact him, while others forgot him.

Theme Page: Courage, page 160

1. Students may take this opportunity to reflect on the relationship of courage to other virtues and to consider if and how courage exists when one is not being actively challenged.
2. Answers will vary. Students' opinions will depend on how they interpret "mighty." If they would consider such things as running a drug rehabilitation program or adopting a foster child—activities with noble possibilities but a great risk of failure—as "daring mighty things," then they will be more likely to consider the statement as a good guide to life. If they consider "glorious triumphs" to be those which gain fame and media attention, they may have a different view.
3. Students may not have previously reflected on Lee as being courageous in publishing the book. Accept reasonable responses.

Theme Page: Status and Reputation, page 161

1. Answers will vary. Accept reasonable responses.
2. Answers will vary. Accept reasonable responses.
3. See the History of Social Thought Pages for information on hierarchies in the South in the 1930s. The most influential factors are race and "background," which is connected to job, culture, and relative wealth.
4. Professional people like Atticus, Judge Taylor, and Dr. Reynolds have status, as do Mrs. Merriweather ("the most devout") and Aunt Alexandra.
5. Answers will vary. Accept reasonable responses.
6. Boo Radley (and his family), Atticus, and Bob Ewell are examples of characters talked about "behind their backs." Boo Radley is accused of crimes and bizarre behavior; Atticus is called names; Bob Ewell is accused of neglecting children, and there are other stories about his losing a job and threatening Atticus. Boo is ostracized; Atticus is still elected to the legislature; Ewell's disgrace spreads.
7. Students will likely report changes in their ideas of Boo Radley, and possibly of Bob Ewell and Atticus as going from reputation to character at some point (for Atticus in Chapter 10; for Bob Ewell when he appears in court). They may also mention the idea of the separation between character and reputation for Boo and Atticus. You may wish to invite students to consider the risk Boo ran of reviving all the stories about his going around town with murderous intent when he went to Jem's and Scout's aid.
8. Students should discuss bad language (one of the items for which Boo was originally sentenced to jail, p. 10), gossip, insult, lies, accusations, labeling people (prejudicial language, p. 108), and our legal system (trial/argument).
9. Answers will vary. Accept reasonable responses. Students may note that Bob Ewell's influence through violence, threat, and neglect was more dramatic and traumatic, whereas Atticus's influence through example, reason, and words was subtler (but perhaps broader and longer lasting).